Teacher Preparation for Early Childhood Education

Special Aspects of Education

A series of books edited by Roy Evans, Roehampton Institute, London, UK

This book is part of a series. The publisher will accept continuation orders which may be cancelled at any time and which provide for automatic billing and shipping of each title in the series upon publication. Please write for details.

Teacher Preparation for Early Childhood Education

Edited by

ROY EVANS
Roehampton Institute, London, UK

and

OLIVIA N. SARACHO
University of Maryland, College Park, USA

GORDON AND BREACH SCIENCE PUBLISHERS
Switzerland Australia Belgium France Germany Great Britain
India Japan Malaysia Netherlands Russia Singapore USA

Gordon and Breach Science Publishers

Private Bag 8
Camberwell, Victoria 3124
Australia

3-14-9, Okubo
Shinjuku-ku, Tokyo 169
Japan

58, rue Lhomond
75005 Paris
France

Emmaplein 5
1075 AW Amsterdam
Netherlands

Glinkastrasse 13-15
O-1086 Berlin
Germany

5301 Tacony Street, Drawer 330
Philadelphia, Pennsylvania 19137
United States of America

Post Office Box 90
Reading, Berkshire RG1 8JL
Great Britain

The articles published in this book first appeared in the journal *Early Child Development and Care*, Volume 78.

Library of Congress Cataloging-in-Publication Data

Teacher preparation for early childhood education/edited by Roy
Evans and Olivia N. Saracho.
         p. cm. — (Special aspects of education; v. 15)
''The articles published in this book first appeared in Early child
development and care, volume 78'' — T.p. verso.
  Includes bibliographical references and index.
  ISBN 2-88124-882-9
  1. Early childhood teachers — Training of. I. Evans, Roy.
II. Saracho, Olivia N. III. Early child development and care; v.
78. IV. Series.
LB1732.3. T43 1992
370'.71'22—dc20

92-23011
CIP

Contents

Introduction to the Series

Increasingly in the last 10 to 15 years the published literature within the field of care education has become more specialized and focused: an inevitable consequence of the information explosion and the wider scope of theoretical and practical knowledge being required of students in both the traditional and developing areas of professional training. Students within initial and post-initial training evidently need to have ready access to specialized theoretical and pedagogical resources relevant to the context of their future professional involvements which also develop special aspects of an area of study in a critically evaluative way.

In the study of education and pedagogy, the analytical and experimental approaches of psychology, philosophy, sociology, social anthropology, etc. have provided insights into teaching and learning, into schooling and education. Historically these disciplines have focused their attention on relatively homogeneous populations. Increased worldwide mobility has created a need for a more pluralistic approach to education — particularly in Western countries — and a more broadly based concern for educational issues related in particular contexts. Hence, further literature has developed in recent years that is concerned with the pedagogical and curricular issues raised, for example, in connection with the "urban school", minority ethnic groups, disadvantaged and handicapped groups, and children who live apart from their families.

What is frequently missing from discipline-oriented studies is a real appreciation of context beyond the "general". What is often not present in the contextual study is an interdisciplinary analysis of the issue that provides a framework for practice.

The present series — "Special Aspects of Education" — is intended to bridge the gap between the problems of practice, as perceived in a variety of contexts, and theory, as derived from a variety of disciplines. Books accepted or commissioned for inclusion in the series will manifestly be expected to acknowledge the interdisciplinary nature of the issues and problems in the field of education and care, and, addressing themselves to particular contexts, to provide a conceptual framework for identifying and meeting special educational needs.

Roy Evans

Foreword

This edited work has evolved over a number of years as a result of conversations with early childhood educators and teacher trainers in many different national and cultural settings. A major question for us has been 'what drives practice?' By this we mean the practice of preparing adults to work with young children in contexts that are either overtly educational or where children's learning and development form important goals of the institutional context. Recognising the difficulty with which 'care' and 'education' issues can be untangled, at points in the span of early childhood, we have nevertheless made a conscious effort to focus on the 'professional' educator. For some, this will mean 'teacher' and carry legal and procedural requirements in respect of preparation for 'teaching' as a career. For others, working professionally with young children will find its meaning through the varying social philosophies, demographic patterns, cultural values, beliefs, traditions and economic well-being which collectively characterise nations and countries. We have made two assumptions which on the surface do not appear unreasonable.

Firstly, that the process of enabling adults to develop as 'professionals' requires some decisions as to what counts as appropriate or legitimate knowledge. Taking a fairly conventional view of 'teacher' the introductory chapter raises some issues connected with the nature of teacher knowledge, in the light of current trends, to bring into sharper relief the 'good enough' or 'competent' teacher. In the UK as elsewhere, the drive for improved standards of performance across the span of compulsory schooling has reopened the debate on the management and organisation of learning, teaching style and pedagogical decision making. What do teachers need to know in order to respond contingently to children's individual learning needs and assure progress through a pre-set curriculum?

Secondly, that this process of education and training must have regard to the means by which the aspiring professional develops and acquires the skills, abilities, attitudes and dispositions which in different national contexts are regarded as appropriate to the early childhood programme. Starting from the assumption that knowledge about practice will, in some measure, be developed through practice, the second chapter focuses on the theory–practice interface by considering issues connected with the trainee professional in the 'school' or early childhood setting. We are concerned here to raise questions connected with the extent to which the processes of training, notably during the practicum, are reflexive in so far as the quality of discourse on practice provides trainees with a solid foundation on which to build a theory of practice. If the early childhood programme is pinned to a particular ideology, to what extent does the supervision experienced by the trainee generate information contingent with their professional development needs? Are there limitations to existing models of practice when examined against desiderata of 'craft knowledge'? Are there benefits to be derived from a reconceptualisation of the basis of training? The major thrust of the book is to explore issues, models and requirements of training in a variety of national contexts. Contributors have reflected in their own way and from their own cultural perspectives significant features of national provision towards the preparation of professionals in the field of early childhood education. Our priorities have been more towards and countries of the Pacific rim and the South Pacific Basin than north-west Europe. This partly followed our own interest in presenting cultural contexts that are perhaps less well-known and partly because we were interested to better understand the points of similarity with conceptions and priorities that have been influential in the West, notably the UK and North America. The extent to which Froebelian practice has harmonised with evolving conceptions of childhood in Japan is particularly fascinating as indeed is the widespread influence of Montessori and Pestalozzi.

This book is not a comparative analysis. Common threads relate descriptively to the organisation of training provision, the goals of provision in relation to goals for young children's development and issues connected with 'professionality'. We believe that there is a powerful case for elaborating a code of ethics in respect of work with young children and an equally powerful case for making it explicit during preservice training.

Roy Evans and Olivia N. Saracho

Empires of the mind: Professional education or training?

ROY EVANS and PHILIP ROBINSON

Roehampton Institute, London, UK

(Received February 1992)

The teacher as 'scholar' is frequently underplayed in much current writing on teacher preparation. This paper seeks to raise issues connected with teacher competence in so far as one can explore what it is that teachers 'do'.

Key words: Professional Education or Training

"The empires of the future are empires of the mind."
Sir Winston Churchill, Harvard, 1943

"Student teachers need more time in classrooms guided by serving teachers and less time in the teacher training colleges."
Secretary of State for Education, UK, 1992

In recent months in England and Wales the practice of primary and early years education has been the subject of sustained and increasingly virulent attack. Teachers, blamed for their slavish adherence to the progressive principles enshrined in the Plowden Report of a quarter century ago, are castigated for failing to raise standards of literacy, numeracy and scientific understanding . . . particularly amongst 7 year-olds. Not only did the publication of the first cohort of National Assessment results on 7 year-olds in school in 1991 provide ammunition for the attack by Central Government, further ammunition emerged by way of the publication in late Autumn of the report by Robin Alexander of an investigation into primary school practices in Leeds. The latter, in common with some other studies claims to show how common primary school practices, including group work, topic work and "enquiry" modes of teacher-pupil interaction, may present teachers with problems of classroom organisation which "subvert the quality of children's learning and frustrate teachers' monitoring of that learning." (1). The summary paper issued on behalf of the Leeds project goes on to note how the investigation "highlighted the prevalence and power of certain orthodoxies about primary teaching methods and the extent to which many

1

teachers feel obliged to conform to these while in some cases being all too conscious of the problems they pose." (2). Junior Education Minister for Schools, Michael Fallon picked up on the Leeds findings in his address to the National Association of Head Teachers' Primary Conference in York on November 1st 1991. "At worst, this kind of practice turns primary schools into pro-school playgroups where there is much happiness and painting but very little learning." (3). Again, "Some topic-work can stimulate and interest . . . But exploration is no substitute for instruction."

Much has also been made of a brief report of a visit by four of Her Majesty's Inspectors of Schools to twelve primary schools in and around Orleans in France. After one week as the guests of the French Education Service the Department of Education and Science in London issued a National News bulletin headed "HMI Find High Standards in French Primary Schools." The key aspect of the Report (4). picked by the Secretary of State for Education was . . . "it highlights the effectiveness of whole class teaching and the importance of a National Curriculum."

The powerful and recurrent theme which has emerged from Government, is the need to seek reform of primary practice. Since the prevailing orthodoxies of the primary classroom are perpetuated by the training Institutions through their commitment to child centred ideologies and constructivist views on the nature of significant learning, then the initial training of teachers must also be reformed. "Theory can be no substitute for this practical training in professions that give person to person services. Student teachers need more time in classrooms guided by serving teachers and less time in the teacher training colleges." (5). What the Secretary of State proposes is quite explicitly an apprenticeship model where the role of training institutions in influencing practice is reduced to a peripheral extent. For almost a decade the study of Education has been increasingly squeezed out of programmes of teacher preparation to the point where the study of the traditional foundation disciplines has all but disappeared. The emergence of "teaching studies" within the curriculum of teacher education at all levels has been in response to the perceived need to create a synthesis of roles and responsibilities previously carried by "education studies" and "curriculum studies" faculty. In essence, and partly but not entirely, in response to the Council for the Accreditation of Teacher Education (CATE), the aims for almost a decade have been, to enable all primary teachers including those of young children, to acquire a competency in one or more subjects at undergraduate level, to develop pedagogic models appropriate to the subject and its educational context, including, since 1988, the subjects of the National Curriculum, and through practical experience in schools to observe and develop an appropriate repertoire of classroom skills. Across all phases of initial teacher preparation the model to be pursued is essentially a competency based model. The general direction of change has been indicated since the early mid-Eighties when the DES published a document titled Teaching Quality. An agenda of change was established which focussed sharply on the need to improve the quality of "output" from training institutions and addressed key issues connected with initial selection, on-course experience and final evaluation. The most radical change was the establishment of a National consensus on the form and content of initial training courses and the establishment of strictly applied formal criteria for course approval. In a very real sense this constituted a National Curriculum for teacher education which was policed by the Council for the Accreditation of Teacher Education serviced by a matrix of "local" Committees attached to one or more Institutions in various parts of the Country. For Institutions not in the University sector, i.e., Polytechnics, Colleges and Institutions of Higher Education etc., all course arrangements required two sets of approvals: Accreditation was secured through CATE which assured compliance of — aims, objectives, subject content, time allocations of particular required elements, sequence, timing and duration of practicums, existence of cross-curricula issues such as gender, special needs, multi-culturalism, information technology, nature and quality of faculty staffing and the quality of learning resources available to students: Validation was secured through either the Council for National Academic Awards (CNAA) a route required for all Polytechnics and some Colleges and Institutes of Higher Education, or, via academic association with a neighbouring University. Accreditation was backed by formal visitations by members of Her Majesty's Inspectorate and their reports on the quality of provision observed subsequently published. The Department of Education and Science has had in place for more than half a decade the machinery through which courses of teacher preparation may be terminated forthwith, suspended pending required modifications to course arrangements or faculty composition or simply granted provisional approval with clear indications as to improvements to be achieved in the short term. Since ALL teacher education is subject to the requirements of CATE, this includes preparation for early childhood teachers and in particular nursery education teachers. Even though the latter is non-statutory provision in England and Wales, where a local education authority chooses to maintain a nursery school or unit, it is necessary for the person in charge to be a trained and qualified teacher whose qualifications are recognised by the Department of Education and Science. This does not apply to private nurseries, crèches, day-nurseries, playgroups or other forms of other-than-mother part or full time care. Equally, however, the requirement for recognised teaching qualifications in respect of all age groups from 5 to 16 yrs, is strictly applicable only within the state controlled, state funded sector. It is only in respect of the public sector of education that the requirements of the 1988 Education Reform Act applies, that is with particular regard to the National Curriculum and its associated assessment and controlling regulations. Inevitably, the need to prepare teachers for playing their part in *delivering* the "entitlement" curriculum has carried substantial implications for the form and content of initial training courses. The language of education has over the past decade increasingly reflected the pervasive tendency towards the comodification of education. Schools are part of a free market, open enrollment carries the implication for projecting an attractive image into the local community, efficient schools deliver the preset curriculum within budget and have a good showing in local "league tables" of results of the National Assessments at the relevant Key Stages, i.e., 7yrs, 11yrs, 14yrs and 16yrs. Consumer choice is the means by which poor schools will decline and good schools will prosper.

Whilst no one can rationally oppose moves to increase the effectiveness of schools in assuring the meaningful education of all their pupils and consequentially the more effective preparation of teachers, the notion of "delivery" is ideologically at variance with the drift of early childhood education over the past two decades or so. Since we may use the term "delivery" loosely, in the sense that Bruner (e.g., 1966) used the term "instruction" . . . another term inclined to irritate, it is worth revisiting the conceptual framework for any curriculum delivery system. Taking schools to be the institutionalised formal system of curriculum delivery, what lies beneath what schools do and how do they justify doing it? Simplistically we can suggest the following as relevant to any analysis of practice:

Firstly, a theory of Curriculum. It is not unreasonable to assume that this is underpinned by a theory of knowledge and a theory of values. This grows out of the position that the knowledge held to be encapsulated by the formal curriculum of the school is not a Neutral statement.

Secondly, a theory of Organisation, relating to the ways in which the available resource, especially the human resource, is deployed, utilised and supported. Literally, the extent to which current ways of organising for teaching are related to a theory of resource management and the implementation of strategies best suited to the achievement of the school's academic plan and mission. Again, resource utilisation is not value free.

Thirdly, a theory of instruction. It is usually useful to explore this in relation to how teachers teach and how children learn. Within the classroom the teacher has regard to similar issues of organisation and management as exist at the more macro-level of the school. Nevertheless, it is within the classroom that the teachers intentions with respect to each child become manifest as "practice." It is here that we seek the intersection of ideas relating to children's learning with ideas relating to teaching. Following Ausubel, it is often convenient to look at teaching methods as logically separate from learning style: from an epistemological viewpoint this may be helpful but in practice as Tomlinson () points out they are frequently not separated. This makes evaluation inordinately difficult.

Fourthly, a conception of childhood. A conception of the nature of Humanness. A further complicating factor relates to the way in which particular ideologies of childhood dispose teachers, particularly early childhood teachers, to justify not only teaching methods but also forms of organisation for teaching against the embedded values of child-centredness and yet be extraordinarily vague about the way in which their practice is pinned to what we know about the way young children learn. Nowhere is this more clearly visible than in the British penchant for eclecticism in nursery and early childhood education. Because the latter is very process oriented, there has been historically a resistance to an analysis of the driving intellectual structure of the preschool learning environment, fearing an interpretation of "struc-ture" that would do violence to the prevailing ideology. It is interesting to note that much that is re-enacted in the name of Froebel ignores the obvious criticism that Froebelian theory advocates a purposive pedagogy rooted within a speculative supernaturalist philosophy of the nature of humankind. It is not a theory of learning: whilst one may accept the values of Froebel espoused, one is still logically required as a professional teacher to ensure that the learning of every child is effectively managed with the resources available and towards socially valued ends.

We would expect some variation both of the ends to be served and the means to these ends across cultures and nations. Nevertheless, the information explosion of recent decades coupled with dramatically improved communication between early childhood scholars and teachers around the world reveal common concerns to improve the practice of existing earlychildhood educators and a particular concern to secure the effective preparation of future generations of educators. Conceptions of "good" teachers, and in particular perhaps the notion of "good" in relation to "fitness for purpose", carries substantial implications for teacher preparation programmes on the assumption that such notions can be both unpicked and translated into operational criteria. The "professional teacher" carries the connotation of "competent" . . . whatever else may be invoked by the term. It is probably true that the professional teacher is involved in a moral endeavour, some would say in a spiritual endeavour. It is probably true that teaching is a personal activity in a public arena; as such it requires self-knowledge, reflection on personal action, and the ability to hold to the long view whilst attending to the here and now. All these things it is, and many more, but wherein lies competence?

Competency-based models of teaching are not new to many states in the USA. They are new to England and the rest of the United Kingdom. Here the term "competency" was last in vogue in teacher education in the mid-sixties when teacher educators set about embracing Chomsky's views on generative grammar into the prevailing orthodoxies. Debate on the utility of the distinction between competency and performance and the need for the prior development of the former to ensure the latter, is according to Devlin (1991), finding echoes in the current National debate on teacher competency. This is especially so when the competency is spelt out in terms of a disposition to perform and where teacher competency is seen as reducible to a series of graded competencies. The origins of the term "competence" refer to the overall suitability of the individual for a particular occupation. In the UK there has been a tendency in the recent discussion of teacher competence to use the term to refer to both the overall and the specific. Devlin (op. cit.) refers to the terminological tangle that is evident in Circulars from Central Government, e.g., Circular No. 24/89 from the Department of Education and Science and suggests that the current moves towards profiling teacher competencies at initial training level and subsequently, would benefit from a clearer elucidation of the whole in relation to its parts by adopting a more appropriate vocabulary. It may be helpful at this point to explore the notion of teacher competence from a slightly different perspective.

Teachers with a Variety of Competences

It has been commonplace in Teacher Education institutions for decades to evaluate a student teacher's fitness to teach on the basis of observation based, performance oriented, criteria. These criteria often find somewhat perfunctory expression in brief aide-memoire or advice to practicum supervisors on "points to mention" during periodic on-course reviews and at the end of the final placement. The conceptual map of the good-enough teacher is of course more explicit in course documents for accreditation and validation purposes. Such documents have, until recently, been useful as statements of intent pervaded by the rhetoric of conventional wisdom, but without the degree of explicitness that would have allowed final competency to be judged through agreement on an exit profile. This is not to suggest that decisions on fitness to teach were reached by training institutions on a less than rigorous basis. Indeed the agenda of fitness could and often was made quite extraordinarily explicit. Interestingly, such sharpness of focus was evidenced at internal meetings of faculty examiners at times of conflict or dispute over a recommended grade following a student practicum or more routinely, in justification of a particular recommendation. The exposition of a practicum supervisor was "public" in so far as the detailed analysis of observed practice was made in front of several dozen experienced and senior colleagues. Such colleagues were, particularly in the Voluntary Church teacher training colleges, the heirs to more than a century of involvement in initial training. Whatever other induction tutors received into life in a training institution, some of the powerful formative influences on judgement and analysis of teacher competence was achieved through discourse in such a "public" forum. Such discourse was evidently not public in the sense that it was accessible directly to external interested parties. It was available indirectly through the professional references and testimonials that the training institutions provided to each of its students for employment purposes. Most such documents were quite general and tended to focus on the main subjects of study, age range of experience, significant performance either way, and comments on personal qualities.

Since the early mid-eighties overarching aims, main and subsidiary objectives have necessarily become increasingly explicit. Specifying the desired characteristics of teachers in terms of the skills, knowledge, attitudes and dispositions required to discharge the tasks perceived as necessary in the schools of the Nineties, has set the agenda for teacher preparation. In a very real sense, targeting competencies and assessing teachers' performance in relation to such competencies carries substantial implications for course design and implementation. Importantly, the competency in question needs to be described in such a way that agreement can be reached on appropriate performance criteria; moreover, that agreement can be reached on what will be taken as evidence of the individual's success in relation to particular criteria, and that opportunity exists for the evidence to be observed. If competencies are to be acquired, planned opportunities must exist for the student to engage in appropriate experiences. Sensible debate on the proportion of the students' time to be spent in schools and College en route to acquiring recognisable competence, can only take place in the aftermath of context analysis. Unfortunately in England and Wales, teacher preparation has come to be seen by Government as "training", which in and of itself has invoked most of the hackneyed cliches concerning low level skills training, the most damaging being that such skills can be acquired "on the job". If this is a problematical view, why is it so?

Despite protestations to the contrary, it is probable that we could sustain an argument for teaching as the oldest profession, provided that we see within the compass of this activity all intentional acts which are designed to socialise infants and young children and to fit them for life in the contemporary society. Whilst public education in its mass formulation, and certainly in relation to "entitlement", has a relatively short history, there has been throughout that history a recognition that teaching is essentially an interpersonal activity. What has been less clear is the recognition of its transactional character as well as the pivotal significance of transaction to the social construction of knowledge. The late twentieth century has been marked by an increasing tendency to first question and then reject the assumptions regarding "truth", "knowledge" and "reality", which grew out of determinism and logical positivism. Increased attention to the power language wields in shaping individual conceptions of the social and material world have provoked observations concerning the negotiability of "truth" because of lack of economy in the use of language. Reality lies at the intersection of interpretations, the latter growing out of transactions unique to the individual. This highlights the problem many educators have in dealing with transmission models of teaching where the term "instruction" becomes associated with the teacher "giving" children relevant knowledge and where the teacher's effectiveness is gauged by the metric of children's subsequent ability to be successful in terms defined by national standard assessment. Commonly perceived tasks of early childhood educators relate to the creation of learning environments in which children are encouraged to develop their representational competences. The latter is developmental, experiential and hence negotiable. The teacher cannot "give" young children adult conceptions of the world; at best they can work within their understandings of individual children's existing level of representation and use the resources at their disposal to progress understanding and the refinement of appropriate skills and abilities. Teacher characteristics regarded as desirable include empathy, versatility, communicative ability and the capacity to motivate children to learn. We can clearly extend this list to reflect the requirements that are made of teachers as a consequence of the particular form of organisation for learning that constitutes "public" education. The requirement on most teachers to function with large groups of children from increasingly diverse cultural backgrounds interposes the need for layers of organisational and management skills which in turn become criteria by which the individual's "effectiveness" is judged. For instance, the requirement of versatility and flexibility grow out of the diversity of contexts and learning environments that the "public" control of education spawns. Huge variations in the state of the physical fabric of school buildings, in the range and quality of learning resources available, in the stability and sense of corporate purpose of the human resource both within and between schools, in the social cohesion of neighbourhoods, in the driving ideologies of Headteachers (Principals) and Governors, and in the quality of support available to classroom teachers influence both the pedagogical strategies employed and their perceived effectiveness. The requirement of versatility relates both to the expediency of responding to work-place differences as well as to the professional challenges inherent to any group of children through their varying rates and styles of learning and their differing educational and personal needs. Such versatility grows out of knowledge: craft knowledge which permits the teacher to make judicious use of available resources to achieve desired ends. It is inconsistent with slavish adherence to particular strategies or particular forms of organisation. Versatility grows out of the ability to choose; to choose how to operationalise the termly, monthly, weekly curriculum plan; to choose forms of classroom organisation capable of serving the determined pedagogical style; to choose and to choose to vary pedagogical style as a set of intentional acts congruent with perceived relations between means and ends, given the resources available. Versatility demands cognitive competence. Where the teacher is construed as versatile, empathic and knowledgeable, preparation for teaching can never be logically defended as a set of skills to be acquired. In both its construction and its performance, the teaching act is essentially creative. It is also creatively complex: fraught with competing value systems and ideologies the young teacher must be prepared to hold to a position of excellence in an education service where the ground rules are constantly moving and where comodification is the prevailing political goal. In a service moreover which has increasingly been required to take over functions previously provided by other social institutions, notably the family. Whilst the basic organisational model employed by "primary" schools is not markedly different now from what it was 100 years ago, the expectations of schools has altered dramatically. Most teachers are only too painfully aware that the ills of society are generally laid at the door of the education service and the quality of teaching therein.

Teaching quality has increasingly been scrutinised in the United Kingdom in an effort to tease out significant dimensions of effectiveness. Reports of enquiries have variously drawn attention to curriculum organisation (e.g., Hargreaves) to institutional organisation (e.g., Rutter et al., Reynolds) and to teacher behaviours in classrooms (e.g., Galton, Bennett). Whilst such enquiry is interesting and instructive, although not devoid of controversy, there is a real sense in which the elucidation of focal competencies in teaching is still more a matter of reflective analysis rather than the fruits of elaborate research. In consequence the publication by the National Curriculum Council (Spring, 1991) which set out the essential knowledge, understanding and skills which all newly trained teachers will need to serve the requirements of the National Curriculum, makes sense because it represents a highly recognisable synthesis of core skills and abilities. Equally, the requirements of DES Circular 24/89 concerning outputs from training puts an emphasis on the students study of subject content which is reminiscent of a long tradition within teacher education including for example, Bruner's report of a conference held at Woods Hole on Cape Cod in September 1959 and published as "The Process of Education". The 24/89 criteria require that subjects studies should develop in students:

1. an understanding of the underlying principles of their specialist subject or subjects;

2. an appreciation of the place of their subject or subjects in the primary or secondary curriculum as appropriate; and

3. a breadth and depth of subject knowledge extending beyond the demands of the programmes of study or examination syllabuses in schools.

In initial training, subject studies must therefore guarantee that a student understands, and can thereby effect, a critique of the presuppositions, assumptions and paradigms that underpin the subjects in which they specialise. There are echoes here of the views expressed by Dewey (1902) in The Child and the Curriculum, where a model of the educational process is advanced in which the responsibility of the teacher is to reinterpret knowledge so that it may be accommodated by the child. What concerns the teacher:

Is the ways in which that subject may become part of experience; what there is in the child's present that is usable with reference to it; how such elements are to be used; how his own knowledge of the subject matter may assist in interpretting the child's needs and doings and determine the medium in which the child should be placed in order that his growth may be properly directed. (Boydston, 1976).

The basis to all teaching, its essential quality, is the teacher's understanding of the matter to be taught. As Shulman (1987) puts it, "Teaching is, essentially, a learned profession". Shulman goes on to argue that there are a number of components to an understanding of content, of subject studies. The first component is an understanding of the substantive structures of knowledge, that is the important ideas and concepts in the area, the second, the *syntactic* component, the understanding of the grounds by which new ideas become accepted in an area and old ones rejected or re-formulated. This implies that in the "subject study" part of initial teacher education students should be aware of the history of a subject, how it was "born" and the changes that have taken place in its explanatory frameworks and the tensions in any competing paradigms. Shulman argues, "Without a firm grasp of the syntax of a discipline, prospective teachers may be unable to distinguish between more or less legitimate claims within a field. Teachers may find themselves unable to counter effectively a specious argument, even if they are aware of its dubious nature." (1989 p. 30)

One of the goals of teacher education must be that of enabling students to understand the scope and procedures, substantive and syntactical, of the subjects they intend to teach. The purpose of this is not that they just acquire expertise, the status of a scholar, but a familiarity with a knowledge area so that they are, "able to elucidate subject matter in new ways, re-organize and partition it, clothe it in activities and emotions, in metaphors and exercises, and in examples and demon-strations, so that it can be grasped by students" (Shulman, 1987, p. 13). O'Hear illustrates the same point in quoting from Michael Oakeshott:

teaching is a variegated activity which may include hinting, suggesting, urging, coaxing, encouraging, guiding, pointing out, conversing, instructing, narrating, lecturing, demonstrat-ing, exercising, testing, examining, criticising, correcting, tutoring, drilling and so on — everything indeed which does not belittle the engagement to impart an understanding. (Quoted in O'Hear, 1988, p. 15)

Maybe in the enthusiasm to adopt "child-centred" methods of learning, (and there can be no other), we forgot that the implications for the teacher is that he or she must have an even greater grasp of the material to be taught than would be necessary in a straightforward "didactic" approach. The central purpose of subject studies in an undergraduate programme is to enable the intending teachers to have an understanding of the principles underpinning their subject areas and be able to locate the specific elements of the programme shared with children within a wider corpus of knowledge. In an adaptation of Shaw's celebrated aphorism, "He who can, does. He who cannot, teaches," Shulman suggests, "Those who can, do. Those who understand, teach." (1986, p. 14)

The recommendation in Circular 24/89 is that students should spend not less than the equivalent of half a year "in the application of students" subject specialisms to the teaching and assessment of pupils' (para 4.6). Shulman labels this as *pedagogical content knowledge*. By this he means the range of different approaches, metaphors, analogies and examples that are used to communicate a subject so as to optimize the learning possibilities for children. It includes specific knowledge of those parts of a subject that conventionally children find difficult to grasp, concepts of, for example, "energy" in science, "negative numbers" in mathematics or "subordinate clauses" in English. The intending teacher would also know the common misunderstandings that children bring to these areas as well as a repertoire of approaches that teachers have evolved over the years to help minimize the lack of comprehension.

"To teach is first to understand", for teachers this means comprehending "the matters, skills and processes which are required to be taught to pupils of different abilities and maturities" (1988 Act Section 2(b). A teacher must comprehend the subject to be taught, understand its relationship to the wider curriculum and to larger educational purposes and values. But more than this, the teacher must be able to transform his/her own knowledge into ways that can be understood by children. Herein lies the essential creativity and professionalism of teaching, the range of pedagogical styles, the endless search for original ways of representing skills and concepts so that the infinite variety of children are enabled to come to terms with the material being taught. Having prepared what is to be taught the teacher must then organize and manage the classroom to give substance to the planning recognising that the process of teaching is not fixed but interactive, guided by the responses children make. The act of instruction requires it be evaluated; the "reflective practitioner" comes into his/her own here as the teacher interprets the consequences of teaching and reformulates both his/her own understanding of the matter to be taught and the future strategies to be adopted.

This cycle of professional development in which there is a continual relationship between the scholarly domain and the practical tasks of teaching is appropriate to a first degree programme. The teacher as "scholar" has been underplayed in discussion of the nature of pedagogy, the opportunities provided by the national curriculum could go some considerable way to re-establishing teaching as an intellectual profession. It is an opportunity to re-plan undergraduate courses of teacher education so that subject studies become an integral part of the process of professional development rather than a separate and too-often, unrelated element.

References

Alexander, R.J. (1991) Primary Education in Leeds. University of Leeds (1)
Ausubel, D.P. (1963) *The Psychology of Meaningful Verbal Learning*. New York: Grune and Stratton
Ausubel, D.P. (1968) *Educational Psychology: A Cognitive View*. New York: Holt, Rinehart and Winston
Ausubel, D.P., Novak, J.D. & Hanesian, H. (1978) *Educational Psychology: A Cognitive View*. (2nd edition)
    New York: Holt Rinehart and Winston
Bennett, S.N., Desforges, C., Cockburn, A. & Wilkinson, B. (1984) *The Quality of Pupil Learning Experiences*.
    Lawrence Erlbaum

Bennett, S.N. (1992) Managing Learning in the Primary School. Assoc. for the Study of Primary Education. UK

Bruner, J.S. (1960) *The Process of Education*. Cambridge, MA: Harvard University Press

Bruner, J.S. (1966) Towards a Theory of Instruction. Cambridge, MA: Harvard University Press

Carnegie Corp. (1986) A Nation Prepared: Teachers for the 21st Century. Washington, DC. Carnegie Forum on Education and the Economy

Central Advisory Council for Education (England) (1967) Children and Their Primary Schools. (Plowden Report). HMSO: London

Department of Education and Science (1982) The New Teacher in School: a Report by HM Inspectors. HMSO: London

Department of Education and Science (1991) Classroom Practice in Primary Schools. Address by Schools Minister, to National Association of Headteachers' Primary Conference. London: DES

Department of Education and Science (1991) Aspects of Primary Education in France: a Report by HM Inspectors. HMSO: London

Department of Education and Science (1991) Primary Education – A Statement by the Secretary of State for Education and Science. DES: London

Department of Education and Science (1992) Address to the North of England Education Conference by the Secretary of State for Education and Science. Jan, 1992. DES: London

Department of Education and Science (1992) Curriculum Organisation and Classroom Practice in Primary Schools. A Discussion Paper. DES: London

Department of Education and Science (1983) Teaching Quality. HMSO: London

Department of Education and Science (1989) Circular 24/89. DES: London

Dewey, J. (1902) The Child and The Curriculum. In J.A. Boydston (ed) 1976, John Dewey: *The Middle Works, 1899–1924*. Vol. 2. 1902–1903. Carbondale: Southern Illinois University Press

Devlin, P.J. (1991) The Roehampton Institute Initial Teaching Competences Project. London: Roehampton Institute School of Education

Galton, M., Simon, B. & Croll, P. (1980) *Inside the Primary Classroom*. London: Routledge

Galton, M. & Simon, B. (Eds) (1980) *Progress and Performance in the Primary Classroom*. London: Routledge

Galton, M. & Williamson, J. (1992) Groupwork in the Primary School. London: Routledge

Grossman, P.L., Wilson, S.M. & Shulman, L.S. (1989) Teachers of Substance: Subject Matter Knowledge for Teaching. In M.C. Reynolds (ed.) *Knowledge Base for the Beginning Teacher*. Oxford: Pergamon

Hargreaves, D.H. (1982) The Challenge for the Comprehensive School. London: Routledge and Kegan Paul

Holmes Group (1986) *Tomorrow's Teachers*. East Lansing: The Holmes Group

O'Hear, A. (1988) Who Teaches the Teachers? London. The Social Affairs Unit

Rutter, M., Maughan, B. *et al.* (1979) Fifteen Thousand Hours: Secondary Schools and their Effects on Children. London: Open Books

Shulman, L.S. (1986) Those Who Understand: Knowledge Growth in Teaching. *Educational Researcher*, **15**(2), 4–14

Shulman, L.S. (1987) Knowledge and Teaching: Foundations of the new reform. *Harvard Educational Review*, **57**(1), 1–22

Tomlinson, P. (1981) Understanding Teaching. *Interactive Educational Psychology*. London: McGraw-Hill

Wilson, S.M., Shulman, L.S. & Richert, E. (1987) "150 Different Ways of Knowing": Representations of Knowledge in Teaching. In James Calderhead (ed.), *Exploring Teachers' Thinking*. London: Cassell

Footnotes

2. Alexander, R. 1991. Primary Education in Leeds. Briefing and Summary. Univ. of Leeds
3. Fallon, M. 1991. Classroom Practice in Primary Schools questioned. Speech to National Association of Head Teachers' National Primary Conference, York. London DES
4. Department of Education and Science. 1991. Aspects of Primary Edudcation in France. London. HMSO
5. Secretary of State for Education. 1992. Speech to the North of England Education Conference. DES.

See also.

Alexander, R., Rose, J. and Woodhead, C. 1992. Curriculum organisation and Classroom Practice in Primary Schools. A discussion paper. London. DES.

Secretary of State for Education. 1991. Primary Education. A Statement. London DES

Developing students' practice through partnership: Improving the quality of field experiences

ROY EVANS and ANNE FINDLAY

Roehampton Institute, London, UK

(Received 1 March 1992)

The relationship between theory and practice, and in particular the role of field experiences in programmes of teacher preparation, is the focus of renewed interest in the light of growing enthusiasm for school based training. This paper explores concepts of partnership between schools and training institutions towards an improvement in the quality of professional support available to student teachers.

Key words: Field experiences, improving quality

In the introductory chapter to this book we sought to assert something of the nature of "teaching" as a professional activity. An activity which may be engaged in differing contexts, in diverse institutions both pre- and post-compulsory schooling, but an activity nevertheless which is characterised by informed intentions and recognisable craft knowledge. It has been argued that teachers' knowledge, gained partly in the future work place and partly in institutions of higher learning, must enable us to sustain a view of teaching as a scholarly activity. Allowing that management and organisational tasks will to a degree be context and age-phase driven and that the prioritisation of actions will reflect developmentally appropriate curricular aims, the essence of teaching is to creatively match each individual to the skills to be acquired and the knowledge to be gained. The teacher is the principal agent in a conscious process of education and socialisation. With any age group of children, but perhaps particularly with young children, the learning environment may include a variety of adults in differing roles and in differing relationship to the children. Parents, care workers, nursery nurses, ancilliary aids, are not uncommonly part of the daily experience of children in preschool, kindergarten or nursery. This cooperative milieu has increasingly become a feature of early childhood education into the period of formal schooling, within which the professionalism of the "teacher" is distinguished by the demonstrable quality of programmatic decision making and the leadership displayed. In different national contexts it must be recognised however that the designation "early childhood professional" is not inevitably synonymous with "teacher", at least with the meanings that have been used in the earlier chapter. In

13

day nurseries in England it is not the "teacher" who is the principal agent, neither is it so in creches, playgroups and family day-care. These facilities, governed by regulations through branches of government other than education, collectively form a pragmatic and generally ad-hoc response to the substitute day-care and educational needs of a complex industrial society. In most Western democracies, the last quarter century has witnessed an unprecedented injection of young mothers into the labour market with the inevitable consequence of increasing demand for day-care and educational provision. With one or two notable exceptions, the response of European countries to a conception of planned, coherent other than mother care/education has been inadequate. In the USA, Pardeck (1990) argues that the situation is exacerbated by the almost complete lack of family policy at Federal level and its consequential reflection in State legislation.

As later chapters make clear, children in the age group 3 to 6 years, can in countries as culturally, socially and economically diverse as India, Japan, Taiwan, USA, Australia, be placed in facilities where "education" is the aim or in any one of a range of other facilities where "care" is the over-riding consideration, and where the education and/or care are provided by adults with very different backgrounds, levels of personal education and professional preparation. The field is extraordinarily broad. The decision to limit consideration to "teacher" preparation in the present book, and thus to target more educationally oriented interventions, is more a reflection of the state of flux in conceptions of initial training of teachers than any overt statement about the perceived value of one form of provision amongst others. Indeed, with young children it is only with some difficulty that we can make statements that discriminate between their care needs and their educational needs. And only then with a degree of arbitrariness. The Department of Education and Science recognised this in 1976 when in written communication to a conference on Low Cost Provision for the Under Fives, it was observed, "Like all provision for small children, public or voluntary, it is essential that nursery schools and classes should provide a secure and caring environment. In common with day care centres and pre-school play groups, they present opportunities for children to become accustomed to a wider range of their peers and of adults than is ordinarily met at home. They provide physical conditions specially adapted for young children."

In the same communication, the DES began to evoke differences between "nursery" and other forms of institution based preschool experience in ways which carried substantive implications for the skills, knowledge, attitudes and organisational abilities of the "teachers". The clear statement that nursery classes and schools were organised in such a way that children from the age of 2 years through to 5 years should be able to gain the "greatest possible educational benefit from their work" reinforced the view that the organisations leader would be a "qualified teacher". Given the orientation of this book to early childhood education the focus on teacher preparation is appropriate. The purpose of later chapters is to explore the extent to which such preparation is pinned to more broadly conceived models of primary, lower primary, kindergarten or elementary school preparation and the extent to which it may be differentiated from such programmes either partly or completely, and either ideologically or experientially. Later chapters will show that what is common to all programmes of preparation across national and cultural boundaries is the requirement for elements of practical experience within the overall programme of initial training. What is not always clear is how the practicums become congruent with the general thrust of training, and how the competent institution manages the total experience of the aspiring teacher so that extended periods of time spent in schools and classes blend harmoniously into the college based work. Since the practical elements are highly valued by student teachers, and in the UK are likely to form an increasingly large proportion of total time available for training, it is relevant at this point to explore issues connected with quality assurance. The embedded questions relate to the nature of the partnerships established between training institutions and cooperating schools and teachers: the clarity with which the partnership has been unpicked so interpretations of roles, rights and responsibilities intersect in some meaningful fashion; the competence and commitment of each of the partners in respect of the agreed roles and responsibilities: a concept of teamwork which is empowering to team members, enables conflict to be dealt with constructively and sponsors effective communication between all parties: the existence of recognisable and effective mechanisms for sustaining teamwork, supporting individual team members and attending to the professional development needs of those members who find themselves in a mentoring or student support role.

The relationship between theory and practice in teacher preparation programmes is the subject of ongoing debate. One deeply ingrained position views the purpose of practicums as enabling students to integrate previous learning with experiences gained in the classroom and to transform theoretical instruction into reality (Borrowman, 1965). In this context, Gillett 1973 cautioned on the devaluing of "theory" through an overemphasis on the practice component. The danger of moving teacher education to a non-intellectual apprenticeship programme through overemphasis on classroom experience under the guidance of classroom teachers has already been raised in Chapter 1. A similar concern is expressed by Gillett. A more recent position concerning the relationship between theory and practice has grown out of a concern to analyse notions of theory. Whilst Schon's writing has embedded the notion of "reflective practitioner" into the rhetoric of teacher preparation programmes, prior concern for what counted as legitimate knowledge is evidenced in the equally powerful notions of "teacher researcher" and "grounded theory" elaboration of which were much evidenced in the late Seventies in the UK and owed much to the work of Stenhouse at the University of East Anglia. Inevitably, within this newer conceptualisation of teacher development, where an important aspiration is to enable the student to develop a theory of practice through reflection on experiences gained in the field placement, much depends on the reflexive character of the students' total learning environment.

In many of the National programmes examined in this book, the student finds herself in a triadic relationship, with the competent institution on the one hand and the receiving class, school or unit on the other. The quality of experience derived by the student from the field placement is a function of the supervision received from the cooperating teachers and the college tutors. These two key agents in the process of professional development are frequently cited as "partners" within an overarching paradigm of supervision. The success of this partnership in assuring the quality of the student's practical experience nevertheless depends on the operation of a series of factors, some professional, some ideological, some organisational/administrative and some purely pragmatic, driven by expediency in relation to the available human resource. Amongst such factors we may recognise the following as influencing the student's perception of benefit received from the collaborative model of supervision as it operates in practice:

— the supervisory competences of the cooperating teacher. Acting as critical friend and mentor to a student in the classroom situation requires skills, attitudes and abilities that go beyond being an effective teacher of children oneself. It may be argued that being effective in this situation requires an ability to observe the practice of another and to subsequently engage that other in critical analysis of the practice observed. What cannot be assumed here is that the pedagogic feedback loops that teachers routinely employ in their work with children are directly transferable to work with adults. In short, the supervisory competences of cooperating teachers cannot be assumed.

— the degree of explicitness with which the roles and responsibilities of the cooperating teachers and the College tutors have been defined. Moreover the extent to which the defined roles have been rehearsed with partners in the enterprise and clarifications achieved. Practical difficulties intervene for large institutions which routinely interface with many schools. The exercise tends to be paper driven with the success of the enterprise being a function of the quality of the information communicated to schools and teachers. For instance, Roehampton Institute, one of the largest institutions of initial teacher education in the UK, routinely places students in more than 800 schools each year. The majority of these are primary schools. Major institutions of teacher preparation in other countries will face similar problems regarding the development of sound relationships and common under-standings when large numbers of schools and cooperating teachers are involved. An international research literature tends to suggest that the power of the triadic relationship in assuring for the student maximum benefit in the practice situation is put at risk or otherwise limited by a series of factors which have currency and recognisability in different cultural contexts. In one sense or another these factors relate either to poor articulation of the division of responsibility between schools and training institutions or a failure to develop mutuality in the ownership of the students development needs. By mutuality we mean a shared understanding between the college supervisor and cooperating teacher of the professional strengths that each can bring to bear on the students classroom experience, the nature of the feedback that each can provide from complementary perspectives and the support networks that can be accessed. Because the cooperating teacher is at hand, she has the opportunity to substantially influence student teaching experience and mediate the professional learning opportunities as they arise. Grimmett and Ratzlaff (1986) argue however that the potential power of complementarity is frequently lost because the responsibi-lities of the college supervisor and cooperating teacher are often unclear and frequently overlap. More damaging but equally recognisable is Bird's (1984) finding that cooperating teachers felt that college supervisors brought to bear a college perspective which disregarded schools. A major criticism related to the limited opportunity college supervisors took to familiarise themselves with the school, the classroom or the teaching personnel. One consequence of this is, as Saracho and Spodek (1992) argue, that college supervisors have limited opportunity to influence the quality of discourse on practice which occurs between student and cooperating teacher, "because they do not spend the time in the schools necessary to build trust". In a further study, Koehler (1984) reported that the college supervisors impact on student teachers' classroom practices was low in comparison with the cooperating teachers.

One consequence of the failure to articulate roles and resolve the inevitable tensions in the triadic relationship is the diffidence with which cooperating teachers proffer advice to students in their care. The uncertainty resides in a perception many teachers hold of the centre of gravity of expertise residing in training institutions. The college supervisor becomes viewed as an agent of that expertise, which whilst rhetorically benevolental and development is also judgemental and determining in respect of the student's success. A consequence of this conflicted situation is, as Saracho and Spodek (op. cit.) observe, that cooperating teachers frequently feel the need to protect "their" student and excuse problems that the college supervisor may present. In the drive to improve the perceived benefit to students of the field experience, the triadic relationship needs to be configured in a way which is mutually supportive and reinforcing.

A major source of criticism which emerges from American studies (see for example, Little, 1981; Zeichner & Liston, 1987), is concerned with the level and quality of analysis of practice that occurs in discussions between student and cooperating teacher. Reservations also exist in regard to the quality of feedback provided by the college supervisor. On the one hand the teacher in situ has the opportunity to act as close educator to the student, to mediate the learning experiences and promote critical reflection in a context of shared meanings, but perhaps lacks the skills, confidence or commitment to the cause. On the other hand, the college supervisor who arguably has the knowledge and skills to enable her to engage the student in reflective analysis, is constrained by a lack of opportunity to observe critical incidents, and much poorer access to the shared understandings and characteristics of the school and classroom. Teacher educators in Britain would probably agree that these are just and proper concerns, and that whilst the character of the school based element of programmes of teacher preparation has been on the professional agenda for over two decades, a perception of the limitations of past practices has not always been matched by the opportunity to effect significant change. Many of the impediments to change, whilst identifiable have been beyond the scope of influence of the training institutions. Stability, either demographically or professionally has not been the character of the Eighties. Reduction in public expenditure on education, amongst other public services created particular stresses for schools, exacerbated by the unrelenting radical educational reforms which has left many teachers exhausted and bewildered. Until recently, attempts to foster collaborative models of student

teacher preparation competed with an avalanche of innovation and change orchestrated by central government. What is perhaps remarkable is that throughout this
period of unprecedented reform, schools have continued to be generally welcoming of
young students and have continued their historic task of contributing to professional
renewal. Laudably, some attempts have been made to develop models of practice
within a larger school improvement context and interesting examples of IT/INSET
exist. The inability of training institutions to offer effective quid pro quo to schools for
working with student teachers has been a constraint to the expectations that such
institutions can hold of schools in developing the supervision process. The evolution
of a partnership model which overtly contributes to the professional load on
classteachers through an extension of role, cannot fail to take into consideration the
possible effects to the school of rededicating a significant unit of resource. The
acquisition of mentoring skills by the cooperating teacher may have useful spin-off
within the school but there is growing evidence that schools are viewing collaboration
as a service for which payment is required. The progressive comodification of
education to which the existing Government is so firmly wedded has encouraged
schools to adopt the market place philosophy in respect of professional services. The
declared intention of the present Secretary of State for Education in England, to
increase the school based element within the current four year undergraduate initial
training programme will undoubtedly be accompanied by mechanisms for the
reimbursement of schools for services provided. It is likely that training institutions
will be required to funnel financial resources into schools to support the field
experiences of students throughout their training. This shift of emphasis has been
referred to earlier. The policy position is to put the professional training in the hands
of experienced teachers and to provide selected schools with sufficient resource to
enable them to discharge their obligations effectively. The implementation of this
model will require reform of the traditional functions of staff in the training faculties
of Colleges and Universities, whilst still requiring these institutions to retain overall
academic control. By the same token, schools will be required to plan staff acquisition
and deployment in recognition of the demands on them to assure a programme of
continuous mentoring and support. It may appear initially that what is proposed by
Government involves such radical reorientation of current practices that the seismic
waves will be reverberating through the system for years ahead. Interestingly,
however, a number of recent Central Government initiatives have served to improve
the sensitivity of schools to issues connected with the provision of professional support
to teachers. Collectively these initiatives have served to substantially increase the
knowledge and skills of serving teachers in respect of curriculum and assessment and
in addition have provided schools with the opportunity to achieve ownership both of
the process of needs identification and the means by which they can be met in the
short and medium term. In so far as they potentially affect the quality of support
available to young teachers and students in the classroom the following developments
are worth mentioning.

   In the first instance there has been a radical overhaul of the system of Inservice
support to teachers since the late Eighties. Large sums of tax-payers money have been
targeted for professional development and specifically to support policy initiatives. Of

significance has been the requirement on schools to a evolve a "development plan" and to coordinate professional development activities to achieve match between the teaching competencies available and those required to achieve the institution's objectives. The importation into schools of the practice and language of human resource development commonly found in industry and commerce, has had a largely salutary effect on the ways in which individual professional needs are identified. Teachers in the work place have, of necessity confronted issues connected with adult learning modes towards self improvement and increased effectiveness in the class-room.

Secondly, but not unconnected with the first point, the introduction of mandatory teacher appraisal has brought its own benefits as well as its own anxieties. Teacher appraisal, not uncommon in some other countries is new to Britain where it is clearly related to improved effectiveness. Whilst ultimately it is locked into the agenda of accountability and the commitment to the improvement of standards, the appraisal process contributes to institutional development through agreement on objectives for personal development. Classroom observation of the appraisee by the appraiser is a required feature of the agreed procedure as one of the precursers to the appraisal interview. In this context the skills required of the appraiser are not dissimilar to those required of the University supervisor in the analysis of observed classroom behaviour. In both instances the observer must reflect on what has been observed, deconstruct the experience and subsequently encode the analysis so that growth needs can be discussed in an atmosphere of trust and mutual regard. The assumption has not been made that in relation to "appraisal" teachers inevitably possess such skills. Training has been instituted to give meaning to the whole process within schools. The spin-off in terms of the potential for future student support is substantial.

Thirdly, a major step forward has been taken in operationalising the rhetoric of teacher induction. Heavily embedded within the educational agenda of all political parties is a commitment to strengthening the induction phase of professional development. The initial, induction, inservice phases of teacher education are increasingly viewed as a coherent whole in the life of the teacher. The rhetoric has existed for decades but it is quite recently that the reality of provision is beginning to transform the rhetoric into practice. Funds from central government have served to pump prime the innovative actions of selected Local Education Authorities in supporting the induction phase. Links with Training Institutions have in many instance been forged to support two significant areas of development. One of these relates to the establishment in schools of a "mentor" whose responsibility it is to support and coordinate the induction of the new entrant to the profession. In many instances the initial training institutions have provided the necessary "mentor" training. A second significant area of development relates to the professional profiling of teachers in the induction phase and beyond. Practical effect in respect of coherent professional extension is now within reach for two main reasons. Firstly the existence of the national curriculum which applies to all state funded schools. Secondly the existence of the national curriculum of initial teacher education assured by the Council for the Accreditation of Teacher Education. These two factors combine to remove many of the dislocations to experience that young teachers in the past encountered in taking up the first teaching job. The development on of competency profiling by initial training institutions into the Local Authorities' own profiling schemes are features of current collaborative practice.

Fourthly the decision by Government to sponsor alternative routes into teaching. The two traditional routes, i.e., four year undergraduate professional degree and the one-year post graduate route have been extended by the addition of two new schemes, the Licensed Teacher scheme and the Articled Teacher scheme. With their emphasis on school focus with mentor support, such schemes are seen as potentially more attractive to the mature entrant who has already evidenced a minimum of two years personal higher education or who has achieved graduate status. The schemes vary in their training requirements, but an important common feature relates to the need within each for a school based-mentor. The role of Higher Education institutions is substantially to support the mentor in her/his role of supporting the new teacher's practice.

We have noted earlier that it is particularly in relation to the roles of the cooperating teacher and the college tutor that the triadic relationship is most at risk of being less effective than it could otherwise be. Further aspects of this relate to the complementary competences required to serve the different roles as they achieve clarification, and in particular, how they are identified and systematically met within the ongoing process of student support. We have also noted earlier that effective "mentoring" will undoubtedly carry resource implications for both schools and colleges. It is opportune therefore to be able to call upon current evidence from the ongoing monitoring of the pilot Articled/Licensed teacher schemes to examine the professional, practical and logistic issues that are generated when the supervision of practice is established firmly within the responsibility of the schools themselves. Future moves towards increasing the schools' training responsibilities within the traditional four year undergraduate programme and one year post-graduate programme can be expected to generate similar needs and issues.

The Role of the "Mentor" in School-based Training

The following issues are identified substantially on the basis of one institution's involvement in the Articled teacher scheme through a Government approved consortium arrangement with a cluster of local education authorities. The training institution concerned is one of the two largest providers of initial teacher education in the UK with extensive and historic links into inner-city areas of London as well as into the more advantaged areas to the southwest of the city. Ongoing monitoring of the scheme as well as the provision of "mentor" support and training have generated the following observations:

At the level of the coordinating authority, i.e., Local Authority/School District, school-based training requires . . .

1. A total commitment to the notion of partnership to get things working with personnel identified and given time allocation for the tasks. These personnel would need to value sensitive personal interaction skills including aspects of openness and questioning.

2. A willingness to support a viable group of school-based training elements.

3. Support to schools that wish to be involved. The concept of using "excellent" schools, much extolled by Government, is too narrow. There are not enough such schools and it implies a correlation between excellence in philosophy, excellence in reality and in having the facility to convey this to a trainee. Issues regarding the selection of "training" schools need to be addressed. Fundamentally, such schools need to have an active philosophy of participation. This entails openness in decision making and in public scrutiny.

4. Involvement in trainee selection, allocation and perhaps reallocation.

5. A willingness to develop "ownership" of the programme through participation in planning, implementation and assessment of the entire programme.

In return, there are clear advantages to the Authority in so far as school-based training establishes a professional support network for all educational services from Initial Training through to professional development on a broad front and subsequently Higher degree study. Furthermore it is an attractive source of starting-teachers already initiated and inducted into the ethos of Borough/district thinking.

At the level of the individual mentor/teacher, participation provides potential for practising teachers to achieve personal professional development whilst remaining in their own classrooms. Reviewing their own practice, exploring new ideas and developing the skills to communicate principles of good practice to the next generation of teachers will require:

1. Developing a working style that has room for observation, discussion, reflection, tolerance and change.

2. Personal sensitivity and an ability to self-question.

3. Negotiating skills.

4. The encouraging of a paced schedule of professional development consistent with an explicit experienced-based model of personal growth which keeps the competencies to be acquired clearly in view.

5. Evaluation, assessment and record keeping skills.

6. A reasoned judgement, as the commitment develops, of whether the mentor role is appropriate to the individual. The mentor role requires a substantial commitment on the part of the teacher in the classroom. Commitment of time, commitment to the student, commitment to personal development, and commitment to working with higher education in a spirit of true partnership.

At the level of the University or College, the reorientation which will be necessary as the partnership with schools evolves must be pinned to a continuing recognition that there is a body of values, knowledge and professional expectations that need to be upheld and transmitted. For the reasons explored earlier in this paper there is good reason to see within the drive to clarify roles and develop the support and supervision skills of the cooperating teacher/mentor the basis for assuring the quality of the student's practical placement. However it continues to be the function of the training institutions to secure academic rigour, professional standards and ultimately to approve the student for certification. Review of the pilot exercise has made it clear that:

1. The Higher Education elements will need to be tied in more directly and be more responsive to what really goes on in schools than is so at present. We can not afford for the exercise to be driven by a "college" perspective.

2. Links between schools and Higher Education will need to be stronger, with perhaps college staff in Consultancy roles to particular schools, within and across curriculum areas.

3. To secure active partnership, core teams of college staff are best deployed in working with distinct groupings of mentors across a span of time. Continuity of experience within stable teams is a significant prerequisite of improved benefit to the students.

4. Mentor training requires a rigorous and substantial programme of professional development orchestrated by the University/College. Where this can be tied in with institutional arrangements for credit accumulation within a modular system of In-service awards, it can potentially offset the resource implications to schools of offering opportunities for student placement. Mentor training is nevertheless costly where it takes teachers out of schools for "training" purposes.

5. Key areas for training include an examination of what "teaching" and "the potential complexity of classroom life" can mean. Importantly attention has to be paid to the concept of "mentoring", and a shared understanding worked for in respect of the competencies to be developed by the student and the criteria through which they may be evidenced.

One of the fascinating outcomes of the involvement of HE staff in increased school-based training and mentor support, is related to the shift of attitudes that has occurred since the commencement of the pilot programme in 1990. There appears now an enthusiastic realisation of the potential of a well integrated programme of Institution/School collaboration, which contrasts with the muted reception with which the Government's original proposals were met. An important spin-off relates to the possible extension to the traditional models of initial teacher training of the ways of working which have emerged through participation in the alternative scheme. Embedding initial teacher development within a broader context of professional extension and renewal, demands a cooperative model which is characterised by active support from teachers, schools and Local Authorities/School Districts. The operation of such a model is proving to have value in support of the complementary missions of both training institutions and schools.

In all that has just been said, extending the professionality of serving teachers, helping them to become better equipped to contribute to professional renewal, has been conceptualised within the context of a team approach. Collaboration is required both within and across institutions who have a stake in providing quality education for children. In regard to facilities for early childhood education, irrespective of whether they provide full or part time opportunities, serve children of statutory school age or preschool age children, the teachers and carers must see themselves and be seen as part of the corporate endeavour. Opportunities for staff development which exist within the compulsory phases of education must be available to preschool teachers. Too many preschool units lay outside of the culture of improvement that has grown within the primary and elementary school phase. Free of the requirement to deliver the entitlement curriculum, such units are in danger of becoming philosophically and ideologically isolated from the early years of statutory schooling. Private nurseries are at particular risk of such isolation although small nursery schools in the public sector are by no means immune. Where continuity and progression are seen as significant contributory measures in assuring children's healthy adjustment to school, the need for schools generally to embrace the community of preschool facilities within their own corporate vision must remain a matter of priority.

References

Bird, T. (1984) Propositions Regarding the Analysis and Supervision of Teaching. Paper to the Loveland, Colorado School Administrators Workshop, Vail, CO

Borrowman, M.L. (1965) *Teacher Education in America*. New York: Teachers College Press

DHSS/DES (1976) Low Cost Day Provision for the Under-Fives. Papers from a Conference at the Civil Service College, Sunningdale

Evans, R. (1990) Development of an IT-INSET Model for Teacher Education. Position Paper, Roehampton Institute, School of Education

Gillett, M. (1973) Introduction to new directions. In: Laska, J.A. and Gillett, M. (Eds). *Foundation Studies in Education: Justifications and New Directions*. Methuchen, NJ: The Scarecrow Press

Little, J.W. (1987) Teachers as Colleagues. In: Richardson-Koehler, V. (Ed). *Educators Handbook*. New York: Longman

Pardeck, J.T. (1990) An Analysis of the Deep Social Structure Preventing the Development of a National Policy for Children and Families in the United States. Early Child Development and Care. Vol. 57, pp 23–31

Peterson, P.L. & Comeaux, M.A. (1989) Assessing the Teacher as a Reflective Professional: New Perspectives on Teacher Evaluation. In: A.E. Woolfolk (Ed.), *The Graduate Preparation of Teachers*. Englewood Cliffs, NJ: Prentice-Hall

Richardson-Koehler, V. (Ed.) (1987) *Educators Handbook*. New York: Longman

Saracho, Olivia & Spodek, B. (1992) Preparing Teachers for Early Childhood Programmes in the USA. *Handbook of Research on the Education of Young Children*

Schon, D. (1987) Educating the Reflective Practitioner. London: Jossey-Bass

Stenhouse, L. & Verma, G.K. (1981) Educational Procedures and Attitudinal Objectives: A Paradox. *Journal of Curriculum Studies*, **13**, 4

Zeichner, K.M. & Liston, D.P. (1987) Teaching Student Teachers to Reflect. *Harvard Educational Review*, **57**(1), 23–48

Early childhood teacher education in the United Kingdom

LINDA POUND and MICHAEL BUCKINGHAM

Roehampton Institute, London, UK

(Received August 1991)

This paper presents a review of the roots of early childhood education in England and Wales and the recent pressures on the training institutions in regard to the form and content of teacher preparation.

Key words: Early childhood Teacher Education, UK

INTRODUCTION

Early childhood education is in this country more a concept than a tangible and coordinated entity. The facts that the United Kingdom has a relatively early age of entry into statutory schooling, that schools and teachers at all levels, have until recently maintained a high degree of autonomy of action, and that much pre-statutory provision falls outside the maintained sector in a confusing variety of institutions, have meant that the field of early childhood education is a complex and convoluted one.

The education of young children in the United Kingdom can broadly be characterised as having two distinct strands. One is drawn from nineteenth century elementary schooling, which can be characterised as having an emphasis on behaviourism, instrumentalism, passivity and discipline. It is an approach that arose in particular with the introduction of compulsory schooling and the need for teachers to prepare large numbers of hitherto unschooled sectors of the population for the labour market. The other strand of early childhood education is the so-called nursery tradition, which was rooted in the mysticism and spiritualism of the early writers and practitioners such as Rousseau and Froebel, in the altruism and social concern of those like Robert Owen, Maria Montessori and the McMillan sisters, and in the developmental insights of Susan Isaacs. In the United Kingdom these two strands may be identified as nursery (three to five years of age and non-statutory) and infant (post-statutory, five to seven years of age) provision, although this is by no means a clear-cut distinction.

There are a number of confusing overlaps which make the term early childhood education a more appropriate one than either nursery or infant schooling/ education. The nursery schools and classes offer education to children under five, although the pioneers of the nursery tradition had not envisaged that the methods and philosophies which they were developing would be applied only to the non-statutory sector. Infant schools on the other hand teach children, including many who are not yet of statutory school age, in conditions constrained by numbers and funding.

It is against this background that early childhood education has evolved. Although the American literature has long employed the term and in 1974 Barbara Tizard published a book, in this country, entitled *Early Childhood Education*, the term has only relatively recently been used to any great extent in the United Kingdom. Hitherto nursery and infant education were widely seen as two entirely separate entities, representing non-satutory and statutory fields. Indeed the Plowden Report, published in 1967, and considered to be the handbook of progressive primary education, probably unwittingly had the effect of further separating the two sectors. In the compensatory climate of the day, nursery education was seen as important but, like the involvement of parents, not for its own sake, but because it was thought to prepare children for school. They would thus be enabled to make better use of their opportunities within statutory schooling when the time came.

It is perhaps during the 1980s that the term has gained general currency. Could it be that the climate fostered by the "deschoolers", which led many to favour a non-statutory rather than a compulsory school system throughout childhood and adolescence, meant that attention focussed strongly on the non-statutory element of education widely perceived as the most successful, namely nursery education? Criticisms of nursery education, based on classroom research, e.g., Bruner (1980) and Tizard and Hughes (1984) shocked many nursery practitioners but led them to reflect on their practice and to re-assert and rethink their principles. This process of reflection may have been, in part responsible for a rash of publications on the subject of early childhood education during the latter part of the 1980s (Blenkin & Kelly, 1988; Bruce, 1987; Clark, 1988; Cohen & Cohen, 1988a & 1988b; Dowling, 1988, etc.). Many of these books were written by teacher educators who welcomed the new spirit of reflection within the teaching profession.

Furthermore, American studies looking at the long-term effects of early education (e.g., Schweinhart *et al.*, 1986) cannot easily be interpreted within British schools because of the age differences in pupils commencing compulsory schooling. Similarly as the United Kingdom has turned its sights towards Europe, the early age of compulsory school admission has conflicted with common European practice and made practitioners in this country more aware of some of the anomalies between nursery and infant practice. It may be that current legislation surrounding the introduction of the national curriculum together with widespread concern about the low-level of child care facilities may further blur the edges between nursery and infant education — an event which will undoubtedly be in the interests of early childhood education, and hence in the interests of young children.

The teaching of young children in the United Kingdom differs in other important ways from much of the rest of the world. For example, no distinction is made between training, status and pay according to the age phase taught. Nursery teachers are trained and qualified to teach the age range 3–7, but many may teach children up to 11 years of age and are, in fact at the time of writing, eligible to teach pupils throughout the school system. There are many strengths to this arrangement. It ensures that teachers of young children receive substantial training at a level commensurate with other areas of higher education. This is turn enhances the status and influence of early years provision and ensures that inservice training for the up-dating of skills is treated equally with other age phases. It also ensures that candidates of high calibre seek to enter the profession, and this in turn provides at least the possibility of a pool of expertise for the next generation of teacher trainers in the field of early childhood education.

This apparent equality of provision has, however, disadvantages. The demand for early years teachers was so great in the 1960s that initial teacher training courses often included substantial specialist elements, including nursery education. By the late 1970s however, the huge drop in the birth-rate resulted in a number of newly qualified teachers, particularly those trained to teach young children since that was inevitably the sector first affected by a declining birth-rate, being unable to find jobs. This decline in demand, which incidentally followed hard on the heels of a period of immense expansion in teacher education, led to rapid contraction in colleges of education. This, coupled with the fact that parity of training gave no protection to early childhood education as a specialism, left many education departments of training institutions denuded of early years tutors. As a reaction to these hard and unpredictable times, colleges tended to design courses offering training for a broader age range than had hitherto been the case, both to ensure greater job flexibility for teachers in training and to minimise the effects of the loss of specialist staff.

The education of the teachers of young children was, in many cases, thus grouped with the whole of the primary age phase and thereby lost much of its distinctive qualities. In courses catering for students training to teach children from 3–13 years of age, the study of child development, vital to the teacher of young children, became much reduced in order to allow space for a broad and detailed curriculum content knowledge to teachers of older pupils. Current developments within the Department of Education and Science stipulate that courses should be divided into groups focussing on 3–8 and 7–12 years but even so current political concerns have continued to lead institutions to feel that curriculum content must have priority.

EARLY DEVELOPMENTS IN EARLY CHILDHOOD EDUCATION

Nursery education is in the United Kingdom a relatively scarce commodity. Pre-statutory provision, though difficult to compare because of differing ages of compulsory schooling and different standards of provision, appears to be lower than that in any other European country, with the exception of Portugal (Moss, 1988). Despite its scarcity, nursery education has enjoyed a strong reputation as being, at its best, amongst the best in the world. It is securely based on what Lesley Webb (1974) has called the *common law* of British nursery education, and Jerome Bruner (1980) termed "the extreme dogmatism" of the nursery tradition.

Tessa Blackstone (1971) has suggested that the nursery tradition has both middle- and working-class roots. Working class provision began in the early part of the nineteenth century with the opening of Robert Owen's workplace nursery in New Lanark. More extensive working class provision was not to emerge until preparation for the Boer War convinced government that the nation's future was in jeopardy, the health and well-being of many British children being at risk. Margaret and Rachel McMillan were instrumental in the development of nursery education at this stage, although they did not regard the provision they made as in any sense compensatory. They were clear that the provision they offered was to educate the whole child, body, mind and spirit. This however could only be achieved if all aspects were taken into account — a healthy mind depended upon a healthy body, a healthy body depended upon fresh air, sleep and a nearness to nature. The success of such approaches to the care and education of young children is underlined by the fact that in the 1920s a rich American parent living in London established the Chelsea Open Air Nursery School for "the cripples of Chelsea", children who were so well provided for that their very affluence disabled them. Such was the influence on early childhood education as a whole of these and other socially aware pioneers of nursery schooling that the fact that Montessori schools are today very much the province of rich and middle class families causes no public surprise, despite the fact that their methods were developed with the needs of the socially disadvantaged firmly in mind. Indeed the sons of the Prince and Princess of Wales attended a Montessori nursery school from the age of three. This is of course a very far cry from the compensatory programmes of nursery education which sprang up in the second half of the twentieth century.

The introduction of middle class nursery provision was marked by the first Froebelian kindergarten in the United Kingdom, which was opened in London in 1851. Blackstone (1971) suggests that the middle and working class strands of provision were drawn together during the early part of the twentieth century by the growth of developmental psychology and rising interest in the study of child development, a movement strongly represented by the work of Susan Isaacs, whose own provision at the Malting House School was firmly rooted in the middle classes. This, Blackstone suggests, produced in the United Kingdom a distinctive, though numerically limited, form of nursery education in nursery schools and classes, which is graphically described in Board of Education publications (1933, 1936). What emerges is a picture of smiling, playing children — eager to learn, gardening, singing, receiving a gentle introduction to the aesthetics and being nurtured, body, mind and soul — in short the British nursery tradition.

Infant education has in some senses a quite separate historical background. It derived from the elementary schools and from the dame schools, and is, in the first fifty years of compulsory schooling at least, stereotypically portrayed as adopting rigid, formal and harsh pedagogical approaches. While there can be no doubt that some schools with more liberal styles existed, we can be equally certain that overcrowding, the "payment-by-results" scheme which closely accompanied the introduction of compulsory schooling, and an underdeveloped pedagogy focussing on what had to be taught rather than the learning process, all contributed to a generally harsh system. Indeed at the turn of the century one of the motivating factors for the McMillan sisters to develop alternative approaches to the education of young children was the sight of pupils of three and four years of age tied to serried rows of desks in elementary classrooms. With the introduction of the Revised Code, which related teachers' income to children's attainment, elementary classes contained an increasing number of children of three and four years of age (Whitbread, 1972) whom it was anticipated would be enabled by an early start in school to achieve a higher standard by the time they reached the age of testing at seven. Social factors connected with the Industrial Revolution also played, of course, an important part in this pattern of early school admission. Many mothers needed to work, older brothers and sisters were, with the introduction of compulsory schooling, no longer available to mind their younger siblings, and, neither government nor employers saw the provision of childcare facilities as part of their role.

During the inter-world war period, nursery education began to be recognised as efficacious by the government of the day. The 1933 Board of Education report on nursery and infant schools commented on "the evidence of their eyes" in recognising the worth of nursery education. It was at this period that infant education began to change too, at least in its theoretical approaches. Selleck (1972) has very thoroughly researched the rise of progressivism, and its impact on elementary schooling during this period up until 1939.

In many important respects developments in early childhood education and the appropriate training of teachers have gone hand in hand. Teacher training courses in the earlier part of the century generally had a strong philosophical base coupled with dedicated and close attention to practice. This ensured high quality practitioners who had a clear idea of what they were doing and why they were doing it. The early years (3–7 years) in teacher education often led the field in terms of prestige. Teachers holding a Froebel certificate were highly valued.

The post war era in higher education brought about many changes, especially in public perceptions of the teachers' role and what constituted "professionalism". The growth in academic fields such as behavioural psychology with its emphasis on measurement and objectivity increasingly exposed a lack of "theoretical" underpinning in much of teacher education. At the same time the works of Jean Piaget were beginning to be translated into English and their significance to the early years was immediately seized upon. Therefore a variety of conflicting factors brought about a gradual transformation in teacher education.

Early years trainers had always been vulnerable to the rather repressive and instrumental views of childhood. Existing theories of learning did not sit comfortably with progressive views of education. The new climate of academic studies, heralded in particular by the work of Susan Isaacs and her appointment as head of the newly formed Department of Child Development at London's Institute of Education in 1933, led them to seek support and justification through focussing on children's learning, linked to mainstream schools of psychology. Thus the important insights of early practitioners, like Froebel and the McMillan sisters, came to be linked with the theoretical insights of Klein, Burt and Piaget. Not only did this marriage add intellectual weight to the Froebelian movement, but the relationship was responsible for the enormous impact of Piagetian theory on teacher training in this country.

DEVELOPMENTS POST-1960

In 1975, what was to become known as the William Tyndale affair broke. It was to have an inordinate impact on British education. A member of the staff of the William Tyndale Primary School in London joined with a group of parents in voicing anxieties about the teaching style and approaches of the headteacher and some of the staff. From small beginnings, levels of disquiet grew, eventually prompting the local education authority to instigate an enquiry. The Auld Report (1976) which enquired into events at William Tyndale School was critical of the low level of control exercised by the local education authority itself, and the whole incident is therefore widely viewed as sounding the death-knell of the high degree of autonomy which British primary schools had hitherto enjoyed. In the same year, 1976, the Prime Minister, James Callaghan, spoke publicly at Ruskin College in Oxford of "the secret garden of the curriculum" and it was this speech which was to pave the way for demands from politicians of all shades that education should be more accountable to the public at large.

The William Tyndale affair was preceded by a range of circumstances which contributed to its impact. The first of these factors was the phasing out of a selective, two- and, in some cases, three-tier system of secondary education, in favour of a comprehensive system in the late 1960s. This government decision gave primary schools the opportunity to try out a range of theoretical and philosophical ideas and to investigate their practical application. As the constraints and pressures placed on primary schools by secondary schools lessened a period of experimentation ensued.

It was during this period too that the Plowden Report was published. Its publication, a further factor leading up to the William Tyndale affair, is widely believed to have been the signal for the widespread expansion of child-centred ideology. As Sylva and Halsey (1987) have pointed out, however, the Plowden Report has had a much stronger influence on educational theory than on classroom practice.

Primary schools, thus freed from the pressures of testing children at the age of eleven, with the official blessing of a government-instigated report and with the relative autonomy which British schools had enjoyed over many years, rapidly filled, since school rolls were expanding, with teachers whose training rested heavily on widely differing interpretations of Piagetian theory. The United Kingdom's reputation for child-centred education gradually evolved. During the 1970s certain British primary schools were inundated with a stream of overseas visitors, in particular from the United States, seeking the holy grail of child-centred ideology in action. Oxfordshire and the West Riding of Yorkshire formed the epicentres of these visits with their strong reputation for active learning, an integrated day, project-based work, vertical grouping, open plan schools, aesthetic display and close observation of natural materials. These pedagogical elements were widely viewed as fundamental to child-centred education, the schools employing such techniques as representing the essence of British infant education.

In the 1960s examples of the successful application of child-focussed psychological theories — and the freedoms brought by the abolition of selection to different status secondary (high) schools — created an atmosphere of renaissance in British primary teacher education. The government report in 1967 chaired by Lady Plowden gave widely publicised blessing for all teacher training colleges to adopt Piagetian ideology. Unfortunately, Piaget was interpreted in as many different ways as there were institutions of training. Since his concern was not pedagogy but epistemology, Piagetian theory was not informative on language and reading development, but it was widely interpreted as though it were. Although Froebelian teacher training was not alone in adopting Piagetian ideas, it was there arguably seen at its best. The philosophical harmony of Froebelian ideas appeared to ensure that the application of Piagetian concepts were appropriately thought through. Neither the ideas of Froebel nor of Piaget matched their popular image. Neither theory was "child centred" in the way that they are widely perceived to be. Neither theorist held sentimental views about children nor did they see the role of the caring adult as being passive in the learning situation. Both, in their separate ways, emphasised the need for structure in the experience and in the reflection of that experience.

During this period, training courses were still widely organised into the history, philosophy and psychology of education, and it is undoubtedly this structure which led many colleges to place great emphasis on the study of Piagetian theory, rather than the practical settings with which they sometimes conflicted. It has been suggested that colleges with a behaviourist background were ideologically ill prepared for this task. Here Piagetian concepts were sometimes taken too literally, for example, gearing the teaching of reading to rigid interpretations of staged development. Thus if children did not display the appropriate "readiness" behaviour, popular interpretations of Piaget's views led many teachers to suppose that the children were to be simply left until they were ready.

This orientation was reflected in teacher education, where the study of "Education" expanded to consider these issues. In most colleges, disciplines tutors received a significant boost to their status and position and successfully reinforced the view that students be initiated into the ways of disciplinary thought before they could appreciate the full complexities of what they were looking at. By the mid seventies, early years trainees could spend their final "honours" year studying the disciplines and subject study with no practical application at all.

The study of the disciplines included not only those of instrumental value, e.g., psychology and sociology, but also philosophy which it was argued was essential to understand *before* one could get on the inside of other disciplines. But philosophy did not just provide intellectual tools, it explored ideas about education, the nature of social order and underlying value systems.

These academic differences unhappily coincided with long standing differences that had grown up between nursery (non-statutory) and infant school reception (statutory) classes. Nursery schools were widely perceived as offering informal and largely unstructured experiences with a heavy emphasis on play and fresh air. This perception lingers despite the fact that much of the earliest nursery provision was by current British perceptions quite heavily structured. Imaginative play was not regarded by the followers of Montessori, for example, as being an appropriate vehicle for learning. The early practitioners had not seen the basic skills as being outside the domain of the nursery teacher. A government report published in 1933 had suggested, citing Froebelian principles, that the child should begin reading when he or she appeared to be ready "whether this be 3 or 6". The emphasis on didacticism in primary schools at that time together with the fact that theoretical understandings of neither reading nor children's learning were sufficiently well-developed to give most practitioners insight into how such learning might be achieved in ways which did not violate the philosophies underpinning nursery education led to a form of protection-ism or isolationism. Many nursery teachers sought to protect those children who were lucky enough to have a nursery place from an instrumentally based curriculum. They sought also to protect children from a pedagogy prevalent within the elementary tradition which intuitively felt to many inappropriate at that time. Their view is, incidentally, given support by current and recent research into children's learning and the effects of early education which would seem to underline the importance of a curriculum which offers children the opportunity to initiate their own learning (Schweinhart et al., 1986; Osborn & Milbank, 1987; Wells, 1985).

Thus, perhaps not surprisingly, the then dominant areas of the curriculum, reading, writing and arithmetic, came to be seen as the province of the infant school teacher, and not the domain of the nursery. This polarisation led to a strange anomaly whereby the teaching of certain curriculum areas such as reading were deemed appropriate for children in reception classes, who might not yet be five years of age, but inappropriate for children in nursery classes, who might indeed be five, although not yet of statutory school age. In like manner, as recently as 1982 (Cleave et al.), teachers were being advised that children entering reception classes would benefit from "pre-school materials", namely sand, water and the like. In other words, what is being suggested conveys the message that what is appropriate material provision for four and five year olds in nursery classes is not to be necessarily viewed as appropriate material for children of the same age in reception classes.

In parallel with the developments in the study of children's learning were new curricular developments that exploited these perceptions. Mathematics was one such area, where schools adopted elements of what was termed *new mathematics*. The fundamental difference between the new and the old was that the former was designed for an active enquiring child who investigated open-ended, problematical situations, whereas the latter required the child to correctly respond to proscribed solutions. Not only was the role of the learner very different; so was the role of the teacher. The new curriculum required the teacher to be a guide, an appraiser who helped the children develop their own ideas through skilled interpretation of the children's reactions and a detailed knowledge of the content of the material being studied. Whilst the *method* was commonplace in nursery schools the new curriculum objectives were not. At infant school level neither applied.

Teacher trainers were then confronted by a number of connected problems: to create an effective link between theory and curriculum practice, to reorientate the curricular thinking of students who themselves had been raised on the "old" system, and not least to inform themselves of all that was going on. Attempts to instigate approaches to teacher education which more closely linked theory and practice often ran up against the now entrenched "disciplines" approach that had become institutionalised in much of teacher education. Lecturing staff had been appointed with an educational discipline, appointed as history, philosophy or psychology lecturers, and therefore felt constrained to protect and enhance their disciplines' standing. They insisted that students had to "get on the inside of the thinking" of the discipline before they could apply it to integrated contexts. Constraints of time often reduced or fragmented this integration, thus leaving many students with a feeling that much of their course had been not entirely relevant.

This is a good point at which to exorcise the ghost of British primary school "progressivism". As was mentioned above, British primary schools had become a mecca for many overseas educators, whose perceptions were not entirely accurate. As Simon (1985) and HMI surveys (1978, 1982) have indicated, child-centred education as exemplified in these heavily visited schools was very far from the norm nationally. Most teachers in most primary schools, it appeared, continued to operate in "traditional" ways, devoting most classroom time to writing and computation, drill and practice.

Many colleges had moved ahead with the few progressive schools, thus losing touch with much of mainstream British education. Indeed, many classroom teachers not only distrusted what students were being asked to undertake while on teaching practice but found themselves quite out of sympathy with what was being taught in colleges. Attempts were made on all sides to try to communicate but fundamental differences in outlook made progress difficult. Parents were affected too. A curious phenomenon meant that primary schools were widely perceived as offering new and markedly different curricula and pedagogy, at a time when we know that in general neither had changed much from pre-war practices. This perception, as we shall see was to have immense consequences throughout education. Of course, there were innovations, particularly in the classrooms of young and newly trained teachers, but when challenged by older colleagues or by parents worried about their children's progress, changed approaches were difficult to sustain. Where the training had been inadequate or at odds with the practice in the school the young teachers were in a weak position to justify their practice, and even some of those whose training had been sound found it hard to explain the theoretical underpinning, especially to lay persons. This became even more true when high-powered academics produced a series of papers, known as the Black Papers which decried changing approaches to teaching, and were in particular critical of those aspects of education supported by the Plowden Report.

A further strand of change in education emerged, or, more accurately for the early years, re-emerged, in the form of concern about deteriorating conditions in many city centres. Concern for equality and justice in the euphoric post-war United Kingdom which fathered the National Health Service and the 1944 Education Act, soon faltered on class issues. Wells and Nicholls (1985) have given a helpful overview to this, in relation to research into language development and its impact on educational

success. The impact of a period of intense growth in teacher education, at a time when
the social deficit theories of Bernstein were first mooted, is still being felt. As Wells
and Nicholls (1985) write:

The comforting notion that some children were failing to learn in School because they spoke a
"restricted code" — assumed to mean "working-class" language — spread much more rapidly
in educational circles than do most theoretical ideas.

To the challenges facing a teaching force largely convinced of the value of deficit
theories and compensatory provision must be added the dimension of race. Although
there have been black workers in the United Kingdom since the time of Elizabeth I,
the 1950s saw an influx of invited low paid immigrant workers whose children entered
inner-city schools in increasing numbers during the 1960s and 1970s, alongside
working class white indigenous children who were already widely perceived as
requiring compensatory programmes of education. The combination of Black and
Asian parents, who had expected much of the British education system, and white
teachers, products of an endemically racist society, brought up on books like *Little
Black Sambo* and *Dr Dolittle*, who had very low expectations of their pupils, was to
prove to be of great concern within the education system.

The underlying assumptions engendered by the climate of teacher education in the
1960s and 1970s, with its emphases on sometimes simplistic interpretations of the
work of Piaget, created in some inner city teachers, the view that the inner city
children they taught were not "ready" for curricular activities. Ensuing concern
about the widespread failure within school of black and working class children
triggered further concern about traditional classroom approaches. The late 1960s and
early 1970s saw, for example, the emergence of the writings of the "deschoolers", a
diverse group of educationalists, mainly though not exclusively American, who
regarded many existing statutory school practices as harmful to children, and in need
of radical reform or abolition. Perhaps a tiny minority of teachers shared, or even
knew about their views, but the public and media perception was that vast numbers
of the teaching profession were radical extremists at pains only to undermine the
public schooling system.

The changes in infant practice which triggered the William Tyndale affair, though
they may in many cases have been more imagined than real, more theoretical than
practical, helped to narrow the gap between the nursery and infant sectors of
education. Over many years infant teachers have increasingly adopted many of the
practices, more widely regarded as nursery practice. The involvement of parents,
vertical as opposed to horizontal grouping, integrated day organization all owe much
to the nursery tradition. The gap has also been narrowed by developments in
theoretical understandings of the teaching of reading. The writings of theorists like
Smith (1972), Butler (1979), and Meek (1982) have led many nursery and infant
teachers to reassess their classroom approach to literacy (Pound 1984). This has
resulted in a far more coherent policy across the two sectors, and is closely related to
the increasing concern for continuity (Cleave *et al.*, 1982; Blatchford *et al.*, 1982).

The effect of this coming closer together in the schools coincided in the mid 1970s
with a dramatic drop in the birthrate. Many nurseries were absorbed into reception

classes, as space became available in primary schools and pupils were wooed with offers of nursery places. The effects on teacher supply, as has been indicated, were such that nursery provision almost ceased to be a separate study and was absorbed into courses on primary teaching.

THE "GREAT EDUCATIONAL DEBATE"

The anxieties that followed the Tyndale affair and the Prime Minister's Oxford speech did not go away. There was an intuitive feeling, promoted by the tabloid press, that all was not well with the Education service; this concern was not only about the schools and who controlled them, it was also about the quality of teaching and what teachers knew.

There had long been a view that teachers were often poorly educated in their own right, and as such functioned more as technicians than professionals. In 1960, the rise in expectations after the war, increasing pressure from government, the inspectorate and the unions led to a change in teacher training from two to three years. An important element in this lengthened course was to be the "subject study", taken at the students own level (e.g., history, science). By the 1970s continued pressure brought about the introduction of teaching degrees with their optional "honours" year at the end. Tension grew between the subject departments and education as to where the extra time was to be spent. The uniformity that had characterised much of initial training for half a century was eroded; some courses had as much as fifty percent on subject studies, others had none. This conflict became a major issue in the controversial reforms of teacher education in the following decade.

In 1972 a government report was published (chaired by Professor James) which reviewed the provision in higher education, including teacher training. A major recommendation was that intending teachers should be educated people in their own right; that either they took a degree first before their initial teacher training (ITT) or that the ITT course should include a substantial element of subject study that was geared to the students' academic development rather than the school curriculum. Furthermore, it was considered beneficial if intending teachers studied this subject alongside those who were studying for non-professional qualifications. The report's recommendations on the improvement to inservice education for teachers had some effect but little other than this last provision was taken up at the time.

The sudden cut back in teacher numbers due to the fall in the birthrate caused many colleges to implement the James' proposals, but more from the need for survival than from any great enthusiasm for diversification of course programmes. This coincided with a move to an all-graduate profession. Many colleges of education merged with one another, or with polytechnics or universities. To create viable course programmes teaching students were often shoehorned into general BA/BSc programmes whose structure took no account of teaching practice. Thus within a few short years the broad national commonality of teacher training courses was lost, and wide discrepancies in content and course programmes emerged. Further, resources were often diverted from teacher programmes to help the fledgling diversified courses, thus leading to large teacher training classes and the trimming of programmes of study.

During this period the outside pressures detailed above which called for improvements to teacher training put additional pressures on course programmes. Ever reluctant to abandon anything, colleges added new courses, e.g., special needs, multicultural education, sex education, inner-city education, information technology, equal opportunities and so on. In some cases this resulted in further trimming or dilution of traditional areas of curriculum study, in others it resulted in the adoption of professional studies "option" courses where students chose from a wide range of offerings. This meant that the early years student could graduate having "opted" not to study the teaching of science or music.

The Department of Education (DES), worried about public concern over teaching standards in schools, and about the multitude of directions in teacher education, set up a committee in 1981 to review the whole procedure of teacher training. A draft consultative document appeared in 1982 and the final — and little altered version — came out in March 1983.

The ensuing White Paper (a proposal to Parliament) argued for three main reforms:

(a) the setting up of a national Council for the Accreditation of Teacher Education courses (CATE)

(b) the setting up of "local committees" — comprising school teachers, local education officers, business persons as well as college tutors

(c) the construction of criteria which had to be met before the local committee and Council could recommend a course for DES approval.

Much of the White Papers recommendations were clearly sensible, especially those requiring college tutors to periodically spend time out in school refreshing their own expertise. Minimum hours spent studying mathematics and language teaching, minimum hours for other subjects in the curriculum were generally welcomed moves. However, an almost universal condemnation came concerning the criterion which required *two full years* subject study (of which a quarter was to include its application in the classroom). The declared intention behind this proposal was to improve the depth of subject understanding in the student, so that he or she not only effected a better content in his or her own lessons, but could also act as a curriculum leader within the school. The effect of this proposal would be to cut the study of Education to a bare minimum, thus extinguishing the disciplines and reducing the study of educational contexts to a minimum.

Critics claimed that this proposal was completely irrelevant to the teacher of the early years; courses needed to be broadly based with a great deal of attention to child development and practical application. Furthermore, as, on average, British primary schools comprised four teachers only, and most teachers studied liberal arts or humanities as their subject at initial level, how did this "reform" do anything for the sciences? Such arguments however proved ineffectual.

It became clear at conference after conference that the model of the teacher in the minds of the government and some members of the inspectorate was that of a secondary (high school) teacher whose stock-in-trade was their main subject. The principal role of the primary school was apparently seen by these sectors as essentially an instrumental one, providing the grounding in subject studies for later work at secondary level. Fundamental questions about the nature of early years education were not addressed at this stage. The expectation was, that like all other teachers, early childhood specialists would undertake the role of curriculum consultant within the school.

So concerned were many primary teacher trainers that they set up a national organisation to represent their views to government and lobby on behalf of the primary movement. Despite their efforts, the White Paper became law and every college had to submit its courses for approval. The "rejection" rate was predictably high, for few were easily able or willing to initiate such change. However, the total inflexibility of the CATE committees eventually convinced all that the changes had to be complied with, though it was rumoured that much "creative accounting" was done with course titles!

THE NATIONAL CURRICULUM

Following their election success in 1987 the Conservative government returned with renewed vigour and sought to reform the curriculum of all state maintained schools, to introduce a "national" curriculum for all state schools. It had been one of the more interesting characteristics — if not idiosyncrasies — of British education, that the curriculum was largely determined at local level. The only previous directive occurred in the 1944 Act requiring religious knowledge to be taught in every school. Thus the government could lay some claim to entitling their proposals as the Great Education Reform Bill, which was immediately dubbed by a largely hostile teaching profession as GERBILL (sic).

The Bill, which became law in the summer of 1988, laid down curricular requirements, including a substantial element of science and technology, and programmes of assessment at 7, 11, 14 and 16 years to check that the curriculum was being "delivered". Results of these assessments are to be made public (in the case of seven year olds publication is advised but has not been made a legal requirement) and available to help parents in making the choice of school for their offspring. As the schools revenue — and hence, teachers salaries — will depend on their recruitment success, the pressures to "succeed" in attainment terms are clear.

The National Curriculum begins with the early years, though to be fair, most teachers would now admit that the programmes of study are not in themselves antipathetical to the present view of early years education. There are some signs that the government's declared intention to provide an entitlement curriculum for all children may be having an effect. Children are to be taught science and technology, subjects which have hitherto had a relatively low profile in infant classes. Current concern lies with the application of market forces which the Act intends to unleash, together with the associated model of assessment. Many teachers fear the return of pressures being fed down from older age groups thus distorting the processes of education towards a product model, and away from the process model of early childhood education which has been evolving throughout this century.

Two principal factors have now emerged in government thinking. The first is to train teachers (that term has now slipped back into fashion in the DES) to "deliver" the National Curriculum. This implies that such training must be provided at both inservice and initial levels. Even before all the colleges have been inspected by the CATE, the criteria which colleges have been struggling to achieve need revision. In a consultative paper published in May 1989, the criteria have been amended to include a substantial element of science and technology (now equal to language and mathematics). Early schoolers will be required to study these subjects for around 60% of the time, and their teachers, although willing, will need help in achieving this.

A second problem to emerge was foreseen in the last decade, namely that the large drop in the birthrate would work its way through to create a serious labour shortage in the 1990s. Teacher shortages, in the field of early childhood education, are already present in the London area because of high housing costs and low salaries. An inevitably worrying state of affairs is being taken seriously by those responsible for state education since teacher shortage will do more than any other single factor to threaten the National Curriculum. For early years provision, at least, there is a very tempting solution in the offing. The country has long had a scheme for minimally qualified school leavers to train from 16 years of age as nursery nurses. The output qualification after two years of further education (NNEB) does not provide them with access to higher education. The careers thus currently open to them, mainly in the field of day care, offer little prospect of promotion and very little status. Many of these nursery nurses have a great deal of valuable experience in work with young children. Many have worked alongside highly trained nursery teachers, and in nursery schools in particular, have received in-service training. As mature and experienced entrants, NNEB qualified students could cope well with the professional part of the teaching degree. Various access schemes have been experimented with to enable such practically experienced but under-qualified people to have the opportunity to train as teachers. These schemes have not as yet met with great success but at the time of writing at least two additional strands are being developed.

The first is the government's licensed teacher scheme, whereby any adult with two years' higher education can apply through a local education authority for qualified teacher status. The second involves an organisation, The National Council for Vocational Qualifications, set up by the government whose role is to develop a system of accreditation which will enable professional and vocational qualifications to be accumulated over a period of time, taking account of practical experience. Accreditation of qualifications for work with young children and possible links with teacher education are being considered.

CURRENT ISSUES

Early childhood education in the United Kingdom currently faces a number of important issues. Some have only an indirect link with teacher education, all have some relevance since they inevitably will face newly qualified teachers going into the classroom for the first time.

Amongst the most important of these issues is the age of entry into school. The statutory age of entry into school in England and Wales is the start of the term after children have reached the age of five. An increasing number of local authorities (Cleave et al., 1985) have adopted a policy of admitting children only at the start of the academic year during which they will be five. Policies do vary from one authority to another — some have one admission date each year, some two (generally in September and January), and some have three (at the beginning of each of the three terms of the academic year). Some admit children before and some after their fifth birthday and, as Clark (1988, p. 35) indicates, this means that children are receiving markedly different amounts of time in school.

Many parents like their children to start school early. In most cases this is undoubtedly because they believe that an early start will give their children an academic advantage, although there is no evidence that early admission into primary school enhances children's attainment in the long term. In many cases it is also because of the absence of appropriate day care and other forms of non-statutory provision for under fives. Working parents, or parents who want their children to have the opportunity to mix with their peers may regard early admission into primary school as their only choice. Local education authorities and administrators favour simplified admission policies. Because the provision is non-statutory it can be used, at times of a low birth rate, to fill empty classrooms and thus have the political expediency of meeting parents' demands. When birth rates rise the policy can be shifted to accommodate more children of statutory school age, fewer under fives. The element of political expediency is further supported by the fact that under fives thus accommodated in primary classrooms appear in statistics as enjoying the benefits of nursery education, with none of the usual costs to the local education authority.

Some teachers also support the early entry of children into primary school. Some, sad to say, are nursery teachers who feel unable to sufficiently extend children's learning. This may be a terrible indictment of training in some institutions. It is also in all probability the result of the low status with which nursery education is endowed and the consequent low self-esteem of many nursery teachers. Infant teachers may feel that the pressures on them to ensure children's high achievement require an early start to their formal schooling.

This erosion of statutory ages of school entry has, as Margaret Clark (1988) points out occurred over many years, and it should perhaps be seen as positive that there is public concern about the position of four year olds in primary classes. The National Foundation for Educational Research has completed a research project to look into provision for children below the statutory age of school admission in statutory classrooms (Cleave & Brown, 1991), and their work is echoed by that of Bennett and Kell (1989). What can be learnt from international studies of the long-term effectiveness of early education (Schweinhart et al., 1986; Osborn & Milbank, 1987; Woodhead, 1987) is the fact that, in particular for some socially disadvantaged groups, provision in the early years which allows children to initiate and control much of their own learning, with low adult-child ratios, with the involvement of parents in their children's education and a reflective attitude on the part of the teachers has important long-term positive effects. These lessons have not yet been learnt by society.

A second area of concern is closely related to this. Early childhood education, at its best and as it has developed in this country, has much in common with what we know about effective early education. This by no means suggests we can be complacent, for as was pointed out in considering the development of early childhood education in this country, the theory is more highly developed and more widely understood than the practice. However at the stage when empirical evidence is lending support to the theory, and when teachers, in particular through the growth of action research and collaborative research are developing their classroom practice, there are perceived pressures towards a more instrumental system. The National Curriculum, together with the introduction of a unique national system for testing specified levels of attainment is causing immense anxiety amongst a teaching force demoralised by rapid change, by the removal of negotiating rights over pay and conditions of service and by media representation which has undermined status and morale. In addition, D.E.S. attention has now focussed on school effectiveness and classroom practice (D.E.S. 1992), suggesting a need for greater subject specialist teaching in Primary schools, if the National Curriculum is to be successfully delivered. There are slim but interesting indicators (Pound, 1986) that teachers who enjoy higher status, either through managerial responsibility or through further study are less likely to value instrumental purposes of education, and may be more likely to have more broadly based aims. National Curriculum legislation has by no means purely instrumental aims, but there is a grave danger that a teaching force perceiving itself as under threat will see its task in such terms.

The third area of concern, and a major one since it has a number of corollaries, is the separation of care and education in under-fives provision. Within the nursery tradition no such gap existed historically; the McMillan sisters for example were clear that children were only able to learn if their physical needs were being met. Infant education, as has already been indicated, had since its inception been regarded as fulfilling in part a baby-sitting role. It was only at the end of the Second World War that these kinds of differentiation were made, as Bowlby's theories captured the spirit of the time (Riley, 1983) and paralleled the financial wishes of the British administration.

The result, in very broad terms, has been a segregated provision with education for children under five being offered in somewhat idiosyncratic ways by local education authorities, mainly on a part-time basis, and day care, offering full-time provision financed by local councils and available only to children categorised according to social need. In this way, children who are at risk of abuse, physical, emotional or sexual, are the ones receiving the highest priority and therefore tending to take up almost all the available provision. Since nursery provision is, at its best labour-intensive and therefore expensive, offering priority to carefully selected and designated groups looks, at first glance, an attractive proposition. Research on the long-term effectiveness of early education tells us that nursery education is beneficial to the socially disadvantaged. The Warnock Report (1978) suggests that nursery education would be beneficial to children with learning difficulties, and as the inspectorate (1983) remind us, helpful in the *identification* of such children. Equally, the Swann Report (1985) underlines the importance of nursery education for black children and for those for whom English is a second language. Targeting of services to children at risk, and to specific groups of children will, as it already does in many cases, result in a segregated service which is not in the best interests of children.

The separation of care and education which has arisen, it can be argued, has, on the other hand, facilitated the growth of an education based service for children below the age of statutory schooling. Nursery *teachers* enjoy the same conditions of service, the same pay scales and the same level of qualification and education as all other teachers within the maintained sector. This has undoubtedly added to the status of nursery education, provided continuity for those children lucky enough to have nursery school or class places, and has ensured that the principles of nursery education have influenced the development of primary education, since the same teachers may be working in both the statutory and the pre-statutory phases. It has also meant of course that British nursery education is expensive.

Demographic trends, greater awareness of women's rights and concern for the quality of service available for young children are bringing about renewed demands for higher levels of day care. This, in turn, brings concerns about the role of expensively educated teachers within such a service, at a time in British political history when public sector spending is severely constrained. There are a number of workers with lower levels of academic qualifications who act as classroom assistants within the education sector, but who within the social services sector entirely staff and manage day care centres. In addition, some local authorities employ a number of unqualified workers as a matter of principle regarding their policy as an important strand in equalising opportunity. Further separation of care and education might make the employment of teachers across the two sectors difficult. HMI seem very much aware of this danger and at pains in a number of recent publications (1989a,b) to draw attention to the importance of nursery education, particularly in its role as a catalyst/model for good quality provision and in its ability to provide continuity of learning opportunity for young children. The Report of the Committee of Inquiry into the Quality of the Educational Experiences offered to 3- and 4-year-olds (DES 1991) recommended better overall co-ordination of services for the under fives, and the further development of combined centres, where day care and teaching staff can work closely to provide an integrated, flexible service.

Education in the United Kingdom is facing a period of immense change and challenge, as we move into the 1990s. Early childhood education inevitably provides the foundation for each child's future education. The education and training of teachers of young children must enable them to move out into schools and community aware of their immense responsibility, proud of their heritage and anxious to continue the pioneering tradition of British early childhood education. Only in this way can teacher education ensure that the quality of education will be safeguarded for all children.

References

Auld Report (1974)

Bennett, N. & Kell, J. (1989) *A Good Start?: four year olds in infant schools*: The William Tyndale School. HMSO, Oxford, Blackwell

The Plowden Report (1967) *Children and their Primary Schools*. London: HMSO

Blackstone, T. (1971) A Fair Start; The provision of preschool education. London. Penguin

Blatchford, P. et al. (1982) The First Transition. Windsor, NFER

Blenkin, G. & Kelly, A.V. (eds) (1988) *Early Childhood Education* London: Paul Chapman

Board of Education (1936) *Nursery schools and nursery classes* Educational Pamphlet No 1072, London, HMSO

Bruce, T. (1987) *Early Childhood Education* Sevenoaks: Hodder & Stoughton

Simon, B. (1985) *Does Education Matter?* London: Lawrence & Wishart

Bruner, J. (1980) *Under Five in Britain* London: Grant McIntyre

Smith, F. (1972) *Understanding Reading* NY: Rinehart and Winston

Butler, D. (1979) *Babies Need Books* London: Bodley Head

(The) Swann Report (1985) *Education for All* London: HMSO

Clark, M. (1988) *Children Under Five* London: Gordon and Breach, London

Sylva, K. and Halsey, A. (1987) Plowden: history and Prospect, Oxford Review of Education 13(4) 3–12

Cleave, S., Jowett, S. & Bate, M. (1984) *And so to school*. Windsor, NFER-Nelson

Cleave, S. & Brown, S. (1991) *Early to School* Windsor: NFER-Nelson

(The Warnock Report (1978) *Special Educational Needs* London: HMSO

Cohen, A. and Cohen, L. (eds) (1988a) *Early Education: the pre-school years.* London, Paul Chapman

Cohen, A. and Cohen, L. (eds) (1988b) *Early Education: the school years* London: Paul Chapman

Department of Education and Science (1982) The First School Survey. London, HMSO

Dept. of Education and Science (1978) *The Primary School Survey* London: HMSO

DES (1991) *Starting with Quality* (The Rumbold Report) London: HMSO

DES (1992) *Curriculum Organization and Classroom Practice in Primary Schools: A Discussion Paper* London: HMSO

Dowling, M.M. (1988) Education 3–5 yrs. London. Paul Chapman

Osborn, A. and Millbank, J. (1987) The Effects of Early Education, Oxford, Clarendon Press.

Pound, L. (1986) An Exploration of Nursery School Teachers' views of the Curriculum. Unpublished M.A. Thesis, University of Wells

Riley, D. (1983) War in the Nursery. London, Virago

Tizard, B. and Hughes, M. (1984). Young Children Learning. Fontana

Tizard, B. and Hughes, M. (1988) Young Children at School in the Inner City. Lawrence Erlbaum

Wells, G. and Nicholls, J. (1985) *Language and Learning: an interactional perspective.* Falmer Press

Wells, G. (1985) Language Development in the Pre-school years. Cambridge, CUP

(The) James Report (1972) *Teacher Education and Training* London: HMSO

Meek, M. (1982) *Learning to Read* London: Bodley Head

Early childhood teacher certification and credentialing in the United States

OLIVIA N. SARACHO

University of Maryland, College Park, Maryland, USA

BERNARD SPODEK

University of Illinois, Urbana Champaign, Illinois, USA

(Received August 1991)

This paper explores the requirements of certification and credentialing – aspects of a process which attempts to assure that individuals who work with children satisfy basic requirements in respect of training and experience, whether as teachers or child care personnel.

Key words: Early Childhood, certification, credentialing

INTRODUCTION

Teachers in early childhood education have a tremendous impact on society. Because of this importance, society, the state, teacher education institutions and other education agencies have established professional standards for being admitted into the teaching profession. These standards are embedded in the process of certifying or credentialing teachers. Unfortunately, the certification or credentialing of teachers has also been perceived as a weak procedure.

The purpose of this paper is to examine the certification and credentialing of early childhood personnel. In addition, a focus is placed in analytical suggestions which offer a promising future for teacher education programs.

Certification[1]

Certification is a "legal admittance to the profession." Its major purpose is to provide evidence that personnel possess the minimum competencies which they need for successful teaching. A teaching certificate attests that professionals have a "safe level"

---

[1]The term "certification" or "credentialing" refers to licensure.

43

of beginning teaching skills (Howsam, Corrigan, Denemark, & Nash, 1976) to initiate a prosperous teaching career. These are merely minimum qualifications which individuals must meet before they are permitted to teach. Policy control over teachers is mainly practiced to identify responsible competent individuals. Some standard qualifications for certification or credentialing are required to guarantee that early childhood educational personnel achieve a degree of professional competence.

The state establishes standards to certify competent teachers and keep the inferior and the poorly prepared out of the profession. Individual states usually offer teaching certificates for different levels of education (e.g., early childhood or elementary teachers) and for different subjects taught (e.g. science, reading). In some cases an initial teaching certificate, or "provisional certificate," is offered to beginning teachers. In order to receive a permanent certificate, teachers may be required to successfully complete a probationary period and pursue additional studies. The state legislatures consult with state departments of education (or state department of public instruction) before approving the qualifications which professional personnel must meet in order to become certified in a particular state. Standards and qualifications vary in each state, but a general agreement exists on the following (Hughes & Schultz, 1976):

1. Authority for the teachers' certification is centralized in the state department of education;
2. Certificates are issued based on subject fields or specified grade levels;
3. Certificates usually have to be renewed periodically;
4. A baccalaureate degree is required to attain a teaching certificate;
5. Certain courses in education and a specific number of semester hours in a subject matter or teaching field are required.

Acknowledging state and national standards, colleges and universities are the primary source of authority for the preparation of professionals. Most of the teacher preparation processes occur at the college or university level as the teaching certificate or credential usually has a baccalaureate degree as a prerequisite. Programs of teacher education include three types of courses: (1) courses for background education, (2) specialized courses for background education, and (3) specialized courses related to the individual's field.

Teacher candidates must attend and pass the courses which are prescribed in their educational plan, student teach under professional supervision, and provide evidence that they have acquired the minimum competencies to be certified by the state. Although the process of becoming a professional teacher has existed for some time, the process needs to be improved.

Levin (1980) proposes a number of stages for establishing out a policy for certification:

1. Specify educational outcomes or desirable teacher behaviors;
2. Establish a value or social utility for educational outcomes or teacher behavior;
3. Indicate teacher characteristics in relation to each outcome;

4. Identify alternative methods to assure the presence of the teacher characteristics.

This possibility has been challenged. Many states do not require a certificate of teachers who teach in non-public schools. Teacher certification is needed for public school teaching in all states. Many times standards do not exist for teachers in those schools which serve children below the age of public school entry. In addition, since child care centers are generally not perceived as schools, the requirements for teachers in these settings are not under the jurisdiction of education authorities. Qualifications for those working in nursery schools and child care centers are embedded in licensing standards of those institutions, established by the state agencies regulating those institutions (Spodek & Saracho, 1988).

The absence of certification standards for child-care workers and nursery schools equivalent to those for kindergarten and primary schools may be rooted in the economic as well as the academic interests. Child care practitioners are the lowest paid child welfare workers. Raising entry requirements for these practitioners would raise the pressure for higher pay and thus raise the cost of child care service (Spodek & Saracho, 1982, 1988).

Severe problems emerge in constructing systems for teacher education. Each teacher education program varies in its components and desirable outcomes. Such differences and a lack of knowledge based on teacher characteristics, which can be objectively assessed, create major obstacles for the present approach in teacher certification. Obstructions may be alleviated through a system which is based on some agreed goals and reasonable knowledge about the relationship between measurable teacher characteristics and outcomes.

Credentialing[2]

In 1971 the United States Office of Child Development (OCD), which later changed to the Administration for Children, Youth, and Families (ACYF), responded to the increased need of competent early childhood personnel who directly work in early childhood programs. OCD appointed a task force to explore the possibility of initiating a credential for early childhood staff. The task force suggested a process to assess basic competencies which will provide competent child care according to national standards leading to an acceptable national "credential" or "award" (Child Development Associate (CDA) National Credentialing Program, 1988, p. 41). To promote the acceptance of the new credential, a consortium was created, representing 39 professional organizations that were directly interested in early childhood education and child development. The consortium was responsible for assessing and awarding the credential.

---

[2]Certification system to assure that individuals who work with children in child care centers are qualified and have the right training and job experience.

The Child Development Associate Consortium (CDAC) is a credentialing agency without any responsibility for training. However, the purpose for this credential is to upgrade the quality of care for young children, whose ages range from three to five. This private and non-profit organization was funded by a division of the Office of Human Development, United States Department of Health, Education and Welfare. Its total membership consists of more than half a million persons who were directly concerned with the education and development of young children.

The CDAC developed and implemented a Credential Award System (CAS) to assess the caregivers' performance and to grant credentials in early childhood education/child development to competent individuals, as perceived by the profession, in caring for young children. The individual receiving this credential is called Child Development Associate (CDA). The CDA is considered a national credential and a new profession. However, the CDA Credential is not a professional award nor a license. Although several states endorse the CDA Credential as one way to upgrade the quality of child care, in other states the CDAC is working closely with officials of agencies (e.g., departments of education and child care licensing bureaus) to get them to recognize the CDA Credential. However, the CDAC is the only one authorized to award the CDA Credential, which has made it possible for some child care professionals to have received training and which has generated a thorough innovative method to credential personnel working directly with young children. The CDA program benefits the educationally disenfranchised (Peters, 1988), and offers the possibility to influence the hundreds of thousands of individuals who work with children but possess restricted levels of formal education. Individuals are assessed to verify they are competent enough to assume responsibility for a group of young children and to work with their parents. Formal or informal training may be required. The credential procedure utilizes competency standards as the reason to improve training and prepare assessment techniques.

Some colleges and universities, who are using the competency-based modular approach, have adopted the CDA competencies as part of their early childhood teacher education program. However, the CDA Credential is not interchangeable with any type of degree. Founders of the CDA clearly indicated that the credential is not equivalent to a standard associate or baccalaureate degree. They strongly believed that a college degree does not guarantee that a person can demonstrate the competencies which are essential to foster intellectual, social, physical and emotional growth in young children. The CDA Credential is based upon a performance-based assessment where an individual demonstrates to be able to assume primary responsibility for a group of young children rather than solely passing courses taken or academic affairs, earning credits or receiving any degrees.

Many educators urge that the CDA Credential be related to a degree. Since the CDA Credential enforces a competency-based approach, the consortium suggests that the teacher education programs modify or add requirements to their standard educational curriculum in order that AA or BA degree candidates can acquire both the degree and the CDA Credential.

Postulated Decisions

In considering a rational approach to teacher education preparation, certification and/or credentialing, the following decisions on the following questions must be finalized:

1. *What are the tasks which need to be done to support the education and care of young children?* Teacher education programs wanting to develop techniques to prepare people for a particular profession must carefully examine it using one of two methods:

A. *A Job Analysis.* A continuous observation at different times and on different dates of the individual can identify the teacher's tasks, while an analysis of the teacher's function can define the job.

B. *A Conceptual Analysis.* A well-planned analysis of the various role dimensions, which are usually apparent, in the early childhood teacher's performance.

Early childhood teachers provide more than classroom instruction or child-teacher interactions. Their professional functions outside the classroom include planning curriculum, organizing materials, evaluating learning, holding parent-teacher conferences and attending professional meetings. These types of activities may become part of the job analysis or conceptual analysis technique by conducting an interview with the teachers to inquire about the teaching behaviors which occur outside the classroom.

2. *What does a person need to know in order to perform the essential teaching tasks? What kind of skills, abilities, understanding, and the like are required for effective teaching?* The job analysis or conceptual analysis can be used as a prerequisite to a task analysis and then an analysis of requirements to each task. Thus, subdividing the larger dimensions of teachers into smaller tasks and determine their prerequisites.

3. *What kind of persons are effective in working with young children?* Teachers play a powerful role in the education of young children. Although there is no evidence that individuals with certain qualities or characteristics become effective teachers, the skills, abilities, understandings, basic human qualities and personal characteristics of people who are interested in working with young children need to be examined. This assessment can help screen the applicants in a teacher education program. Selection procedures can identify persons with required basic qualities and those individuals who have the potential to learn those which are learned.

4. *What means would be used to judge whether people who are completing a teacher education program have the knowledge and personal qualities which are required to become effective teachers? How can these people's capability to become effective teachers be assessed?* Some teacher preparation programs assess their students in terms of professional competencies, which were originally developed from observing and analyzing the teaching behavior of a teacher whom the program considered to be effective. The program teaches those behaviors and assesses them, based upon observable behavioral objectives. There are two problems with this process:

One, is that only part of the teaching behaviors can be observed in the classroom.

Jackson (1966) and Shulman (1986a), for example, describes two different phases of teaching: the pre-active and interactive phase. The interactive phase is the part of teaching which occurs in classrooms when teachers interact with children. The pre-active phase is everything which takes place prior to those interactions: the planning, the preparation, the provisioning, the organizing, the evaluation. These tasks occur when the children are not in the classroom and very often take place in a manner which is non-observable. If observable behaviors are the only ones assessed, two important components are neglected: (1) the behaviors which take place before and after school starts and (2) the most rational part of teaching. Although reason does not go out the window, once the teachers begin interacting with children, they do not have time to reflect upon spontaneous situations. Often times the teachers have to make instantaneous decisions. There are many demands on them and a large number of interactions which they have to respond to automatically and intuitively rather than in a rational mode. If two children are fighting, the teacher would not have an opportunity to say, "Let me look at the alternative ways I could respond to the children. Let me think about what the probability is of each of these alternatives in terms of change which might come about in that child's behavior. Then I shall make a decision." By the time the teacher analyzed the problem and made a decision, one of the children could be bloodied and bruised. The teacher needs to intervene and immediately respond.

The phrase "teacher behavior" are two words that have been paired almost automatically for many years in academic discussions of research on teaching, and have been deliberated to teaching policy. Research on teaching measures and manipulates these variables, and the focus on behavior has been the cornerstone of American psychology. Studies on teacher characteristics have failed to provide replicable results, the focus has turned to describing teachers' behaviors in the classroom, ways their behavior relate to student behavior, and ways training can modify their behavior (Shulman, 1986b).

The second problem with focusing on the observable is that many of the teachers' functions are not critical. The deviations in performance are often variations in style than differences in technique.

Saracho and Spodek (1981) describe two types of teaching styles: (1) field dependent (FD) in which teachers enhance interpersonal relations using discussion and discovery techniques and field independent (FI) in which teachers maximize interpersonal relations utilizing lecture, an indirect instructional strategy. FD teachers have a social interest and may emphasize social goals, while FI teachers are oriented towards striving and may focus on achievement goals. The children's and teachers' interactions in the classroom are supposed to affect the learning outcomes. Saracho (1980) found that the teachers' cognitive style (FD versus FI) made a powerful impact in the students' achievement scores. The students who were in the classroom with the FI teachers obtained higher scores than did the students who were in the classroom with the FD teachers. Although some educators affirm that teachers can be taught to function in a particular style, a great range of styles is legitimate and research has not fully shown that one style is better than others.

5. *What issues have emerged in relation to the preparation, certification and/or credentialing of*

teachers? While the preparation of teachers in a four year institution has been an accepted practice, a number of issues challenging the process have emerged recently. The teacher education program for the early childhood professional usually includes completion and passing of liberal arts and science courses as well as professional courses without a four year degree program. The passing of courses does not guarantee that candidates have achieved a minimum competence to teach effectively. However, a college degree does help the teacher candidate to become certified and qualified for a teaching position.

A Definition of the Teaching Process

The importance of what lies behind the abstraction called "teaching" is referred by Gage (1978) as the concerns people have when adults take care of children in an educational setting. Teaching is a form of art which is a useful or practical art rather than one dedicated to the creation of beauty and the evocation of aesthetic pleasure. However, teaching is also a science. Gage (1978) differentiates between the science of teaching and a scientific basis for the art of teaching. The science of teaching implies that good teaching will be attained by closely following rigorous rules which are highly predictable and controllable. For instance, chemists practice science, not art, when they use available knowledge to obtain almost completely predictable results. They manipulate certain variables under specified conditions. On the other hand, scientists practice an art when they conduct research. Agreeing with Gage (1978), Schwab (1983) defines teaching as an art and discusses art characteristics:

Every art, whether it be teaching, stone carving or judicial control of a court of law . . . has rules, but knowledge of the rules does not make one an artist. Art arises as the knower of the rules learns to apply them appropriately to the particular case. Application, in turn, requires acute awareness of the particularities of that case and ways in which the rule can be modified to fit the case without complete abrogation of the rule. In art, the form must be adapted to the matter. Hence the form must be communicated in ways which illuminate its possibilities for modification. (p. 265).

If teaching is an art, its practice requires a minimum of three forms of knowledge: (1) knowledge of rules of principles, (2) knowledge of particular cases, and (3) knowledge of ways to apply rules appropriately to discerned cases. Successful process-product research usually generates propositional rules. These general rules consist of propositions regarding the assigning of praise or blame, allocating turns, sequencing instruction, checking for understanding, and the like (Rosenshine & Stevens, 1986). In addition, there are general maxims that do not necessarily derive from research on teaching, but are part of the traditional wisdom of the practitioner (Shulman, 1986a).

Teaching can be examined to obtain knowledge of classroom practice through a role analysis. According to Katz (1973, 1974), the different role dimensions of early childhood teachers include caretaking (that is, caring for children, providing emotional support and guidance, instructing and facilitating). Research-based practices found in the literature consist of activities embedded within theoretical frameworks. A teacher uses an activity within a classroom, which is embedded within the teacher's set of premises, that framework does not relate to learning but to classroom management and control or student testing, and to notions of the roles of teachers and students. Therefore, the research-based activity and the implemented activity may look somewhat similar, but in reality differ, because the activities are embedded in different belief sets, intentions, and theoretical frameworks (Richardson, 1990).

Practice as an activity embedded within a theoretical framework is important in the modification of teaching practice. Since teachers continuously change, the focus should be on teachers' dialogue concerning warranted practice and control of their classroom activities and theoretical justifications (Richardson, 1990; Wildman & Niles, 1987); and the extent such justifications relate to the socially constructed standards of warranted practice. In Richardson's (1990) study, the school-level culture in two schools provided justifications, which encouraged their teachers to ignore questioning their own beliefs, understandings, and activities. For example, the school district imposed the use of basal readers and their workbooks, therefore, teachers could disregard their internal conflict between believing that these materials offer an easy way to teach reading and maintain control over students, and the belief that these materials are not the best materials to teach reading.

The perspective to modify teachers' practice based on research data indicates a different strategy in preparing teachers. Teacher education programs must permit teachers to interact and discuss standards, research, theory, classroom activities, and teachers' own conceptions of warranted practice (Richardson, 1990). Opportunities for teacher candidates to test in their classrooms derived practices from research on teaching. This process must be implemented in a trusting environment, using extreme care of the beliefs and premises. Otherwise teachers will disregard the research-practice relationships.

Teacher education programs vary in their preparation approach. Some teach their students the knowledge which they need to learn in order to teach, others socialize their students as they learn to teach by working under the supervision of mature professionals. These educators assume that teaching is intuitive and the best teachers are natural teachers. This idea is that what is important is "caught rather than taught."

Teaching is a creative process; not a mechanical art. Several reasons support this assumption: (1) It demands more than just to assimilate the behavior of a role model. (2) There are several methods of teaching and not one is better than the other. (3) The rational basis to teaching is definitely not learning through modeling. (4) Insufficient research evidence fails to support that some teacher behaviors increase pupils' outcomes or that a particular standard, a specific model of acceptable behavior for good teaching performance is independent of outcomes.

There are a number of alternative approaches to early childhood education. Presently, several of the different program models are available. Each program model requires different teaching behaviors. Although teachers should not be prepared to work in a specific program model, they need to know about each model such as the Piaget-oriented or Applied Behavior Analysis. Teachers need to be independent thinkers as well as nurturing and warm.

According to the Child Development Associate Consortium (1976), a competent child-care worker meets the specific needs of a group of young children in a child development setting by nurturing the children's physical, social, emotional and intellectual growth, by establishing and maintaining proper child care environment and by promoting good relations between parents and the child development center.

The consortium's broad description of a competent professional does not respond to the question of what teacher needs to know in order to teach effectively. Teachers should value and respect diversity and individual differences. Performance skills should be interrelated with a body of knowledge and theory in which teachers need to be immersed.

Teachers apply this knowledge in the classroom as they plan and evaluate instruction. In addition, knowledge facilitates the selection and sequencing of approaches and methods of instruction as well as the development of educational goals for young children. Knowledge must be integrated and understood to create a broad perspective and must be made relevant to teach (Saracho & Spodek, 1983).

Assessing Teacher Candidates for Credentialing and Certification

Credentialing

The Child Development Associate Consortium (CDAC) credentials individuals based on a competency-based assessment. It has designed Competency Standards to be used as the basis for assessing candidates for the CDA Credential. These are composed of six Competency Areas, which are then divided into 13 Functional Areas. For each Functional Area, the CDAC provides examples of the performance behavior of a competent child-care worker. The indicators are a sampling of behavior, which changes under the different circumstances the candidate is working. Six basic competency areas include:

1. to establish and maintain a safe, healthy environment;
2. to advance physical and intellectual competence;
3. to support social and emotional development and provide positive guidance;
4. to establish positive and productive relationships with families;
5. to ensure a well-run, purposeful program responsive to participant needs;
6. to maintain a commitment to professionalism.

These competency areas were field tested and received input from the task force and approximately 1,000 early childhood practitioners.

According to the CDAC, the CDA Credential is only awarded to persons who demonstrate competent performance in the Competency Areas: (1) who are sensitive to children's feelings, able to perceive individuality and make positive use of individual differences within the group; and (2) who are committed to building on the strengths of individual children and their family.

The CDAC awards the CDA Credential after the Local Assessment Team (LAT) successfully completes the assessment and the team decides to recommend to the consortium that the Credential be awarded.

The four-member team assesses the CDA Candidate's performance with children, staff and parents. The team is composed of the following:

1. The Candidate, who shares knowledge of self and a personal perspective on her/his own performance with children;

2. A Trainer/Advisor, who shares the professional experiences of the Candidate and is knowledgeable in the areas of early childhood education/child development in the region;

3. A Parent-Community Representative, who shares the perceptions of the community in which the Candidate is being assessed;

4. A Consortium Representative, who provides an outside perspective to the team and knows the CDAC's assessment procedures.

These assessment team members gather all types of data to obtain the appropriate information about the Candidate's performance. For example, the Candidate compiles evidence in a Portfolio such as samples of work with children, curriculum materials, examples of home-center coordination planning charts and the like. The Trainer/Adviser writes a detailed report on the Candidate. The Parent-Community Representative observes and records the Candidate's performance to investigate the Candidate's relationships to a group of children, and then conducts a follow-up interview with the Candidate. The Parent-Community Representative also surveys the parents of the children in the classroom to find out their reactions to the Candidate's work. All information is kept confidential.

All the information is combined and is examined by the four LAT members during an assessment team meeting. At the meeting the team votes whether or not to recommend that the Candidate be awarded the CDA Credential. In addition, the LAT prepares a profile of the Candidate's strengths and weakness in working with young children. The profile is issued later to the Candidate.

Presently, the CDA Credential is granted for three years and may be renewed every five years (CDA National Credentialing Program, 1988). Procedures to renew it have not been developed.

Certification

A means to assess that people entering the profession have the knowledge and personal qualities for effective teaching is essential. In the United States admission to the teaching profession is controlled by a state certificate or state credential. Each state provides a certificate or a credential which serves to protect the client and the profession. A school system will not employ people without a certificate. The certificate indicates that the individuals are able to teach and provides a protection for the children against gross incompetence in the classroom.

Certificates also protect the teachers. Once teachers attain this credential, they are not required to be examined yearly in relation to their teaching competency. That license certifies minimum competency. However, some states are reuniting the CAT test where teachers are tested for basic academic skills. They also have to take the National Teachers' Examination.

Certification has been awarded based upon successful completion of courses in a degree plan. Some educators believe that teaching should not be certified merely on the basis of courses. They advocate a set of tests for teachers in order that after students have graduated from a program, they would receive their diploma. They then would have to take a test, much like those needed to become a lawyer or a doctor or a certified public accountant, in order to teach. This test could be a national teachers' examination or a local one and would require that teachers demonstrate knowledge and performance about teaching. Teacher education programs should assess teacher candidates to ensure that they can manifest basic minimum competencies in terms of classroom behavior.

State certification certifies teachers, but the system has not designed a renewal process. The reason may be that several state levels are involved in the certification process, which can create difficulties in decision-making.

Most major national reports on the status of education in America express concern about the quality of the teaching profession. For example, the Carnegie Commission raises issues such as who is entering the profession and who is leaving: "The caliber of new teachers is low and is getting worse" (Feistritzer, 1983, p. 105), and "Not only do poor students enter the profession, but those who leave teaching often are the ones the schools can least afford to lose" (Boyer, 1983, p. 172).

States' concerns about teacher quality are reflected in the way they are restricting standards for certification, such as testing teachers. Gorth and Chernoff (1986) reported:

. . . Between 1977 and 1981, 16 states enacted legislature or state board of education policies of this sort. More states, have joined the trend of late. In fact, keeping track of policy and legislative initiatives and changes in teacher certification testing requires full-time attention. Only four or five states remain that have neither a testing program nor serious plans to test (p. 20).

Regardless of some individuals' fears, government leaders may need to move further on this issue. As early as 1980, *Time* (1980) magazine in "Help! Teachers Can't Teach!" reported that 85% of the adults in this country supported teacher testing for certification. Wise, Darling-Hammond, McLaughlin, and Bernstein (1984) recommended that education policy makers must consider better teachers and better teaching as the key to better education.

According to McNergney, Medley, and Caldwell (1988), in February 1982 the Virginia governor (Charles Robb) persuaded the State Board to pass the following resolution:

BE IT RESOLVED, that certification regulations for public school teachers in Virginia shall include a requirement that beginning July 1, 1984, all beginning teachers satisfy a provisional period of not less than two years and that the Department seek the necessary financial assistance to establish and validate the standards upon which the provisional certificate may be elevated to full certificate status.

Testing only measures knowledge of basic skills through a paper and pencil test. Unfortunately, the new teacher certification examination fails to assess teacher competence. A passing score on the examination qualifies teachers to become certified as competent teachers; therefore, the examination should assess teacher competence in relation to professional knowledge about teaching and learning. Most educators have defined teacher competence as the ability to diagnose students' needs, design and implement instruction, and manage a class.

The states of Virginia, Georgia and Florida developed a procedure to assess teacher competence. The Georgia's Teacher Performance Assessment Instrument (TPAI) is used to assess teachers' performances for certification (Capie, Anderson, Johnson, & Ellet, 1979). The TPAI is a behaviorally anchored rating scale where the observer records the extent to which a teacher demonstrates each of a set of indicators of competent performance. The TPAI has been empirically refinement and is believed to be a sophisticated example of a behaviorally anchored rating scale (Capie, 1985). Florida adopted the Florida Performance Measurement System (FPMS) to assess the performance of beginning teachers. Dade County in Florida selected a different instrument, a modified version of the TPAI. The FPMS, a low inference observation instrument (Coalition for the Development of a Performance Evaluation System, no date), allows the observer to select from two sets of indicators of "competent" classroom performance. The observer records whether the teacher has demonstrated a positive or negative classroom performance during a five minute observation period. The TPAI and the FPMS assess a beginning teacher's performance. The observer records the presence or absence of specified indicators of competence behavior. However, assessment of teachers needs to include the teachers' professional behavior the public expects teachers to model for students, and minimal expectations such as teachers' abilities to acquire and apply professional knowledge, self-efficacy, creativity, and the ability to make spontaneous decisions. However, the assessment of certification standards and teacher preparation are affected by teacher shortage. Many states are having problems filling teaching positions. Reformers and researchers predict severe teacher shortages in the future.

In the past, teacher shortages caused certification standards to be loosened. Individuals entered the profession by obtaining emergency certificates; teaching subjects certified teachers were not prepared to teach; taking advantage that teacher education programs switched to colleges, universities and public schools; entering programs which helped decrease the teacher shortage (federal government established a national Teacher Corps program), and the like. If necessary, multiple strategies must address the teacher shortage. Such strategies must be balanced with new vigorous certification standards.

Arnstein (n.d.) states, "In describing the existing system, with its remarkable similarities from coast to coast despite the variations among the 50 jurisdictions, a common characteristic is the attempt to impose the authority of state by creating some intermediaries. While the State may have the last word, the actual operations have been conducted by a group of accrediting agencies colleges, private efforts and the various inputs of professional associations" (p. 5).

Arnstein (n.d.) adds that many are unhappy with the process of certifying teachers for three reasons. One is a demographic problem. The second is a political problem. There are pressures in the United States to redistribute the power, the authority and the responsibilities for the preparation and credentialing of teachers. In the past, colleges of education "owned" not only the preparation of teachers but the certification or credentialing of teachers. Now the organized profession, the teacher association, the National Association, the Teachers' union and the American Federation of Teachers are seeking greater control over admission to the profession. The professionals themselves, including the classroom teachers, are trying to become the gate keepers and not just leave it to the professors or to state legislature. Finally, Arnstein (n.d.) says the problem is epistemological. "The state of the art of teacher education does not permit the assertion of those skills and competencies that every teacher must have. While the teaching certificate is an evidence of competence, of having mastered a body of knowledge which reflects a genuine member of a profession, in point of fact this assertion is shaky and debatable. This quality control moves to a political level because the epistemological problems are essentially unsolved." Arnstein (n.d.) adds that teacher education programs do not know how to describe the knowledge they should require of all teachers, what it is that teachers need to know, and to do in order to be considered competent.

The teacher education program must evaluate its goals, content and field experiences. The goals must be restated to reflect the accountability issues of preparing effective teachers. Similarly, the program must be reviewed in light of the changing society and a program developed to reflect the integrative nature of teaching behaviors instead of fragmented courses often taught in isolation.

A variety of evaluation techniques must be used for different situations and to determine the teacher candidate's progress at various phases of the program.

Conclusion

In the years immediately ahead, teachers and those concerned with children will indicate their priorities as the issues of quality and control become more important to them. Educators will take stands and demonstrate what they believe to be right, true and good for young children. These stands will determine the future of teacher education in the United States and will provide an educational framework.

Teacher education programs need a new conceptual framework of the programs. The content, practice and methodology must be altered. The accumulated faculty enterprise on the instructional processes needs to be transformed. A modified teacher education program can certify or credential effective teachers only if it is responsive in preparing teachers for their multifaceted roles within our society.

References

Arnstein, G. (no date) *Teacher certification: Is it an art or a science?* Mimeograph paper

Boyer, E.L. (1983) *High school: A report on secondary education in America.* New York: Harper & Row

Capie, W. (1985) *Teacher performance assessment instrument.* Athens, GA: University of Georgia

Capie, W., Anderson, S.J., Johnson, C.E., & Ellet, C. (1979) *Teacher performance assessment instrument.* Athens, GA: University of Georgia

Child Development Associate Consortium. (1976) *The Child Development Associate Consortium's credential award system: A report on its development and evaluation of its first year of operation.* Washington, DC: Author

Child Development Associate National Credentialing Program. (1988) *Child Development Associate assessment system and competency standards: Preschool caregivers in center-based programs.* Washington, DC: Author

Coalition for the Development of a Performance Evaluation System. (no date) *Participant's manual of the Florida performance measurement system.* Tallahassee, FL: Florida Beginning Teacher Program, Office of Teacher Education, Certification, and Inservice Staff Development

Feistritzer, C.E. (1983) *The condition of teaching: A state by state analysis.* Hillsdale, NJ: Erlbaum

Gage, N.T. (1978) *The scientific basis of the art of teaching.* New York: Teachers College Press

Gorth, W.P., & Chernoff, M.L. (Eds.) (1986) *Teaching for teacher certification.* Hillsdale, NJ: Erlbaum

Howsam, R.B., Corrigan, D.C., Denemark, G.W., & Nash, R.J. (1976) *Education a profession.* Washington, DC: American Association for Colleges for Teacher Education

Hughes, J.M., & Schultz, F.M. (1976) *Education in America* (4th ed.). New York: Harper & Row

Jackson, P.W. (1966) *The way teaching is.* Washington, DC: Association for Supervision and Curriculum Development

Katz, L.G. (1974) Issues in education. In B. Spodek (Ed.), *Teacher education.* Washington, DC: National Association for the Education of Young Children

Katz, L.G. (June 1973) *Nature and nurture of teachers of young children: issues and concerns.* Paper Presented Interdisciplinary Conference on Early Childhood Teacher Education Programs, Chicago, IL.

Levin, H.M. (1980) Teacher certification and the economics of information. *Educational Evaluation and Policy Analysis*, **2**(4), 5–18

McNergney, R.F., Medley, D.M., & Caldwell, M.S. (1988) Making and implementing policy on teacher licensure. *Journal of Teacher Education*, **39**(3), 38–44

Peters, D.L. (1988) The Child Development Associate Credential and the educationally disenfrancised. In B. Spodek, O.N. Saracho, & D.L. Peters (Eds.), *Professionalism and the early childhood practitioner* (pp. 93–104). New York: Teachers College Press

Richardson, V. (1990) Significant and worthwhile change in teaching practice. *Educational Researcher*, **19**(7), 10–18

Rosenshine, B., & Stevens, R. (1986) Teaching functions. In M. Wittrock (Ed.) *Handbook of research on teaching* (pp. 376–391). New York: Macmillan

Schwab, J.J. (1983) The practical 4: Something for curriculum professors to do. *Curriculum Inquiry*, **13**(3), 239–265

Saracho, O.N. (1980) The relationship between the teachers' cognitive style and their perceptions of their students' academic achievement. *Educational Research Quarterly*, **5**(3), 40–49

Saracho, O.N., & Spodek, B. (1981) The teachers' cognitive styles and their educational implications. *Educational Forum*, **45**(2), 153–159

Saracho, O.N., & Spodek, B. (1983) The preparation of teachers for bilingual bicultural early childhood classes. In O.N. Saracho & B. Spodek (Eds.), *Understanding the multicultural experience in early childhood education.* (pp. 125–146). Washington, DC: National Association for the Education of Young Children

Shulman, L.S. (1986a) Paradigms and research programs in the study of teaching: A contemporary perspective. In M. Wittrock (Ed.), *Handbook of research on teaching* (pp. 3–36). New York: Macmillan

Shulman, L.S. (1986b) Those who understand: Knowledge growth in teaching. *Educational Research*, **15**(2), 4–14

Spodek, B., & Saracho, O.N. (1982) The preparation and certification of early childhood personnel. In B. Spodek (Ed.), *Handbook of research in early childhood education*, (pp. 399–425). New York: The Free Press

Spodek, B., & Saracho, O.N. (1988) Professionalism in early childhood education. In B. Spodek, O.N. Saracho, & D.L. Peters (Eds.) ( ) *Professionalism and the early childhood practitioner* (pp. 59–74). New York: Teachers College Press

Time (1980, June 16). Help! Teachers can't teach! *Time*, pp. 54–60, 63

Wise, A.E., Darling-Hammond, L., McLaughlin, M.W. & Bernstein, H.T. (1984) *Teacher education: A study of effective practices.* Washington, DC: National Institute of Education

Wildman, T., & Niles, J. (1987) Reflective teachers: Tensions between abstractions and realities. *Journal of Teacher Education*, **38**, 25–31

Wise, A.E., Darling-Hammond, L., McLaughlin, M.W., & Bernstein, H.T. (1984) *Teacher evaluation: A study of effective practices.* Washington, DC: National Institute of Education

Calling the tune or dancing to it: Early childhood teacher education in Australia

GEORGE F. LEWIS, WENDY SCHILLER and JAN DUFFIE

Macquarie University, Institute of Early Childhood, Macquarie University, Sydney, New South Wales, Australia

(Received August 1991)

Issues relating to the quality of teacher education have dominated educational debate. There has been a proliferation of reports addressing issues of low morale, career opportunities, preservice and inservice education, and matching supply to demand. Early childhood teacher education in Australia is experiencing a crisis of identity reflecting its ambivalent position within a nationally funded centralised system of higher education. Recent amalgamations between the research-oriented university system and the vocationally oriented colleges of advanced education have produced a system increasingly responsive to government economic priorities.

In the flurry of reports there has been a noticeable absence of articulation about the role and nature of early childhood teacher education which reflects an assumption that early childhood personnel preparation mirrors elementary and secondary teacher education. At the same time early childhood field staff responded to changed community needs through changed roles. There is an expectation that graduates from early childhood programs will provide sensitive and skilled leadership in the preschools, long day care centres, elementary school grades K-2, family day care, occasional care, out of school hours care, and any other setting where there are children from birth to 8 years of age.

The chapter seeks to explore the constraints placed on early childhood teacher education by the centralised higher education system, by the research-oriented universities which now are responsible for teacher education, and by the expectations being placed on the graduates by children's services staff who value practical skills in working with young children. The chapter seeks to identify the consequent tensions underlying the decisions being made by early childhood teacher educators on the nature of preservice programs, induction as teachers, and inservice provision and argues:

1. That early childhood teacher education in Australia must of necessity respond both to government policy for higher education for continued funding and program accreditation and to government policy for children's services for credibility and employability of its graduates.

2. That early childhood teacher education is interactive with government in the process of policy development.

3. That early childhood teacher education has considerable freedom within the orbit of the higher education system provided that funding and academic criteria are satisfied.

4. That government policy development has been uncoordinated and inconsistent in regard to the relationship between early childhood teacher education and children's services.

The major issues that the chapter considers are:

1. Where is early childhood teacher education within Australian higher education? The change from small, private, employer run colleges to the university

system has resulted in an imperative to be responsive to government policy and taken away independence. Yet how much consideration is given to the needs of early childhood teacher education in the context of government policy for the higher education system or for teacher education?

2. What is the nature of the skills needed by the graduate seeking employment in children's services in Australia? There is enormous diversity in the professional roles of the early childhood educator reflecting the historic division between the roles of education and social welfare fulfilled by children's services. Yet there is a consequent uncertainty about what constitutes early childhood teacher education in relation to the structures of teacher education, to elementary education, to school systems, to community development, and to social welfare.

3. What are the points of tension between the conflicting views of early childhood teacher education? The focus of early childhood teacher education varies with the predominant model of children's services in the different states because the training cannot be all things to all people because of, (a) the role of K-2 preparation, the need for quality specialised practicum, and preparation for administrative roles, (b) the need to provide a range of student choice to allow specialisation within the program to produce a competent graduate on career entry, (c) the continuum between preservice and inservice education and opportunities for postgraduate study and research in the university setting, and (d) decreased attractiveness of the working conditions in the profession.

Key words: Early Childhood Education, Australia

The debate in Australia on the quality and development of teachers reflects issues that have dominated educational debate at the international level for at least five years. A number of recent reports such as *Schools and quality: An international report* (1989) by the Organisation for Economic Cooperation and Development, the National Commission on Excellence in Teacher Education *A call for change in teacher education* (1986) in the US, and the House of Commons Education, Science, and Arts Committee report *The supply of teachers for the 1990s* (1990) in the UK address issues of improving the status and attractiveness of teaching, building new career structures and opportunities for teachers, developing teachers' knowledge and skills through preservice and inservice education, and matching supply to demand in a coordinated way. A major OECD conference held in Sweden on teacher education policies for the 1990s noted the pivotal role of the teacher in achieving high quality education and the consequent need to redefine teacher professionalism in terms of the new accountability to the community, the politicisation of teaching, and the effects of economic constraints on education.

Early childhood teacher education in Australia in the 1990s is experiencing a crisis of identity as it seeks to respond to different demands from different stakeholders and yet to maintain its distinctive approach to education. Although state governments have constitutional responsibility for education, the national government, as the source of funding, has taken the position that higher education should reflect national government policy. The recent amalgamations of the vocationally-oriented former colleges of advanced education (which were responsible for early childhood teacher education) into the research-oriented universities produced a unified national higher education system responsive to the national government's economic priorities. First, there is a clear mandate from national and state government and from the children's services field to provide quality preparation for teachers of young children to work in a variety of roles in a range of services. Second, early childhood teacher education within the university system depends entirely on continued government funding for higher education in a climate of economic restraint producing competition between universities for the available resources. Third, early childhood teacher education depends on the university both to accredit the courses and to provide the necessary resources for teaching, supervision of practicum, research, and administration. Fourth, early childhood teacher education must compete each year with other types of teacher education and with other faculties for allocation of sufficient study places at the university to supply the increasing demand for early childhood teachers.

In Australia, there have been four major reports on teacher education in twelve months, three at the national level and one at the state level in New South Wales. *Teacher quality: An issues paper* (1989) is a report prepared by the Schools Council of the National Board of Employment, Education, and Training, the principal advisory body to the national Minister responsible for education. The report proposed four year training as the necessary minimum qualification for teachers and pointed to the importance of practicum, internship, and induction as part of the process. *Teacher education in Australia* (1990) is a report to the Australian Education Council from its working party on teacher education. The Australian Education Council consists of the national and state Ministers responsible for education and the state Directors General of Education. The report considered issues of the structure and content of preservice teacher education, and the nature of the continuum between preservice and inservice teacher education recommended a decade earlier by the *Report of the national enquiry into teacher education* (1980), known as the Auchmuty Report. *Teacher education in Australia* (1990) recommended a one year internship (as a half time associate teacher supervised by both university and employer and undertaking further concurrent study) following preservice education in order to become a fully qualified teacher. *Quality of teaching — an issue for all: An initial statement* (Department of Employment, Education, and Training, 1990) by the national Minister responsible for education also promoted quality preservice and continuing education courses to improve teachers' working conditions, and self-image. Finally, *Teacher education: Directions and strategies* (1990) is a report on the recruitment, education, and professional development of teachers prepared by the New South Wales Ministry of Education, Youth, and Women's Affairs.

Each of the reports has made significant recommendations for reform in Australian teacher education reflecting the proposition by national and state governments that if Australia's future is to depend on improving the efficiency of industry through an increasingly skilled work force then education must be the engine of that economic development (Ramsay, 1988; 1990). The paper *Quality of teaching — an issue for all: An initial statement* (Department of Employment, Education, and Training, 1990), for example, argued that if efficiency of learning is to be a function of the quality of teaching then quality of teacher education must be improved by a combination of, (a) basing the curriculum on an in-depth understanding of the subjects and disciplines, (b) involving employers, and (c) providing on-the-job training. The lack of comment about the role and nature of early childhood teacher education seems to reflect an assumption that early childhood personnel preparation mirrors the nature of primary and secondary teacher education. It also reflects a lack of understanding of the diversity of children's services in Australia. Only *Teacher education: Directions and strategies* (1990) addressed early childhood teacher education directly and with understanding in recognising the diverse and complex role of early childhood teachers.

In the 1990s early childhood educators in Australia have been responsive to changes in their role. The children's services field requires quality teachers who can provide sensitive and skilled leadership in the preschools, kindergartens, long day care centres, elementary school grades K-2, family day care, occasional and out-of-school hours care, playgroups, and other settings where there are children from birth to 8 years. The nature of that leadership requires not only skills in curriculum development for all children including children with disabilities, children from non-English speaking backgrounds, and Aboriginal children, but also skills in administration, working with families, and in advocacy (Ebbeck, 1990; *Teacher education: Directions and strategies*, 1990). Teachers at the point of career entry are expected to be skilled practitioners. There are implications for the range of experiences in the teacher education curriculum and for the consequent diversity of practicum placements allowing a range of choices and experiences within preservice preparation and reflecting early childhood career opportunities.

The chapter will explore the effects of the different demands and expectations on early childhood teacher education through, (a) analysing the constraints placed on early childhood teacher education by a centralised higher education system responsive to national government economic priorities, (b) identifying the expectations of early childhood teacher education being placed on graduates by children's services which value practical skills in working with young children, and (c) identifying the consequent issues and tensions underlying the decisions being made by early childhood teacher educators on the nature of the preservice programs, induction as teachers, and inservice provision. The chapter concludes that early childhood teacher education in Australia must, (a) respond of necessity both to government policy for higher education for continued funding and program accreditation and to government policy for children's services for credibility and employability of its graduates, (b) interact with government in the process of policy development, (c) use its autonomy in developing appropriate courses within the higher education system provided that academic and funding criteria are satisfied, and (d) advocate for government policy that is coordinated and consistent between departments in matching the supply of early childhood teachers to the demand for children's services.

What Are the Constraints of Higher Education on Early Childhood Teacher Education? A Sense of Deja Vu

With a new round of amalgamations, underfunding, economic belt-tightening, tension, and debate by national and state governments, questioning of teachers' professional standing in the community, and proposals for reforming the teacher education curriculum, early childhood teacher educators are experiencing a sense of the wheel having come full circle in 1990. They have seen it all before, or have they?

Where is teacher education in Australian higher education?

Australia's rapidly growing economy in the 1950s and 1960s resulted in an increased demand for higher education. In 1957, *The report of the Committee on Australian universities* (1957) by the Murray Committee, recommended an increase in the number and size of universities. Seven years later, the report *Tertiary education in Australia* by the Martin Committee (Committee on the Future of Tertiary Education, 1964) recommended an even greater increase in higher education than that envisaged by the Murray Committee. However, Parry (1989) pointed to two reasons for opposition to unrestricted university expansion. First, the British view of the university as an elite institution was a powerful one. The special role of universities in undertaking research and scholarship, it was argued, could not be maintained with a massive increase in undergraduate rather than postgraduate teaching without academic repercussions. Therefore higher education for all would have to be achieved in some other way. Second, financial prudence demanded a cheaper alternative to the university system. The Martin Committee recommended that funding for non-university, non-research, tertiary teaching institutions (the new colleges of advanced education) be increased from 45% of university expenditure per full time student in 1962 to 60% by 1971.

The new, economical colleges of advanced education providing higher education, existed alongside but separate from the universities. The first colleges established were Institutes of Technology whose courses were based on technical college associate diploma and diploma courses. The qualifications were not at degree but at diploma level. The financial responsibility for the new binary system rested with the Commonwealth through two separate and unrelated bodies (the Australian Universities Commission and the Advanced Education Commission). The educational responsibility for university courses remained with the university while college of advanced education course accreditation and certification became the responsibility of a state Board of Advanced Education.

The Martin Committee identified a need to increase both the number and the quality of teacher education students and a role for the new College sector in the process of upgrading teacher education. The report recommended that the national government assume financial responsibility for upgrading teacher education by providing funding for recurrent and capital expenditure in cooperation with the States, a minimum of three years preparation for elementary school teachers, removal of teachers colleges from the control of the state departments of education, and the establishment of Boards of Teacher Education in each state to assume the educational responsibility for course accreditation and certification. However, in 1965 teachers colleges had no powerful constituency to lobby for them and they remained within the state departments of education and separate from the newly created colleges of advanced education.

Secondary teacher education remained mainly the responsibility of the universities through a three-year degree program followed by a one-year Diploma of Education. Elementary teacher education remained mainly the responsibility of the state Department of Education through a two-year program to prepare teachers for state schools. Financial and educational responsibility lay with the state Department of

Education. Privately funded teachers colleges trained teachers for non-state schools. It was not until 1973–74 that the state teachers colleges moved from the state departments of education to become independently incorporated colleges of advanced education as suggested by the Martin Committee to offer a three year Diploma of Teaching qualification.

Where Is Early Childhood Teacher Education in Australian Higher Education?

Early childhood teacher education in Australia developed differently from elementary and secondary and was well established before the state teachers' colleges started. The Sydney Kindergarten Teachers College took in its first student teachers in 1897 while it was not until 1906 that the Sydney Teachers College was established to train elementary teachers for the state school system. Early childhood teacher education was both financially and educationally independent of other teacher education institutions. Kindergarten Teachers' Colleges were established in the capital city of each state largely on the initiative of the state-based voluntary associations of kindergartens which operated the centres and needed trained teachers. There was no need for regional or national planning since graduates of the kindergarten courses were only employed by the organisation which owned the training college. The money to provide the training came from the general funds of the organisation and represented fund raising, student fees, and philanthropic support, as well as limited State government financial support (for all aspects of work).

The nature of the education reflected a deep ideological split between education and care. Kindergarten experience for preschool aged children were seen as having educational value. The Sydney Kindergarten Teachers College established a two year training program (with a third postgraduate year added in 1898) to train teachers in Froebel's methods for the free kindergartens operated by the Kindergarten Union (Harrison, 1985). Day nurseries and nursery school education (influenced by McMillan's work) were seen as primarily providing care during the extended hours the children spent at the centre. The Melbourne Kindergarten Teachers College in Victoria first introduced nursery school training in Australia in 1930. It was then offered in New South Wales by Sydney Day Nursery and Nursery Schools Association in 1931 just one year after it was established. Subsequently the Association founded the Nursery School Teachers College to provide trained teachers for the nursery schools (Kelly, 1988). All training was privately funded. Practical aspects of early childhood teaching were provided by experienced staff from the sponsoring organisation, while the more academic aspects were given by guest lecturers from the university or state teachers college. Certainly, to this point the nature of early childhood teacher education was directly controlled by the early childhood employing organisations which provided three years of training (as indeed were elementary and secondary teacher education by the state departments of education which owned the state teachers colleges and provided two years of training).

That young children in care require high quality, well-trained staff was not accepted in all States. The view that the needs of children could adequately be met by "warm-hearted people who are fond of children" had some credence (Stonehouse, 1988). As the number of centres outstripped the number of suitably qualified staff many programs were implemented by teachers qualified in other areas of education, by other professional staff (such as nurses), or by persons without any formal qualifications (Kelly, 1988). The Sydney Day Nursery and Nursery Schools Association in New South Wales was the only organisation in Australia which has always employed trained teachers to work in their long day care centres. The Fry Report *Care and education of young children* (Australian Pre-schools Committee, 1973) expressed concern at the division between pre-school and long day care being perpetuated by separate training programs. Teacher education, the report argued, should equip staff to meet all of the education and care needs of children from birth to 8 years of age. The Report recommended an integrated approach to training all staff working with young children while allowing for specialist backgrounds such as teacher, nurse, or social worker. There were no prescriptions about the type of program that was desirable but rather a recommendation that the training institutions develop and teach courses to suit local or state circumstances in the light of the nature of the work. The Report noted the long experience of the training colleges in preparing staff and recommended extending the scope of the training to include training directed towards the full day care of children under six. Consultation with the state Boards of Advanced Education was to be part of the process. The training was to be three years full-time or its equivalent with the same status and nomenclature as other awards for courses of similar length and standing.

The Fry Report (Australian Pre-schools Committee, 1974) analysed the increasing financial involvement of the national government in early childhood teacher education as a result of community pressures to increase the quantity and type of child care available. With national attention, increased finance and the consequent expansion in the provision of early childhood places, came a corresponding expansion of early childhood teacher education facilities in all States, using both state and voluntary agency funds. The national government first provided financial support in the period 1966–1972 by awarding scholarships to students in the pre-school teachers colleges. In 1973 the national government introduced the Pre-school Teacher Education Scholarship to cover fees and a living allowance for all students on a more favourable basis than that provided by the States to students attending state teachers colleges. Capital funds were first made available in 1968 through the State Grants (Pre-school Teachers Colleges) Act. The unmatched grants were designed to assist the six mainland pre-school teachers colleges and the Tasmanian Department of Education. A Special Committee on Teacher Education in 1972 made recommendations on the future development and funding of the colleges. No longer were the pre-school colleges to be maintained by voluntary agencies but by the national government as autonomous institutions funded on the same basis as Colleges of Advanced Education.

The early childhood teachers colleges continued to function as independent institutions providing specialist education until the end of 1975 when they were incorporated as separate Colleges of Advanced Education within the binary system. What was to follow was to test the resolve and the unique identity of early childhood teacher education! Rationalisation and amalgamations of institutions became the order of the day. Faced with a perceived over-supply of teachers (at least of elementary and secondary teachers), a plethora of separate education institutions, and the first winds of economic recession, the national and state governments moved towards a series of forced amalgamations within the college of advanced education sector in the interests of efficiency and economy. Shades of the 1990s and the unified national system formed from the amalgamations with the universities!

Briggs (1984) noted the differing perceptions of what constituted early childhood teacher education. By 1984, after the amalgamations, there were three programs that retained a distinct structural identity within their institution and some academic autonomy (the Brisbane College of Advanced Education Division of Early Childhood Studies in Queensland, the Sydney College of Advanced Education Institute of Early Childhood Studies in New South Wales, and the Melbourne Institute of Early Childhood Development in Victoria). These courses were convinced of the need for a discrete program to maintain an early childhood specialisation and a methodology that took into account the needs and developmental stages of the individual child. As well, the early childhood specialised course contributed towards diversity in higher education and, in addition, had a contribution to make in the context of the state elementary school K-2, and rural, ethnic, and community projects. In the other states the early childhood courses were attached to departments, schools, or faculties housing other disciplines or primary and/or secondary teacher education. Where new early childhood courses were established in colleges of advanced education (either in provincial towns or in outer metropolitan areas) they had neither educational nor geographical affinity with the established courses. Faced with severe reductions in funding and with reduced teaching practice many early childhood teacher educators felt pressure to maintain the early childhood orientation of their programs but also voiced concern that they had lost control of early childhood education programs to academically well-qualified senior staff with little understanding of or sympathy for what the early childhood course was trying to accomplish.

Early Childhood Teacher Education in the Unified National System

The Williams Committee report *Education, training, and employment* (Committee of Enquiry into Education and Training, 1979) failed to address the problems of the binary system other than to recommend cross-contracting between the sectors, and continuation of external accreditation of College of Advanced Education courses. Successive reports of the Commonwealth Tertiary Education Commission between 1980 and 1985 did not address the issue of creating a single, better coordinated, national system while maintaining the benefits of the practical, vocational, and accessible higher education provided by the college sector. The first move towards developing coordinated policy for the university and the college sectors at a national level came in 1985 with the merger of the two separate advisory bodies (the Universities Council and the Advanced Education Council). The Commonwealth Tertiary Education Commission recommended that funding for the two sectors could best be managed if it were a unified rather than a binary program (Commonwealth

Tertiary Education Commission, 1985). However, as Parry (1989) pointed out, what the Commonwealth Tertiary Education Commission did not understand was that distinct university and college of advanced education sectors could not adequately cope with the type of higher education needed. So, in some States, the Advanced Education Board merely became absorbed within a Higher Education Board, which performed the role of coordinating all higher education programs at state level. The *Review of efficiency and effectiveness* (Commonwealth Tertiary Education Commission, 1986) supported maintaining separate university and college sectors and recommended that doctoral programs be established in colleges if the subject area was not available in a university. The Report also suggested that technical education cooperate in providing higher education where it was not otherwise available. During 1981–82 the national government, as a means of reducing expenditure, required a restructuring of all colleges with an enrolment of less than 2000 students through merging with other institutions. All the institutions involved were colleges providing only teacher education.

The Commonwealth Tertiary Education Commission, however, had seriously misread the extent of national government concern about the binary system. Ramsay (1989) suggested that the factor underlying government concern was the lack of usefulness of the binary system as a means for organising higher education as the factor underlying government concern. Its ineffectiveness stemmed from several factors. First, it was difficult to maintain differentiation in status between the traditional universities and the colleges of advanced education. The colleges had degree granting status for many years. They were awarding Bachelors, Masters, and Doctoral degrees, and offered courses in the same areas as the universities (except in medicine, dentistry, and veterinary science) without the necessity for the provision of additional funds for research and its associated infrastructure. Increasingly, academic programs were able to stand up to national and international scrutiny as being of comparable standard to those offered by the universities. Many of the programs were produced by staff with higher academic qualifications. The standard of the academic programs reflected a system of course accreditation by state Boards through a standard set of external assessment procedures. The external assessment committees making recommendations consisted of representatives of employers, other colleges of advanced education and universities with expertise, and professional bodies. Second, the colleges which were involved in research and higher degrees were attracting outside research funding. Third, the states showed little interest in promoting developments in a college sector for which they were not paying while they were also not able to include the universities in planning. Fourth, the Commonwealth found itself funding a dual higher education sector from a single pool of funds. Fifth, even though the 1982 mergers had reduced the number of colleges of advanced education, by 1984 their enrolments were higher than the university sector. Finally, the separateness of the structures had broken down. One new university had been formed from two colleges. Three universities had shown that they could accommodate former colleges into their structures. Two colleges of advanced education had used state legislation to rename themselves as universities while still being funded at college level.

The Federal election in 1987 marked the retirement of a long serving national Minister for Education. Her replacement was a Minister with an agenda for change. The restructured Department of Education, Employment and Training (DEET) combining the formerly separate departments of education and of employment pointed to a strong commitment to rationalise higher education to make it meet government economic objectives. A government discussion paper, or green paper, (Department of Employment, Education, and Training, 1987) was followed by a policy paper, or white paper, (Department of Employment, Education, and Training, 1988) which proposed the establishment of a unified national system of higher education funded in terms of its actual teaching and research activities. The new system would require fewer, larger, and more efficient institutions (of not less than 8,000 students). The national government would further require the universities to develop strategic plans by 1990 reflecting its economic and educational priorities.

Early childhood teacher education again became involved in amalgamations as Colleges of Advanced Education (to which they belonged) became part of existing universities or formed new universities. Some early childhood teacher programs retained a separate identity within their Faculty of Education, others remained merged within an existing primary teacher education program. Only one amalgamated as a separate faculty of early childhood within an existing university. The wheel had come full circle for early childhood teacher education in 1990 from amalgamating with colleges of advanced education to amalgamating with universities!

The change from small, private, employer run colleges to colleges of advanced education to university has resulted in an imperative to be responsive to government policy. Little consideration has been given to the needs of early childhood teacher education in the context of government policy for the higher education system or for teacher education. There may well be either lack of knowledge or interest in early childhood teacher education on the part of the decision makers!

What Are the Constraints from Children's Service? The Field-based Dimension

There is a degree of uncertainty about what constitutes early childhood teacher education in relation to the education and care of young children provided by the community, by social welfare, and by school systems. The way early childhood is defined determines what children's services expect from the graduate of an early childhood teacher education course.

Care or education: diversity or division

One issue that early childhood teacher education must address consciously is the division in early childhood between education (which by state regulation requires trained teachers) and care (which by state regulation, except in New South Wales, does not). Drake (1990) pointed out that the development of child care services in Australia originated both in education and in welfare, a difference still evident in the distinction between preschool and long day care in all states of Australia. A complex mosaic of services has developed involving national, state, local government and voluntary organisations in often uncoordinated funding and policy development, with responsibility being divided between education, welfare, and health departments. Preschools, catering for children between 3 and 5 years traditionally provided education whereas long day care traditionally provided care for extended periods of time. The services were operated by voluntary organisations and by state Departments of Education. Little interest was shown by either national or state governments in funding long day care services. However, by 1979 both national and state governments had developed policies which supported increased child care, based either on government sponsorship or community management and a wide range of services was planned including preschools, long day care, family day care, playgroups and alternate forms of before and after school care. In the 1980s, the national government created child care places in long day care services for children 0–3 years and more recently family day care, without considering the problem of undersupply of trained staff to be the directors and coordinators of the services.

Avenues for employment of early childhood graduates are predominantly in long day care and preschools, in the K-2 grades of the elementary school, and in other children's services. The major employers for long day care and preschools include community managed groups, private owners, councils, government authorities, religious groups, industries, and other voluntary non-government organisations, whereas the major employers for school settings are the Education Departments in each state and the religious and private school systems. A plethora of career opportunities exist in other children's services such as family day care, neighbourhood centres, mobiles, outreach programs, and out of school hours care. There are also career opportunities in advocacy for children's services, and in media corporations. Early childhood graduates may have similar responsibilities regardless of the settings within which they work, yet they are employed under a wide range of working conditions. Remuneration and conditions vary between service types (long day care, preschool, and school) and within service types (depending on whether the employer is a local council, state education authority, or non-government organisation). In some settings teachers work a 30 hour week while in others they work a 35 hour week. In some settings teachers have 4 weeks annual leave while in others they have 10 weeks. In some settings teachers are on duty between 9 a.m. and 3 p.m. while in others they work shifts between 6.30 a.m. and 7 p.m. With unions, the national government is working towards agreements for a national scale of teacher salaries and for reform of work practices to achieve the greater efficiency and productivity which is planned to lead to improved teaching (Department of Employment, Education, and Training, 1990).

The *Report of the Committee of Review of New South Wales Schools* (1989), known as the Carrick Report, highlighted a number of issues of concern in relation to the diversity of children's services and early childhood teacher education. The undersupply of early childhood teachers led to a pressing need to provide sufficient numbers of trained staff who can provide high quality education and care and liaise effectively with the home, school and community. The Carrick recommendations were, (a) to articulate an agreed set of principles on which policy decisions relating to children's services could be based, (b) overcome the problems of discontinuity of programs offered by preschools, long day care centres, and schools, (c) develop a coherent set of aims, expectations and values relating to early childhood programs be developed, (d) provide parenting programs, and (e) coordinate and provide quality programs for children from birth to 3 years. Without resolution of such issues the Report noted that early childhood teacher education may be operating without any clear direction.

Who decides on the qualifications for quality care?

There has been debate about the adequacy of standards in child care and the capacity of state regulations to mandate quality care for children. In the absence of a national set of regulations governing minimum publicly acceptable standards for young children's programs each state sets its own standard. Marked variation between states occurs. On the one hand early childhood professionals have advocated improving the standards within regulations to reflect knowledge gained from recent research on high quality programs. On the other hand, funding and licensing bodies have resisted regulating for quality standards. Since funding levels are often tied to the regulations, there is great pressure to contain government costs by resisting improvements in standards. In all states other than in New South Wales, regulations for long day care settings do not require trained early childhood teachers to be employed. However, in all states regulations for preschool settings do require early childhood teachers to be employed. Therefore, regulations do contribute in a very real way to the split between care and education. Australia is also disadvantaged by lack of a national data base on users of children's services (Edgar, 1990) and research data justifying the presence of early childhood teachers in programs (Ebbeck, 1990). Evidence is dependent on US research in noting the positive effects of teachers with backgrounds in child development and early childhood education.

The profile of the graduate needed to meet the demands of such a diverse field is awesome (Ebbeck, 1990). As a teacher, there is a need for a strong background in child development and an ability to plan an individualised curriculum, in particular for children with special needs, for children who are Aboriginal, for children from a non-English speaking background, or children in rural and isolated areas. To meet the challenges of most early childhood career opportunities the graduate needs not only to be a proficient teacher but also a politically aware professional who is also skilled in the areas of personnel management and administration (*Teacher education: Directions and strategies*, 1990). How can any preservice teacher education course fulfill such requirements?

What are the key professional roles?

Graduates entering the realm of the 0–5s outside the major educational systems embark on a career path which very quickly leads to the position of Director/Coordinator. In this leadership position responsibilities are many, extending towards children, community, parents, staff, funding bodies, licensing bodies as well as the profession generally. These services demand the administrative skills of small business management. In order to survive and flourish, the director must have considerable administrative skills or must support community committees with a charter to do so. The skills required for personnel management and quality control in these settings are complex. In some cases, the early childhood professional is designated as non-teaching Director. More frequently, however, the Director is employed as a teaching Director so that teaching must compete with the management components of the role. In the area of staffing, centres may hire the least expensive staff to save costs. However, these personnel may require more on-the-job training and support and add to the responsibility of the director.

Motivation: money or morale?

With the acknowledged low morale amongst teachers, the industrial climate is characterized by friction between employer bodies and unions reflecting the deterioration of conditions and salary in comparison to comparable professions. An increase in teacher resignation rates, particularly of experienced teachers, seems attributable to low morale. Reviews of schools at the national and state levels have prompted revised curricular expectations, increased accountability, and new challenges in adapting to school management structures that are locally not centrally based (Scott, 1990). More and more is demanded of those opting to remain in teaching positions in schools. In children's services (from birth to 5 years) the low morale has produced an image problem. It is difficult to attract and retain suitably qualified staff (Department of Community Services and Health, 1990). The turnover rates for early childhood teachers are reported as being 58% over a two year period (Ryan, 1989). Some graduates never actually work in the teaching profession as their skills are highly marketable and they move to better paid careers in other fields. The loss of graduates before career entry and the high attrition rates suggest a more detailed study of early childhood teacher supply and demand be undertaken in order to ensure that current and projected vacancies can be filled.

The Australian public needs to value the work of the early childhood graduate (*Teacher education: Directions and strategies*, 1990). A system of national accreditation of children's services may provide a means of ensuring accountability but also a means of encouraging children's services to gaining recognition for the quality of the service. There are hopes for the potential to raise the interest and respect of the community towards the profession of early childhood by breaking the poor image cycle. More teachers may opt to stay in the profession and more suitable candidates may be attracted to the profession if indeed the image is improved. However, the effects of poor monetary remuneration cannot be underestimated. Within current negotiations with unions about changes in work practice lies an opportunity to pursue claims for salaries and conditions which reflect an accurate understanding of the nature of roles and responsibilities of the early childhood professional. There is of course no easy answer to the dilemma. Should early childhood teachers working with children under 5 years be successful in improving salaries and conditions, the cost of children's services will rise. Then either parents or government will need to pay more. In economically restrained times the cost of children's services is a contentious one and leads to arguments for reducing cost through employing untrained staff since anyone can care for young children.

What constitutes early childhood teacher preparation?

By international definition, early childhood encompasses the age span from birth to 8 years, but in Australia there is no national policy on what constitutes early childhood (Schiller, 1989). Therefore, deciding on the parameters of early childhood preparation has become a fundamental problem for early childhood teacher educators in their quest to prepare quality graduates. There are real difficulties in adequately preparing graduates to enter settings differing so markedly from informal programs for children from birth to 5 years to the more formal K-2 settings. This raises the question of whether early childhood teacher education should plan for career entry or for career flexibility. In most Australian states, quality preparation in the students preferred area of choice (such as birth-to-3, 3-to-5 or 5-to-8 years) seems to have been the emerging trend. However, in the light of recommended national and state directions in reports such as *Teacher education in Australia* (1990), *Discipline review of teacher education in mathematics and science* (Department of Employment, Education, and Training, 1989), and the *Report of the Committee of Review of New South Wales Schools* (1989) such specialisation may be lost in the search for maximum flexibility in teacher education. Ramsay (1988) questioned the teacher education categories of early childhood, primary, secondary, and TAFE arguing that restructuring of teacher education was inevitable in order to provide flexibility. He suggested that teachers should be prepared to work in any two adjacent age ranges (e.g. 0-5, 5-8, 8-12, etc.).

In working with children from birth to 5, it is acknowledged that the early childhood professional needs basic preparation in far more than teaching skills (Brennan & O'Donnell, 1986; Ebbeck, 1990). In programs for this age group, the graduate must accept responsibilities which include managerial aspects (if only at the level of working with an assistant, forming parent relationships, or networking with other professionals) whereas preparation for the K-2 area would involve more emphasis on subject-content curriculum. However, in striving for quality preparation for specific settings, universities must be mindful not to create or perpetuate a care versus education dichotomy!

In search of a structure: Fundamentals or flexibility

The dominant early childhood teacher preparation model of the 80s has been three years of preservice preparation for the award of a Diploma of Teaching (Briggs, 1984). In some States, it was then possible after a minimum of 120 days teaching to undertake one year's further full-time internal study (or equivalent part-time external study) for the award of a Bachelor of Education (Taylor, 1990). This model was challenged by *Teacher education in Australia* (1990) which proposed a first degree after three years (equivalent to 7 semesters of study rather than 6) followed by a two year internship as an associate teacher on a half teaching load with concurrent study leading to a professional degree of Bachelor of Education. There seems to be a consensus among teacher educators that the first qualification should be a four-year degree for all teachers, including an induction period with contractual (or other) obligations between employers and higher education institutions. However, the question of affordability and funding remains unresolved as does portability of qualifications between states. No doubt the availability of funds at the national level will determine whether there will be three or four year degrees.

Elementary and early childhood teacher education: Nexus or focus?

One tension underlying decisions about the nature of early childhood teacher education concerns its relationship to elementary teacher education. Many Australian early childhood teacher education programs exist as downward extensions of an elementary teacher education program, often as specialised options during the later years following a common core with the elementary program. Early childhood may be a department within a faculty of education to provide the specialisation. Shared staff and courses with other teacher education students provide the common components; components which may have little light to shed on the problems of early childhood in their focus on the school. The interest of the national government in teacher education has also focused on the problems of the school rather than the preschool years. The national government's paper *Quality of teaching: An issue for all* (Department of Employment, Education, and Training, 1990) shows little if any understanding of the nature of the complex early childhood field in its comments on the benefits to the nation of improving the quality of teaching as well as conditions and image of teachers, or providing career paths for teachers, or pre- or in-service teacher education (Walker, 1990). The outcomes of primary and secondary school education, not early childhood education are the focus for the national report. Battersby (1990) argues that early childhood teacher education is a handmaiden of elementary teacher education. Despite paying lip service to access and equity issues, early childhood teacher education has largely been neglected in the national government's proposed reforms to teacher education. There has been no attempt to analyse the nexus between elementary and early childhood teacher education or to define the nature of the different approaches to the common K-2 area. "Little, if any, analysis was completed on the differences in the workforce profile of those employed in the early childhood field compared with those employed in other education sectors" (Battersby, 1990, p. 2). There has been no account taken of either the national government initiatives increasing funding for child care or pressures to move towards privatisation and deregulation of child care, both of which have training and employment implications for early childhood teacher education. The terminology of the Australian Education Council has always referred to schools and school systems. Early childhood teacher educators become alienated by the exclusive use of such terminology. While the direct provision of children's services has been on the political agenda in 1990 the provision of qualified staff for those services has not! Early childhood teacher education as part of the wider scope of teacher education seems to be perceived as the least powerful sector!

There is an alternative view of early childhood teacher education that would seek to maintain the uniqueness of early childhood as a discipline in its own right and separate from the school system. Brennan argued in a national report on child care, "Training courses which prepare students to work with children aged 0-8 years should be separate from programs which train teachers within formal schooling systems" (Brennan & O'Donnell, 1986, p. 86). Some support has come from a state perspective. The *Report of the Committee of Review of New South Wales Schools* (1989) pointed to the powerful influence of parents on the motivation for learning and educational success of their children and the profound positive effects of quality early childhood education on the development of the child. The Report showed an awareness of the complexity of children's services in terms of types of service, range of employing bodies, and lack of coordination between the education, welfare, and health departments of government sector and between government and non-government service providers. The Report also highlighted the need for well-trained early childhood educators as an important quality component and suggested that students should identify a focus of interest and gain a set of career entry skills which could then be extended to meet the demands of career flexibility through continuing study. An alternative was to prepare only for the birth to 5 year group and let traditional elementary teacher education programs prepare for the K-6 grades. It would however be unfortunate to separate the knowledge and expertise that early childhood education can contribute to in K-2 settings because of enforced fragmentation between the community sector and the education system and consequent industrial fragmentation. Yet the issues must be resolved!

Community development and education systems models

The early childhood teacher educator must try to juggle two complex models of education in preparation of teachers. The community development model encourages flexibility and direct response to local community needs and focuses on the early childhood worker as a member of a team of professionals involved with children's services. The education systems model is school-based, regionally organised and more prescriptive in its curriculum and pedagogy. There is conflict between the philosophy of a discipline-based acquisition of knowledge (appropriate for adult learners) or an experience-based integrated approach (common in early childhood settings). Who should offer such courses in the early childhood teacher education faculties which are discipline-based, such as mathematics and science, or the faculty of pedagogy in the faculty of education which is based on the methodology of teaching, or a specialist early childhood faculty? How can teacher preparation be reconciled with research as a basis for teaching? How can early childhood teacher education courses impart the knowledge and methodology that graduates need to give them confidence in planning curricula for early childhood centres? Such issues have been debated at meetings of the deans of education from all Australian universities as well as at meetings of the deans within states. Can this only be done by specialised early childhood teacher educators? It is interesting to note that in 1990 only one university Chair in early childhood exists in Australia. This is, in fact, the first recognition in Australia of early childhood as a discipline.

The practicum: fundamental or a frill?

Historically the practicum has been seen as an important focus within early childhood teacher preparation, allowing the student the unique opportunity to demonstrate understanding of young children and to integrate theory with practice.

The practicum has been viewed as an essential component of preparation. In the 1990s the issues for the practicum are cost (Taylor & Williams, 1989), placement of practicum within the university calendar, and appropriateness of practicum models. In Australia, higher education institutions must pay cooperating teachers to undertake the work and supervision associated with student teaching. Cuts in the funding base have placed enormous pressure over time on the amount and nature of practicum experiences. Educators are now being faced with the vital questions about the scope, breadth, depth, and diversity of practicum experiences required to adequately prepare graduates. All learning areas in traditional teacher education programs are being pressed to reduce student contact time so that they may fit in with the traditional university model of teaching and calendar. To capitalize on the benefits of amalgamating with the universities, programs need to be designed to attract students from other areas within the university and to allow early childhood students to study courses external to early childhood. Hence the placement as well as the length of the practicum is problematic. The credibility of early childhood preservice education may be upheld or lost over the practicum issues currently being debated.

The benefit of the practicum experience is contingent upon many variables including availability of appropriate placements, standards within placements, and the expense of supervision. As the cost of practicum escalates and the supervisory role of university staff is questioned, there is growing interest in rethinking the role and orientation of the practicum in order to demonstrate a more reflective orientation (*Teacher education in Australia*, 1990). Governments are expecting employers to share the costs of preparation through contractual agreements with universities for the induction and internship period by employing students part time for two years as associate teachers (Taylor & Williams, 1990; *Teacher education in Australia*, 1990; Walker, 1990). However, for early childhood such a mandate poses more questions than answers (Goodfellow, 1990). Since early childhood employers are mainly small community-based committees rather than the large state-wide systems of education it is difficult to develop the tripartite arrangements for the associateship between unions, universities, and employers.

Induction, inservice and postgraduate study

Teacher education in Australia (1990) and *Teacher education: Directions and strategies* (1990) both acknowledge the need for induction, inservice and upgrading of qualifications to be part of a teachers career. These areas have been handled badly as funding was inadequate and coordination between universities and employing authorities had not been considered previously. Now, universities and employers are being asked to enter into contractual agreements similar to those in the UK. Much attention is being devoted to planning and rebuilding career paths for teachers through carefully thought out sequences of advanced standing in teacher education courses and dual qualification credit transfer for courses offered by employers towards university qualifications. Joint initiatives between departments of education, other employing authorities, and universities are being encouraged as part of staff development packages.

Support also comes from the national Training Guarantee Act (1 July, 1990) which requires all employers who have a payroll of $200,000 or more per annum, to spend at least one per cent of the payroll on formal training programs for employees, in an attempt to improve the skilling of Australia's workers. This incentive in the teaching area has great possibilities, but for small, isolated, early childhood services where such incentives are needed, there are currently no solutions! However, such moves have encouraged universities to open their doors to graduates, to consider greater flexibility, portability and access, and to plan more effectively for inservice and postgraduate studies.

Access and equity

An issue which has caused grave concern in early childhood education at the tertiary level is the limited access of Aboriginal people and those with English as a second language. Bridging courses have been established to better equip these students for higher education courses. Tutors were appointed to assist students on an individual basis and money was provided by the national government to set up Aboriginal enclaves (or support units) for indigenous groups many of whom reported cultural alienation, unfamiliarity with city living and expectations, and social isolation. Where institutions were sincere in setting up such units and community networks could provide the necessary human resources, the rewards have made the investment worthwhile. Where institutional efforts were half-hearted and programs languished, dropout rates ensured a quick demise. In 1990, there has been a resurgence of interest and funding support at the national level through the Department of Education, Employment, and Training for innovative programs designed to improve participation, access, and equity for all sectors of the community. There is no current support for students from isolated rural communities to study at home although this is technologically possible. However, a negative aspect is that many language laboratories established to assist students who had English as a second language have been converted to institutional money-making ventures in providing English classes for non-English speaking fee paying students from Thailand, Indonesia, and other Asian countries seeking student status in Australian universities.

There are also few initiatives to encourage male student teachers to become early childhood educators but several much publicised child sexual abuse cases allegedly involving male directors in Australia have served as disincentives to male teacher education students to make early childhood teacher education a chosen career. Currently in student teacher intakes, five out of every 200 students in early childhood teacher education are male.

Conclusions

Will the next ten years in early childhood teacher education be as stormy as the 1980s? As Australia moves towards a national curriculum for schools making mobility easier for children will there also be mobility for teachers? What will the impact of the unified national system of universities be on early childhood teacher education? What will be the impact of technology on enrolment patterns, study methods, and course options? Will economic values prevail over educational ones in the decisions about course length, nomenclature, and content as early childhood teacher education moves through the 90s? Will adequate funding be available from government and industry for early childhood research?

Australia is at a crossroad. It will take time for patterns to emerge in relation to the new directions for early childhood teacher education. The opportunity exists for a fresh start and a dynamic approach reconstructing teaching as a career. But the economic forecast is gloomy! From the eye of the storm the changes have been a mixed blessing. Less optimistically, Australia might well witness the decline of a profession.

References

Australian Pre-schools Committee (1974) *Care and education of young children: Report of the Australian Pre-schools Committee.* (Chaired by J. Fry), Canberra, ACT: Australian Government Publishing Service

Battersby, D. (1990) *Early childhood teacher education: Compromises and contradictions.* Paper presented at the Australian Early Childhood Association (NSW Branch) State Conference, University of Western Sydney (Macarthur), Milperra, NSW, September 8–9, 1990

Brennan, D. & O'Donnell, C. (1986) *Caring for Australia's children: Political and industrial issues in child care.* North Sydney, NSW: Allen & Unwin

Briggs, F. (1984) A survey of early childhood teacher education courses in Australia. *Australian Journal of Early Childhood,* **9**(1), 5–13

Committee of Enquiry into Education and Training (1979) *Education, training, and employment: Report of the committee of enquiry into education and training.* (Chaired by B. Williams), Canberra, ACT: Australian Government Publishing Service

Committee on the Future of Tertiary Education in Australia (1964) *Tertiary education in Australia: Report of the committee on the future of tertiary education in Australia to the Australian Universities Commission.* (Chaired by L.H. Martin), Melbourne, Vic.: Government Printer

Commonwealth Tertiary Education Commission (1986) *Review of efficiency and effectiveness.* (Chaired by H.R. Hudson), Canberra, ACT: Australian Government Publishing Service

Commonwealth Tertiary Education Commission (1985) *Review of the structure of the Commonwealth Tertiary Education Commission and arrangements for coordination and consultation with states and institutions.* (Chaired by H. R. Hudson), Canberra, ACT: Australian Government Publishing Service

Department of Education, Employment, and Training (1989) *Discipline review of teacher education in mathematics and science.* Volume 1: Report and recommendations. (Chaired by G. W. Speedy), Canberra, ACT: Australian Government Publishing Service

Department of Education, Employment, and Training (1987) *Higher education: A policy discussion paper.* (by J.S. Dawkins) Canberra, ACT: Australian Government Publishing Service

Department of Education, Employment, and Training (1988) *Higher education: A policy statement.* (by J.S. Dawkins), Canberra, ACT: Australian Government Publishing Service

Department of Employment, Education and Training (1990) *Quality of teaching: an issue for all: An initial statement.* (by J.S. Dawkins), Canberra: Australian Government Publishing Service

Department of Community Services and Health (1990) *NSW State Planning Committee recommendations to the Minister for Aged, Family, and Health Services.* Sydney, NSW: Unpublished paper

Drake, R. (1990) *A study of the relationship between children's services policy and the use of long day care centres in western Sydney and country areas of New South Wales.* Unpublished Masters thesis submitted to Macquarie University

Ebbeck, M. (1990) Preparing early childhood personnel to be pro-active, policy making professionals. *Early Child Development and Care,* **58**, 87–95

Edgar, D. (1990) Personal communication, July 31, 1990

Goodfellow, J. (1990) *Response to the Report of the Australian Education Council Working Party on Teacher Education.* Paper presented at the NSW Teacher Education Conference, Macquarie University Institute of Early Childhood, May 1990

Harrison, R. (1985) *Sydney Kindergarten Teachers College 1897–1981: A pioneer in early childhood education and care in Australia.* Sydney NSW: Sydney Kindergarten Teachers College Graduates Association

Kelly, J. (1988) *Not merely minded: Care and education for the young children of working women in Sydney. The Sydney Day Nursery and Nursery Schools Association 1905–1945.* Unpublished doctoral thesis, University of Sydney

National Commission on Excellence in Teacher Education (1986) *A call for change in teacher education.* Washington, DC: US Government Printer

Parry, R.E. (1989) *Reflections: New South Wales perspective.* In L.M. Koder (Ed.), *In Transit: Sydney CAE 1982–1989.* Sydney, NSW: Sydney College of Advanced Education

Ramsay, G.M. (1988) Commonwealth perspectives on teacher education. In J. Murphy, (Ed.), Teacher qualifications and employment patterns: Implications for teacher education. *Forum of Education Monograph No. 1*

Ramsay, G.M. (1989) *Reflections: Federal perspective.* In L.M. Koder (Ed.), *In Transit: Sydney CAE 1982–1989.* Sydney, NSW: Sydney College of Advanced Education

Ramsay, G.M. (1990) *The context of educational change.* Paper presented at the Restructuring the Education Industry Conference, Darling Downs Institute for Higher Education, Toowoomba, Qld

Report of the committee of review of New South Wales schools (1989) (Chaired by J.L. Carrick). Sydney, NSW: New South Wales Government

Report of the national enquiry into teacher education (1980) (Chaired by J.J. Auchmuty). Canberra, ACT: Australian Government Publishing Service

Ryan, P. (1989) Leaving the industry: A report on staff turnover in New South Wales long day care centres. *Rattler,* **9,** 4–5

Schiller, W. (1989) Towards a "fair go" for children: An early childhood perspective on the Convention for the Rights of the Child. *Australian Journal of Early Childhood.* **14**(2), 15–20

Schools and quality: An international report (1989) Paris: OECD

Scott, B. (1990) *School-centred education: Building a more responsive state school system.* Sydney, NSW: New South Wales Government

Stonehouse, A. (1988) Nice ladies who love children: The status of the early childhood professional in society. In *Looking forward, looking back: Proceedings of the 18th National Conference of the Australian Early Childhood Association,* Canberra ACT, September 4–8, 1988

Taylor, A. (1990) A collaborative model of teacher education. *Independent Education,* **20**(3), 6–9

Taylor, A. & Williams, D. (1989) *The influence of policy on practicum organisation: A New South Wales perspective.* Paper presented at the Fourth National Conference Practicum in Teacher Education, James Cook University, Rockhampton, Qld, September, 1989

Teacher education: Directions and strategies (1990) Sydney, NSW: Ministry of Education, Youth, and Women's Affairs

Teacher education in Australia (1990) Final advice to the Australian Education Council from the Working Party on Teacher Education, May, 1990

Teacher quality: An issues paper (1989) Report prepared by the Schools Council of the National Board of Employment, Education, and Training. Canberra, ACT: Australian Government Publishing Service

The report of the Committee on Australian universities (1957) (Chaired by K.A.H. Murray), Canberra, ACT: Government Printer

House of Commons Education, Science, and Arts Committee (1990) *The supply of teachers for the 1990's* (1990) London, UK: Parliamentary Report

Walker, J. (1990) In the national interest: But who carries the load? *Independent Education,* **20**(3), 26–28

The mosaic versus the melting pot: Teacher preparation in Canada

KELVIN L. SEIFERT

University of Manitoba, Winnipeg, Canada

(Received August 1991)

Set within the context of 'North America', this paper explores similarities and differences between Canada and the U.S.A. in the initial preparation of teachers to serve early education. The specific goal for the paper is to assess the status and future needs of early childhood teacher preparation in the Canadian context.

Circumstances have intertwined Canadian with American history, often making Canadians seem rather American to outside observers. Canadian early childhood education partakes of this confusion, no less than other parts of society. In this chapter, therefore, I will do what many other Canadian writers have done for other realms of life: I will point out similarities between Canadian and American experience, but emphasize the differences (Malcolm, 1985; Lipset, 1990). Unlike the other writers, however, I will focus on an important aspect of early education — the initial preparation of teachers in Canada. I will argue that differences from Americans are greater and more significant than they first appear, and that similarities to them are not necessarily desirable for the early childhood teachers and young children of Canada.

Coming to this conclusion, however, requires three other preliminary steps. First, the chapter must document the extent of actual similarity in early childhood teacher preparation between the United States and Canada. Second, it must assess how well current models of teacher preparation fits Canadian circumstances. And third, it must document the level of public support for present forms of early childhood education in Canada. After looking at all of these points, and only then, can this review reach its goal, which is to assess the status and future needs of early childhood teacher preparation in Canada.

IS CANADIAN TEACHER PREPARATION "JUST THE SAME" AS AMERICAN?

In many ways, the answer to this question has to be *yes*. In Canada, as in the United

States, candidates for initial preparation in early childhood education are largely self-selected females, mostly in their 20s, and tending to lack practical experience working with young children (see Barbour, 1990, for example, versus Seifert, 1975a, 1985, 1988; King-Shaw, 1984). Official goals for Canadian and American training programs differ in phrasing, but not much in underlying content (compare Lero, 1986, to Bredekamp, 1987 or to Read, *et al.*, 1987). In both countries, future teachers are supposed to acquire an understanding of child development, and learn the benefits of play, self-choice and social competence for young children. Then they have to practice providing these benefits to children in a practicum of some sort. Recently, too, future teachers in both countries are supposed to learn about cultural and language differences among children (Mallea & Young, 1984). As explained more fully below, though, Canadian policies of "multiculturalism" are somewhat more concerned with celebrating cultural plurality than on making assimilation possible to a mainstream culture. This difference remains in spite of growing American recognition of the inevitability of cultural differences in that country (Crawford, 1989; Ovando, 1990).

In formal academic structure, initial training programs seem remarkably similar between the two countries. Virtually everywhere in Canada, future early childhood teachers take modest amounts of child development or psychological foundations, combined with larger amounts of curricular methods, usually including the teaching of reading. Greatest energy and status are reserved for practice teaching. Variations among individual training programs occur in the sequencing and amount of contact time given to each type of course; but the choice of elements itself does not vary widely (Irvine, 1990). American programs can be summarized in similar terms, and indeed often have been (among others, see Almy, 1988; Haberman, 1988; Barbour, 1990; Perry, 1990).

Furthermore, the oft-noted split between day care services and school-based early childhood education occurs on both sides of the border, with separate training programs consequently providing for each type of service. In both the United States and Canada, day care training occurs largely in community colleges, and school-based early childhood training in faculties of education. In both countries the training for day care and early childhood education differs in similar, but small ways. Because of more limited training time, community colleges focus somewhat more on professional activities (like classroom methods) than do faculties of education, as well as more on topics unique to day care centres, such as nutrition and financial management (Canadian Task Force on Day Care, 1986; Tudiver, 1986). But these are differences in emphasis only. Initial training in day care and early childhood education resemble each other more than they differ.

FITTING THE AMERICAN MODEL TO CANADA

Given this description, it should not be surprising that Canadians have consciously borrowed ideas from south of the border in preparing early childhood teachers, as in preparing teachers in general (compare Hersom, 1989 with Holmes Group, 1986). Given the vastly larger population and resources of the United States, such a strategy seems understandable. But how appropriate has it really proved for early childhood education? How well are the young children of Canada served by early childhood training programs that resemble American ones strongly?

The answer, in a nutshell, is "not as well as in the United States." Seeing why this is so, however, requires noting three key features of Canadian geography and demography, and how the features differ from comparable ones in the United States.

First, Canada is just as multicultural as the United States, but its cultural groups tend to be more concentrated geographically than those in the United States. Almost a third of the country speaks French as a first language and participates in a French-speaking "community" with several hundred years of history in North America. Another third are of English-speaking, or at least European, descent; and the remaining people are divided among an assortment of smaller, but often very vital cultural and national groups from around the world (Samuda, *et al.*, 1984).

But the existence of ethnic peoples is less noteworthy than their geographical concentration and consequent self-conscious vitality as communities. Most French-speaking Canadians, for example, live in just one province, Quebec; the majority of Chinese-speaking Canadians live in just one metropolitan area, Vancouver (Friesen, 1983); an unusually large number of Native Indians live in one prairie city, Winnipeg (Canada Yearbook, 1990). Because of these concentrations, Canadians often speak of their country as a cultural "mosaic," rather than as a "melting pot," as do the Americans. In spite of some notorious exceptions in the past, Canadian social policy has aimed to preserve and nurture the mosaic of communities, rather than to assimilate them to a single mainstream culture, as American policy still tends to do (compare Lipset, 1990, or Armour, 1981 with Crawford, 1989, or Ovando, 1990).

In these ways, multiculturalism means something different, and perhaps more significant, in Canada than in the United States. Before settling on what that difference implies for teacher preparation, however, a second and third circumstance of Canadian society have to be taken into account. One of these is regionalism: the marked tendency for Canadians to feel loyal to their province or region almost as much as to Canada as a whole (Doran, 1989). The Canadian constitution both creates and reinforces this tendency by giving much more power to the provinces than do other countries which are federally structured. Provinces collect and spend substantially larger shares of the taxes than do American states, for example, and can even set their own policies for immigration and emigration. Not surprisingly, broad provincial powers extend to creating social policies about early education and child care.

While the balance of power in Canada makes for chronic conflicts between the federal and provincial governments, the balance also has the advantage of giving local leaders a relatively small, manageable forum in which to exercise influence. In developing new training requirements for teachers of young children, for example, early childhood educators from Nova Scotia need only persuade a local legislature and premier in Halifax, less than a hundred miles away, to act on behalf of a province of less than a million people — a community therefore similar in size to numerous middle-sized cities in the United States or Europe.

These comments point to a third important circumstance of Canadian life, its unusually low density of population. Most Canadians live within about 150 miles of the southern border; but even within this strip of land, people are especially scarce west of the Great Lakes. Viewed from the air, the land is really an archipelago of settlements: city-islands and farming enclaves interspersed with vast expanses of near wilderness. The geographic balance shifts to cities and farms in southern Ontario and southwestern Quebec, but elsewhere the balance favors the wilderness by a considerable margin. Early childhood education must find a place in this landscape, one that offers proportionately fewer cities and urban concentrations than does the United States or Great Britain, where early education as a profession originated.

EARLY EDUCATION IN CANADIAN CONTEXT

These comments imply that early chilhood education serves different segments of Canada in different ways and to different degrees, and that the variations are both inevitable and appropriate to Canadian society. Reviews of the field's development in this country (for example, Biemiller et al., 1987; Goelman & Pence, 1985) are therefore misleading to the extent that they imply that early education is distributed uniformly and successfully in all parts of the country.

This conclusion follows from Canada's style of multiculturalism, its regionally oriented politics, and its widespread domination by wilderness, rather than by urban settlement. Under these conditions, not all cultural groups have equally welcomed education of any sort — much less welcomed early childhood education. Currently, for example, one extreme example of caution are the Hutterite communities in the western Prairie provinces, who constitute several percent of the populations in those areas, but who have chosen to have minimal contact with non-Hutterite communities (Friesen, 1983). Less extreme, but perhaps just as significant, is the caution of much of the French-speaking community. The Francophone government of Quebec has spent only about half as much on prekindergarten and child care services as the Anglophone government of Ontario, even though the two provinces are about equally prosperous overall (Bates, 1986; Tudiver, 1986).

The reasons for culturally based caution such as this vary. Some groups, like the Hutterites, mistrust the competitive, individualistic attitudes which they feel that public schooling promotes. More moderate groups, including some of the French in Quebec, may object on similar grounds, though their particular caution may also reflect biases against all things Anglophone, based on historical conflicts, more than biases against early education specifically. In any case, culturally based caution frequently makes little sense to leaders in early childhood educators in Canada, who seem more intent on proving the universal applicability of early childhood services across society (Esbensen, 1986).

Another reason for caution about early education outside Anglophone communities has to do with language: in spite of widespread support for multiculturalism in principle, Canadian early education and child care teachers tend to use the politically dominant language of whatever region in which they work (usually English, though sometimes French). But the two dominant languages, and the cultures they represent, do not reflect the language and cultural needs of many young children in Canada. In northern Saskatchewan, for example, most preschool children speak primarily Dene; in northern Manitoba, primarily Cree; in the Northwest Territories, primarily Dene and Inuit. Early education programs in these areas need teachers and caregivers who are bilingual in these languages, educationally qualified, and committed to the local early childhood programs and communities for extended periods without interruption. Unfortunately, though, the combination of Canadian wilderness, regional commitments and multicultural differences often work against meeting this need.

Even in the south, many communities are too small to support early childhood education, at least of the sort which early childhood leaders are currently able to offer. To operate, early childhood programs require groupings of young children — perhaps a dozen for a small child care centre or junior kindergarten, and about five for a family day care home. Arranging groups of this size is comparatively easy in cities and small towns. But not so in the farmlands of Alberta, Saskatchewan and Manitoba: these extend for nearly a thousand miles from east to west, but average only six persons per square mile (Canada Yearbook, 1990). Because these areas have one of the lowest population densities of any settled area in the world, they are challenged simply to group enough children together for a small school of mixed ages, let alone enough children of specifically preschool ages for a nursery, kindergarten, or day care centre.

EARLY CHILDHOOD TEACHER PREPARATION IN CANADIAN CONTEXT

All things considered, then, Canadian circumstances create significant questions about the appropriateness and practicality of current models of early childhood education in this country. What are the effects of the challenges on how early childhood teachers are prepared in Canada? As it turns out, the challenges and needs of teacher preparation reflect those of the early childhood field generally. The challenges suggest, in particular, that Canadians need new models and priorities for preparing teachers of young children, ones not so dependent on the more urban experiences of Americans, or on their associated tendency to prefer cultural homogeneity.

To understand how early childhood services and teacher preparation relate, consider the example of Manitoba. In that province, early childhood education and day care programs are well-established in Winnipeg, a city of about 600,000, and to a much lesser extent in Brandon, a city of about 10,000. Both cities offer a range of program types, from school-based junior kindergarten to privately-financed day care.

Early childhood teacher preparation in Manitoba is also centred entirely in the two urban communities — with two training programs in Winnipeg, one in Brandon. The three programs resemble the generic description given at the beginning of this chapter in their selection of students, content, and academic structure (Stapleton, 1990; Irvine, 1990). Surveys show that graduates of these programs tend either to find teaching jobs in the two metropolitan areas, or not to enter teaching at all (Seifert, 1975b).

So far, so good. What is left out in this description is the fate of early childhood education for the non-urban half of Manitoba's population: what services do the other five- to six-hundred thousand people receive who live in rural areas and the north? These people are scattered over an area as large as five or six average American states. About 10% speak French as a first language, and another 10% speak Cree as a first language (Gregor & Wilson, 1984). In general, these groups have received very few early childhood services. An exception are prekindergarten classrooms in elementary schools that are federally financed by the Ministry of Indian and Northern Affairs; but even these classrooms serve only a fraction of the Native Indian population, and they lack access to trained staff and in-service development activities (Seifert, 1986).

As the experience of Manitoba shows, teacher preparation in early education reflects the pattern of early education itself, which in turn reflects patterns of Canadian society as a whole. In Canada, as in Manitoba, teacher preparation in early education is really not a universal service or profession, but a geographic and cultural patchwork. Some places, like Winnipeg, have access to trained individuals, but others do not, like the Manitoban North. Present early childhood teacher training in Canada therefore remains an urban activity, successful to the extent that it can serve largely Anglicized urban population centres.

In spite of these comments, though, teacher preparation is neither static nor unable to change, in spite of these comments. Further, vigorous development of initial training programs can occur to the extent that Canadian early education begins recognizing and responding to the unique qualities of the Canadian geography and demography. In particular, training programs must make multiculturalism a central priority for future teachers — more than it has in the past. Doing this will mean more than simply teaching future teachers about exotic holidays and some important foreign words and phrases. It also means actively recruiting members of the many Canadian minorities into early childhood training programs, and supporting their efforts to complete the programs and return to serve their communities. Good beginnings at this sort of multiculturalism are already happening at a number of Canadian universities with regard to teacher education in general. At the University of Manitoba, for example, the Winnipeg Education Centre has successfully recruited, trained, and placed several dozen Native Indian and immigrant students in elementary teaching positions through the province, including in the North (Stapleton, 1990). Unfortunately for early childhood education, these individuals have not received training specifically focused on the learning and development of the very young. But the Winnipeg Education Centre project suggests that such training may at least be feasible.

In addition to a fuller multicultural commitment, teacher preparation programs in early childhood education will need to devise ways to serve low-density populations, so that children in widely scattered areas do not need to be gathered every day at great effort and expense. One strategy may lie with greater development of parent-education and parent-visitation programs; another, with greater attention to family day care. These are not new activities in English-speaking early childhood circles, of course; much of the American Head Start program, for example, is committed to them. For parent-education and family day care to work in Canada, though, Canadian early childhood leaders will have to resist the temptation to borrow heavily from programs designed for the United States. With due respect to our colleagues to the south, American ideas for programs tend to assume urban-sized concentrations of children, and to equate multiculturalism with assimilation to a single mainstream society (Powell, 1989; Lombardi, 1990). These are important American facts of life; but they are American nonetheless, not Canadian.

References

Almy, M. (1988) *The early childhood educator revisited*. In Spodek, B., Saracho, O., and Peters, D. (eds.). *Professionalism and the early childhood practitioner*. New York: Teachers' College Press

Armour, L. (1981) *The idea of Canada and the crisis of community*. Ottawa: Steel Rail Press

Barbour, N. (1990) Issues in the preparation of early childhood teachers. In Seefeldt, C. (ed.). *Continuing issues in early childhood education*. Columbus, OH, USA: Merrill, pp. 154–172

Bates, H. (1986) Day care standards in Canada. In Task Force on Child Care (ed.), *Child care: Standards and quality*. Ottawa: Ministry of Supply and Services

Biemiller, A., Regan, E., & Lero, D. (1987) Early childhood education programs in Canada. In L. Katz (ed.), *Current topics in early childhood education, vol. 7*. Norwood, NJ: Ablex, pp. 32–58

Bredekamp, S. (ed.) (1987) *Developmentally appropriate practice for early childhood educators*. Washington, D.C.: National Association for the Education of Young Children

Statistics Canada. (1990) *Canada Yearbook, 1990*. Ottawa: Author

Chenier, N. & Bates, H. (1986) The informal child care market: Public policy for private homes. In Task Force on Child Care (ed.), *Care: Standards and quality*. Ottawa: Ministry of Supplies and Services, pp. 150–186

Crawford, J. (1989) *Bilingual education: History, politics, theory and practice*. Trenton, NH, USA: Crane Publishing

Doran, C. (1989) Contrasts in governing: A tale of two democracies. In L. Lamont and J.D. Edmonds (eds.). *Friends so different*. Ottawa: University of Ottawa Press, pp. 149–159

Esbensen, S. (1986) Effects of day care on children, families, and communities. In Task Force on Child Care (ed.), *Child care: Standards and quality*. Ottawa: Ministry of Supply and Services, pp. 187–250

Friesen, J. (1983) *Schools with a purpose*. Calgary, AL, Canada: Detselig Publishers

Goelman, H. and Pence, A. (1985) Toward an ecology of day care in Canada. *Canadian Journal of Education*, **10**(4), 323–344

Goldberg, M. & Mercer, J. (1989) The livable city: Comparing the urban cultures of Canada and the United States. In L. Lamont and J.D. Edmonds (eds.). *Friends so different*. Ottawa: University of Ottawa Press, pp. 173–184

Haberman, J. (1988) Gatekeepers to the profession. In Spodek, B., Saracho, O., and Peters, D. (eds.). *Professionalism and the early childhood practitioner*. New York: Teachers' College Press, pp. 84–92

Hersom, N. (1989) Teacher education in Faculties of Education: An assessment and strategies for achieving excellence. In H. Stevenson and J.D. Wilson, (eds). *Quality in Canadian public education*. London, UK: Falmer, pp. 47–60

Holmes Group. (1986) *Tomorrow's teachers*. East Lansing, MI, USA: Holmes Group, Inc.

Irvine, J. (1990) *An assessment of training needs for early childhood education*. Winnipeg, MB, Canada: Faculty of Education, University of Manitoba

King-Shaw, E. & Unruh, W. (1984, June) *A survey of early childhood education in Ontario*. Paper presented at the annual meeting of the Canadian Society for Studies in Education, Guelph, Ontario

Lero, D. & Kyle, I. (1986) Day care quality: Definition and implementation. In Task Force on Child Care (ed.). (1986) *Child care: Standards and quality*. Ottawa: Ministry of Supplies and Services, pp. 85–149

Lipset, S.M. (1990) *Continental divide: The values and institutions of the United States and Canada*. London, UK: Routledge

Lombardi, J. (1990) Head Start: The nation's pride, a nation's challenge. *Young Children*, **45**(6), 22–29

Malcolm, A. (1985) *The Canadians*. New York: Times Books

Malea, J. and Young, J. (1984) Teacher education for a multicultural society. In J. Malea and J. Young (eds.), *Cultural diversity and Canadian education*. Ottawa: Carlton University Press, pp. 399–411

Ovando, C. (1990) Politics and pedagogy: The case of bilingual education. *Harvard Educational Review*, **60**(3), 341–356

Perry, G. (1990) Alternate modes of teacher preparation. In C. Seefeldt, (ed.). *Continuing issues in early childhood education*. Columbus, OH, USA: Merrill, pp. 173–200

Powell, D. (1989) *Families and early childhood programs*. Washington, D.C.: National Association for the Education of Young Children

Read, K., Gardner, P. & Mahler, B. (1987) *Early childhood programs: Human relations and learning*. Philadelphia, PA, USA: Saunders

Samuda, R., Berry, J., & Laferriere, M. (1984) *Multiculturalism in Canada: Social and educational perspectives*. Toronto: Allyn and Bacon

Seifert, K. (1975a) Salaries and working conditions of early childhood teachers in Manitoba. *Today for Tomorrow: Journal of the Early Childhood Education Council*, **10** (Fall), pp. 1–4

Seifert, K. (1975b) An evaluation of graduates in early childhood education in Manitoba. *Manitoba Teacher*, September 1975, pp. 9–10

Seifert, K. (1985, June) *Careers of male and female teachers of young children*. Paper presented at the annual meeting of the Canadian Society for Studies in Education, Winnipeg, Manitoba

Seifert, K. (1986) *An assessment of early childhood education in Federally sponsored schools in Manitoba: Final Report*. Winnipeg, MB, Canada: Ministry of Indian and Northern Affairs

Seifert, K. (1988) Men in early childhood education. In Spodek, B., Saracho, O., and Peters, D. (eds.). *Professionalism and the early childhood practitioner*. New York: Teachers' College Press, pp. 105–116

Stapleton, J. (1990) *Faculty of Education Review, 1990*. Winnipeg, MB, Canada: Faculty of Education, University of Manitoba

Task Force on Child Care (ed). (1986) *Child care: Standards and quality*. Ottawa: Ministry of Supplies and Services

Tudiver, J. (1986) *Early childhood education/services*. Ottawa: Council of Ministers of Education

Early childhood teacher education in Indonesia

R. MURRAY THOMAS

University of California, Santa Barbara, California, USA

(Received August 1991)

As a background to understanding Indonesia's system of early-childhood teacher education, it is first useful to learn something of the nation's social characteristics and educational development. Therefore, the following chapter begins with an overview of the country's sociopolitical condition and modes of schooling. Next, attention is directed at provisions for the education of children ages three through six. Subsequently, the preparation of teachers of young children is described in some detail.

Key words: Early Childhood, Indonesia

INFLUENTIAL SOCIOPOLITICAL CONDITIONS

Present-day early-childhood education in Indonesia has been heavily influenced by the country's population distribution, colonial past, and educational policies.

Demographic Characteristics

Geographically the Republic of Indonesia is comprised of thousands of islands that form the world's most extensive archipelago, stretching 3,194 miles east to west and 1,180 miles north to south beneath continental Southeast Asia. More than 900 of the islands are inhabited. Some are crowded, while others are sparsely populated. The most concentrated is Java, with nearly 100 million inhabitants on a land area of 50,000 square miles (2,000 people per square mile). (In area, Java is half the size of the United Kingdom, which has a population of 60 million at 610 people per square mile. Java is one-third the area of California, which has a population of 29 million at 167 per square mile). The most sparsely settled Indonesian province is Irian Jaya (Western New Guinea) where 1.5 million people live in an area of 163,000 square miles at 9 people per square mile (Indonesia, 1990, p. 637).

Such size and population distribution pose a demanding challenge for early-childhood educators. By the early 1990s, the nation's inhabitants would exceed 185 million, making Indonesia the fifth most populous country in the world, exceeded only by China, India, the Soviet Union, and the United States. Of the 185 million, an estimated 11 percent or 20.3 million would be ages three through six, the range from which early-childhood programs have traditionally drawn their clients. At an annual population-growth rate of 1.61 percent, the number of Indonesians is expected to pass 214 million by year 2000, meaning that 23.5 million children would then be potential candidates for nursery-school and kindergarten places (Indonesia, 1990, p. 637).

Over the centuries, the nation's topography of mountainous islands and dense jungles has fostered the separation of the inhabitants into a host of tribal divisions, thereby promoting the evolution of multifarious ethnic groups, languages, and cultural traditions. By the mid-20th century, an estimated 350 languages were spoken throughout the archipelago. However, the Republic also has a national language, a variant of Malay called *bahasa Indonesia* (Indonesian language), that people through-out the archipelago willingly learn as a bond unifying the diverse cultural groups into a cohesive national society. The language that most children learn in their homes is a regional vernacular that is typically used as the medium of communication in early childhood programs. However, the national Indonesian language is the home language in a few regions and in the capital city of Jakarta, and there it serves for instruction in preschools. Generally, not until children enter the primary grades do they begin to learn the national tongue. By grade three or four, virtually all teaching is in bahasa Indonesia.

As for urban-rural distribution, Indonesia's population is overwhelmingly rural, with 78 percent of the inhabitants living outside the cities and major towns. Over 85 percent reside in communities of less than 100,000 residents. In terms of occupation, most Indonesians engage in agriculture and fishing.

Such demographic conditions have meant that leaders of the nation's early-childhood movement face the demanding task of providing educational opportunities for over 20 million children spread across hundreds of widely dispersed, mountainous islands. Most young children grow up in villages, far removed from regular contact with events in the more modern, industrialized urban centers where the preschool movement has experienced its greatest growth.

A Colonial Past

The boundaries that define the Republic of Indonesia today were established by Dutch mercantile and military forces who, from the 17th into the 20th century, gradually gained control of the archipelago to form the Netherlands East Indies colony. The Dutch ruled the area until ousted by the Japanese military during World War II. When the Dutch returned after the war to reclaim their East Indies territory, Indonesian nationalists declared their independence. However, it required four years of fighting against Dutch troops before the Republic of Indonesia became independent in fact.

The legacy of Dutch colonialism has influenced the development of early-childhood education in several ways. For example, the Dutch were the first to set up formal early-childhood centers and to introduce European teaching methods. In the relatively small number of private preschools that the Dutch established during the early 20th century, the methods of Frederich Froebel (1782–1852) formed the principal approach to instruction. Although the methods of Maria Montessori (1870–

1952) were also introduced in the latter 1930s, Montessori's work had little time to affect preschool education in the colony before the Dutch were expelled by the Japanese in 1942. Also during Dutch times, two varieties of native early-childhood movements appeared. One kindergarten that opened in 1922 blended elements of Javanese culture with European educational traditions. This school was the creation of a Javanese aristocrat, Ki Hadjar Dewantara, who labeled his invention *Taman Indria*, meaning "The Five Senses Garden," thereby reflecting Froebel's and Montessori's conviction that early-childhood education should focus on sharpening children's sensory skills (Dewantara, 1962, pp. 241–243). The second indigenous departure consisted of kindergartens set up by Islamic women's associations to promote nationalistic and religious aims in reaction against the Dutch-oriented preschools (Junus, 1962, pp. 234, 259, 277).

Thus, when Indonesians under their free Republic began establishing kindergartens in the 1950s, they modeled their preschools on the Dutch and native prototypes from colonial times. The Dutch models also influenced the form of teacher training that Indonesians would adopt in the early years of the Republic. Although during colonial days the Dutch had provided relatively few schooling opportunities for the indigenous peoples, a small number of Indonesian girls during the 1920s were able to enroll in two secondary-level Froebel Teacher-Training Schools (*Froebel Kweek-school*). Indonesian girls also prepared as kindergarten teachers in a number of home-economics secondary schools operated by private Dutch educational bodies. This provision for training native girls as teachers proved later to be a vital element in the development of preschool education during the 1950s and 1960s, since key leaders of the Republic's early-childhood programs would be women who had been schooled by the Dutch in the 1920s and 1930s.

From Dutch times, the tradition of private groups taking responsibility for early-childhood education was carried over into the Republic. By the 1990s, more than 99 percent of Indonesian preschools were still sponsored by private organizations (Thomas, 1988, p. 40).

Educational Policies and Progress

The pattern of formal educational development found in virtually all societies has been repeated in Indonesia during the four decades of the Republic's existence. In nearly every society, provisions for formal schooling are initiated at the primary level to serve pupils ages 6 to 12. Then, as a growing number of the young complete the primary level, secondary schools are added and, subsequently, higher education institutions. Only after this basic scheme of general primary, secondary, and tertiary schooling has been well established are serious efforts launched to furnish formal learning opportunities for young children, for the handicapped, and for older adults.

In keeping with this scheme, the Indonesian government in its basic education law of 1950 obligated itself to furnish six years of primary education for all children. The law provided for expanded secondary and higher-learning opportunities for graduates of the six-year primary school. In addition, kindergartens were identified as a recognized type of school, but the law did not commit the government to make early-childhood education universal, compulsory, or publicly supported (*Undang-undang no. 12*, 1954).

Because only a minor portion of the islands' indigenous population had attended school under the Netherlands East Indies government, the task now confronting the Republic was enormous indeed. Not only was there a relatively small number of school buildings and teachers left over from colonial times, but the government faced the additional problem of producing a large quantity of textbooks in the Indonesian language to replace the Dutch-language texts that had been used in the better schools during colonial times. To complicate their task, educational leaders were attempting to fulfill their educational commitment in an atmosphere of political turmoil and economic deterioration. Problems with contentious political parties and disastrous economic policies during the 1950s and early 1960s led to civil war in late 1965 and the replacement of President Sukarno's government by the Suharto government that would rule from 1966 into the 1990s.

Three sociopolitical conditions of the Suharto era have boded well for educational progress. These have been general political stability, a significantly improved economy, and an effective family-planning program. Political stability has meant that government programs could be implemented without interference from periodic public disorder and policy change. The economy received a fortuitous boost in the 1970s when the OPEC oil cartel — of which Indonesia is an important member — fixed crude oil prices at a high level, with a large portion of the resulting income budgeted in Indonesia for the rapid expansion of primary and secondary schooling. And in contrast to the previous government under Sukarno, which encouraged parents to bear many children, the Suharto government established a family-planning policy which has reduced the pace of population growth to a more manageable level than was true during the 1950s and 1960s.

The Indonesian government has assigned the education system a crucial role in achieving the goals of the nation's series of five-year national socioeconomic-development plans. Specifically, the country's educational institutions — from the nursery school through the university and adult education — are expected to produce patriotic and skilful citizens, well equipped to enter a labor force that fosters modernization and general prosperity. The preparation of early-childhood teachers is seen as an important component of this mission.

THE SYSTEM OF EARLY-CHILDHOOD EDUCATION

In the Indonesian language, educational programs for young children are identified by the equivalent of the German *kindergarten*, that is, by *taman kanak-kanak* (taman = garden, kanak-kanak = small child). The word *prasekolah*, as a variant of the English-language *preschool*, has recently become popular as well. All programs for children ages 3–6 are designated by these labels. In keeping with Indonesian usage, throughout the following discussion the term *kindergarten* refers to programs serving any segment of the four-year age span 3 through 6.

For several reasons, statistics describing early-childhood education in Indonesia are imprecise. First, figures compiled by the Ministry of Education include only those programs that meet the government's minimum standards for registration. In addition, Ministry figures do not include child-care facilities developed under the aegis of other government departments. Nor does the Ministry report the host of informal child-care arrangements in communities across the archipelago. Therefore, reported data are an underestimate of the extent of early-childhood provisions.

By the mid-1980s, the total number of children served in registered kindergartens exceeded 1.24 million. Of this total, 99.8% were in private preschools and only .2% in public facilities (*Statistik taman kanak-kanak*, 1985, pp. 1–2). These figures illustrate the fact that Indonesia's early-childhood education has resulted almost entirely from the initiative of private women's organizations that represent neighborhood groups, regional associations, religious bodies, or the families of men in a particular branch of the government. Especially in the cities, employees in a government department frequently live with their families in the department's complex of houses or flats, so the wives can conveniently establish a preschool to serve their children.

The extent and distribution of early-childhood programs in the mid-1980s are shown in Figure 1. The 1.23 million children enrolled at that time represented 7% of the nation's children ages 3 through 6. During this same period, over 98% of the country's 7-through-12 year-olds were reported as attending elementary schools. Thus, the government's success in pursuing the goal of universal primary education was in sharp contrast to the ability of the leaders of the early-childhood movement to furnish educational opportunities for the entire population of preschool children.

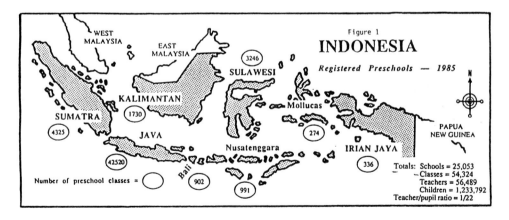

Figure 1

The conduct of early-childhood education in Indonesia has assumed the form of congenial cooperation between private women's organizations and the Ministry of Education. However, over the years the government's contributions to early-childhood education have always been dwarfed by the efforts of the private women's

foundations whose initiative has been the true stimulus behind preschool development. A landmark event in the growth of the movement was the establishment in
1957 of the federation of preschool sponsoring groups, entitled the Indonesian
Preschool Education Association. Since that time the Association — along with its
sister organization, the Kindergarten Teachers Alliance — has grown ever stronger
and more effective in expanding early childhood education opportunities.

   In the division of assignments between the Association and the Ministry of
Education's preschool section, the Association takes responsibility for the quantita-
tive expansion and basic financial support of preschools, while the government is
responsible for preservice teacher training, for the qualitative improvement of
kindergartens, and for support services. Furthermore, the government's 1989–1994
Five-Year National Development Plan has called for establishing of a public
demonstration kindergarten in each county and major city, for refurbishing classrooms that have fallen into disrepair, and for providing more government-paid
teachers in private preschools (*Replita V*, 1989, pp. 20–37).

EARLY CHILDHOOD TEACHER EDUCATION

The preparation of teachers for Indonesia's early-childhood programs has taken three
principal forms — unorganized on-the-job experiences, a formal three-year upper-
secondary-school preservice program, and organized inservice-education sessions.
Teachers whose training consists entirely of on-the-job experiences are ones who
either (1) organize a child-care unit on their own initiative or else (2) enter an
established early-childhood program as a teacher's aide, then acquire their teaching
methods by observing the program's veteran staff members and by learning from
their own trials and errors. Although this informal mode of preparation is rather
common, it is not the type deemed most suitable by either the Ministry of Education
or the Preschool Association. Thus, leaders of the early-childhood movement
endeavor to increase the proportion of teachers who have completed the formal three-
year training program and who subsequently engage in periodic inservice upgrading
sessions. Inservice courses are of several varieties: (1) national seminars sponsored
jointly by the Preschool Education Association, Kindergarten Teachers Alliance, and
Ministry of Education, (2) regional and local workshops that are typically led by
delegates who have participated in national seminars, and (3) supervisory visits to
classrooms by experienced Association members or Ministry personnel.

   We now consider in more detail Indonesia's preservice teacher-education provisions in terms of the evolution of programs and contents of the present-day
curriculum.

The Teacher-Education Secondary Schools

Formal teacher training in the Republic traces its beginnings to the weeks immediately following the end of World War II, when the Dutch sought to regain control of
the islands. In late 1945, a private women's group, under the title Yayasan

Pendidikan Lanjutan Wanita (Women's Advanced Education Foundation), opened the National Kindergarten-Teachers Training School in a garage in the capital city of Jakarta. It was a nationalistic movement in opposition to the return of the Dutch, led by women educated as preschool teachers before the war. In 1951, a year after the Dutch relinquished control of the islands, the training school received a government subsidy and expanded its operation. In 1955 it was officially placed under the Ministry of Education, and the school staff went on the government payroll.

During the 1950s, emergency programs to supply primary and kindergarten teachers included (1) short-term preparation for elementary-school graduates and (2) a junior-high teacher-training program (*Sekolah Guru B* — Teacher School B). A three year senior-high teacher-training school (*Sekolah Guru A* — Teacher School A) was also established. As the number of graduates of the senior-high teacher-training program increased by the end of the 1950s, the emergency programs were phased out, and the three-year senior-secondary training course (renamed *Sekolah Pendidikan Guru* — Teacher Education School) became the standard preservice program for teachers in both elementary schools and kindergartens. By the early 1990s, the *Sekolah Pendidikan Guru* (SPG) continued to be the principal source of accredited primary and preschool personnel and of special-education teachers assigned to elementary schools. However, as Haslam has explained:

Historically, the primary teacher training high schools were created to provide a reasonably well trained teaching force quickly to meet the demands of explosive enrollment increases in the primary schools. Recently, as enrollment has stabilized, the Indonesian parliament has directed the Ministry of Education and Culture to prepare and implement new primary [and early childhood] teacher training programs at the collegiate level. In addition, Parliament's decree also calls for the upgrading of all elementary school teachers who are currently employed. The decree, in effect, mandates an inservice staff development program for more than one million teachers (Haslam, 1989, p. 4).

By the opening of the 1990s, there were 215 SPGs distributed throughout the archipelago for training primary-school teachers (Haslam, 1989, p. 4). Many of these had specializations in early-childhood education. Both the public and private SPGs have been required to adopt the curriculum issued in 1983 by the Ministry of Education (*Kurikulum SPG*, 1983).

The Teacher-Education Curriculum

The training program in the SPGs is divided into three major segments — basic general education, foundations of teacher education, and specific teacher training. The titles of the courses comprising the three segments, and the weekly class hours dedicated to each course (called *credit hours*) are shown in Table 1.

The general-education portion comprises around half of a student's program and the two teacher-education segments the other half. As the totals at the bottom of the table indicate, teacher-training students spend 40 hours each week in class. However, in schools that include regional-language pedagogy in the curriculum, the total becomes 42 hours. For each hour in class, students are expected to spend one-half

Table 1

| | | | Class Hours Per Week | | | | | |
| Basic General Education | Year | I | | II | | II | | |
	Semester	1	2	3	4	5	6	Total
1. Religious Studies		2	2	2	2	2	2	12
2. Moral Pancasila Education		2	2	2	2	2	2	12
3. History of the Indonesian National Struggle		2		2		2		6
4. Indonesian Language		2	2	2	2	2	2	12
5. Social Science		3	3	3	3			
6. Health and Physical Education		2	2	2	2	2		10
7. Art Education		2	2					4
8. Manual Skills		2	2					4
9. Mathematics		4	4	2				10
10. Natural Science		4	4					8
11. English Language		4	4					8
Foundations of Teacher Education								
12. The Science of Education		6	8	4	2			20
13. Psychology		3	3	2	4			12
14. Foundations of Special Education		2	2					4
Specific Teacher Training – Materials, Methods and Evaluation Techniques in the Areas of:								
15. Moral Pancasila and National History				3	4	3	5	15
16. Language Development				4	3	3	5	15
17. Emotional and Social Development, and Environmental Awareness				3	3	3	5	14
18. Creativity				4	4	3	4	15
19. Cognitive Development				2	4	4	4	14
20. Health and Physical Development				3	3	4	5	15
21. Regional Language (only where regional language is used in preschools)		(2)	(2)	(2)	(2)	(2)	(2)	(12)
22. Practice Teaching in the Community					2	10	6	18
Total Student Course Load		40	40	40	40	40	40	240

Source: *Kurikulum SPG* (1983), p. 9.

hour outside of class completing homework assignments and pursuing practical applications of classwork. During the practice-teaching portion of their studies, students receive one credit-hour for every two hours spent in the practicum. Therefore, the amount of combined in-class and out-of-class study time ranges from 60 hours a week during the first three semesters to 65 hours a week during the fifth semester. In schools offering regional-language studies, these totals become 63 and 68 hours respectively. Furthermore, the study hours are distributed across as many as 15 or 16 different subject-matter fields during the early semesters of the program. Consequently, for the typical teacher-education candidate, this heavy, diversified load of expectations has proven to be very burdensome indeed.

Teacher-education students are obliged to engage in three types of learning experiences — intracurricular, cocurricular, and extracurricular. The intracurricular portion is comprised of those activities typically carried out within the classroom — listening to lectures, engaging in question-answer sessions, participating in discussions, taking tests. The cocurricular part consists of out-of-class experiences intended to strengthen and embellish the students' mastery of the objectives pursued in class. Cocurricular study includes such undertakings as reading supplementary materials, carrying out simple experiments, writing essays, and implementing projects that require the application of knowledge and skills the students gained in class. Extracurricular activities are ones pursued outside of the classroom and beyond the cocurricular assignments. The goal of extracurricular applications is to provide students an opportunity to integrate what they have learned in separate subject fields through engaging in educational ventures beyond the school. Extracurricular experience is gained by participation in Scouting, the Red Cross Youth Movement, drama and music societies, hobby clubs, and the like (*Kurikulum SPG*, 1983, p. 9).

Over the years, critics have attacked the SPG curriculum for its multiplicity of subjects. The pattern of having students pursue a large number of subject-matter areas simultaneously was inherited from the Dutch, whose school programs during colonial times consisted of a wide range of subject fields, each studied for one, two, or three hours a week. The problem of requiring students to pursue so many subjects simultaneously has been exacerbated under the Republic whenever authorities have added new topics to the curriculum without reducing the number of old topics. Observers have charged that when teacher-education candidates bear such a heavy burden of studies, the quality of their education cannot help but suffer. This problem of quality is said to result from the SPGs' overly "ambitious — some say impossible — dual missions of completing the academic training of their students as well as developing skills in pedagogy" (Haslam, 1989, p. 4). The government's recent plan to advance primary-school and early-childhood teacher-training to the collegiate level reflects educational and political leaders' recognition that the dual missions of the SPGs have not been satisfactorily achieved.

In summary, the standard and officially endorsed preservice preparation of early-childhood teachers in Indonesia over the past three decades has consisted of a three-year teacher-education high school program built around the type of curriculum displayed in Table 1.

The instructors who staff the SPGs have typically been graduates of the nation's 10 public college-level Teacher Education Institutes (*Institut Keguruan dan Ilmu Pendidikan*) or of the 21 Teacher Education Faculties (*Fakultas Keguruan dan Ilmu Pendidikan*) attached to universities throughout the islands. In addition, some SPG instructors are graduates of the country's private teacher-education institutes and faculties.

CONCLUSION

In 1986, a nationwide seminar of early-childhood educators attracted more than 200 participants from all parts of the Indonesian archipelago. The mission they set for themselves for the remainder of the 20th century was reflected in the seminar theme: *Popularizing Kindergarten Education*. A crucial element of this endeavor would be to correct two current weaknesses of preschool programs — the inadequate preparation of teachers and the lack of sufficient guidance for teachers in the conduct of specific daily activities for children. Steps taken in the latter 1980s to remedy these shortcomings included upgrading the quality of preservice instruction in the teacher-education high schools, widely distributing preschool-teachers' guidebooks by the Ministry of Education, and expanding regional and local inservice workshops. These endeavors, combined with the vigorous efforts of the Preschool Education Association to establish new early-childhood programs in rural districts and remote islands, were designed to achieve the goal set in the government's 1989-1994 Five-Year Development Plan of increasing the number of children attending preschools by an additional 1.1 million by 1995 (*Replita V*, 1989, pp. 20–37).

References

Dewantara, K.H. (1962) *Karja Ki Hadjar Dewantara, bagian pertama: pendidikan* (The works of Ki Hadjar Dewantara, first part: Education). Jogjakarta: Madjelis Luhur Persatuan Taman Siswa

Haslam, M.B. (1989, April) *Teacher selection and placement: A study of Indonesia's policies and practices.* Paper presented at the meeting of the Comparative and International Education Society, Cambridge, MA

Indonesia (1990) *Britannica book of the year.* Chicago: Encyclopaedia Britannica

Janus, M. (1962) *Sedjarah pendidikan Islam di Indonesia* (A history of Islamic education in Indonesia). Jakarta: Pustaka Mahmudiah

Kurikulum SPG — Sekolah pendidikan guru (Curriculum of the SPG — Teacher Education School). (1983) Jakarta: Department Pendidikan dan Kebudayaan

Replita V (Five-Year Development Plan — 1989–1994). (1989) Jakarta: Republik Indonesia

Statistik taman kanak-kanak (Preschool statistics) (1985) Jakarta: Department Pendidikan dan Kebudayaan

Thomas, R.M. (1988) Dividing the labor: Indonesia's government/private early childhood education system. *Early Child Development and Care*, 39, pp. 33–43

Undang-undang no. 12 tahun 1954 tentang pernjataan berlakunja undang-undang No. 4 tahun 1950 dari Republik Indonesia dahulu tentang dasar-dasar pendidikan dan pengajaran di sekolah untuk seluruh Indonesia (Law no. 12, year 1954, concerning the ratification of the earlier law no. 4, year 1950, of the Republic of Indonesia regarding the foundations of education and instruction in school for the entire nation) (1954). Jakarta: Republik Indonesia

Early childhood teacher preparation in Taiwan

YU-WEI LIN

Taipei Provincial Teachers College, Taiwan
BERNARD SPODEK

University of Illinois, Champaign, Illinois, USA

(Received August 1991)

Against the background of early attempts to establish provision for young children in China, influenced by practices imported from Japan. This paper describes the current scene in Taiwan and focusses on issues to be resolved currently.

Key words: Early Childhood, Taiwan

Early childhood education has developed at a rapid pace in recent years in Taiwan, especially during the past decade. The Ministry of Education (1989) notes that there were 570 kindergartens in Taiwan in 1970, compared to 2548 kindergartens in 1989; 91,984 kindergartners in 1970, compared to 248,497 in 1989; and 7,344 kindergarten teachers in 1970, compared to 13,466 in 1989. Thus, the recent growth in kindergarten education in Taiwan has been exponential.

In Taiwan, early childhood education is considered education before elementary school. There are a variety of early childhood programs, including kindergarten, nursery school, and child care, including day care centers and family day care programs. Of these, kindergarten and nursery school are the most popular. The kindergarten is an educational institution that serves children between the ages of four and six. The nursery school is considered a social welfare institution that serves children from one month of age through age six. Day care centers and day care homes, also considered social welfare institutions, serve children from one month of age through age twelve. While kindergartens emphasize education, nursery schools, day care centers, and family day care homes emphasize care.

A distinction is also made in Taiwan among early childhood practitioners. Kindergarten practitioners are called "teachers." Those who work in the nursery schools, day care centers and day care homes are called "caregivers." Practitioners who are qualified to teach kindergarten can teach in nursery schools, day care centers and family day care homes, though the reverse is not true. This chapter will focus only on the preparation of kindergarten teachers. It will first review the history of early childhood teacher preparation, then present its current status, identifying some of the pressing problems in teacher training program. Finally, suggestions for improving early childhood teacher preparation will be presented.

A Brief History

Early childhood and teacher preparation in Taiwan is an outgrowth of early childhood education and teacher preparation in China before 1949. Tracing its history to the beginning of the twentieth century can help to understand the current situation.

Early childhood education in China

In ancient China, most young children were educated at home or in private classes. Private teachers would teach young people the Chinese classics and prepare them for civil service examinations. However, there were no formal schools in China in the western sense until the beginning of the twentieth century (Wang, 1977).

The history of early childhood teacher preparation begins about eighty years ago. In 1903–1910, the last days of the Ching [Qing][1] Dynasty, there was a concern for the lack of modernization in Chinese society and for the need to reform Chinese life in order to allow the country to compete with and defend itself from western nations. The reformers thought that the best way to improve their society was to abolish the civil service examinations that were used to select government officials. These examinations emphasized the recitation and composition of ancient poetry. The reformers also wished to do away with the private-tutor system that was designed to prepare people for these examinations. They hoped to establish modern public schools which would be supported and supervised by the government. In time, the Chinese government responded to these reformers and began to initiate educational reform — including new initiative in early childhood education.

In 1903, the Imperial Chinese government established "Enlightenment Centers" for children ages three to seven. This was the formal beginning of early childhood education in China. The enlightenment centers, designed to help family education, had a curriculum which included play, nursery songs, stories, and handicraft activities. Because women were not enrolled in schools at that time, the caregivers in these centers learned to teach by reading books about childhood education (Wang, 1977). One enlightenment center was established in 1903 in Peking [Beijing] along with a caregiver normal school -- the earliest early childhood teacher preparation institution. The normal school provided a five-year training program. The teachers in the enlightenment center were brought from Japan, as were the curriculum, teaching methods, and materials.

---

[1]Because this chapter is written about early childhood teacher preparation in Taiwan (the Republic of China), the romanization used in here for the names of Chinese persons and places is that used in the Republic of China. Pinyin, the romanization used in the People's Republic of China is presented in brackets.

At about this time, a group of Japanese kindergarten teachers were brought to Hupei [Hubei] Province in China to establish kindergartens for 4- to 6-year-old children and to train Chinese kindergarten teachers. Later, caregiver training centers were established in Shanghai, and Wushi [Wuxi] (Yuan, 1948; Chang, 1933). In 1907, Wu Tsu-Che [Wu Zu-zhe], a Chinese educator who went to Japan to study kindergarten education, returned to establish a caregiver learning center in Shanghai. She offered courses in child psychology and early childhood education to 36 students (Wang, 1980). That same year, the government established guidelines for four-year Girls' Normal Schools, reflecting a new concern for women's education.

The Chinese looked to Japan for educational inspiration because they felt that Japan's culture was close to Chinese than were western cultures. The educational programs they imported, however, were heavily influenced by western culture. The Japanese kindergarten education imported to China was a Froebelian model that had been brought to Japan by American Christian missionaries. During this period, Froebelian kindergartens were also established in China by American missionaries. Programs for young children had been established somewhat earlier, but these were characterized as "observing things around them" schools rather than as kindergartens. These schools were part of a welfare plan to help widows without economic support. The program, called "Mong Yiang Yuan", hired widows to teach young children. In some sense these were similar to the "dames schools" of colonial America. While there seems to be no written descriptions of these schools available, the name suggests either a Pestalozzian influence (Spodek, 1988) or the influence of Kao Cheng [Kao Zheng] scholarship, which was popular during the Ching [Qing] dynasty (Spence, 1990).

In 1912, when the Republic of China was established, the government created a Ministry of Education and established a public education system. According to *the Teacher Education Law and Primary School Organization of 1912*, girls' normal schools and primary schools were to establish enlightenment centers. In addition, girls' normal schools were to include caregiver training programs. In 1916, the word "kindergarten" first appeared in the *Education Law*.

After World War 1, the Chinese resisted Japanese influences in educational and cultural affairs and looked more toward America and Europe. During that period, John Dewey and Bertrand Russell lectured in China and had a significant influence on Chinese educational reform. In 1922, the Ministry of Education promulgated a "New Educational System." The enlightenment centers were renamed "kindergartens." In 1923, the first public early childhood education departments were established in Nanking [Nanjing] Girls' Normal School and Tengching [Denjing] Girls' Normal School. In 1926, the *Teacher Education Law* proclaimed that every normal school should create a two-year early childhood education program. From that time, early childhood education programs, rather than caregiver training programs, became the primary form of early childhood teacher preparation. The caregiver training that remained was delegated to in-service activities in nursery schools and child care centers.

Within a few years, many normal schools established early childhood education departments. In 1929, the Ministry of Education promulgated the *Temporary Guideline for Kindergarten Programs*. Four universities — Yenching [Yanjing] University, Chinling [Jinling] Women's University, Chilu [Qilu] University and Huahsi [Huaxi] University — created early childhood education courses in their home economic and sociology department in 1930. This was the first time that universities offered early childhood education courses. A standard teacher training curriculum was established by the Ministry of Education in 1935.

Chen Ho-Chin [Chen He-qin], a progressive educator, who had studied in the United States from 1914 to 1919, had established five experimental schools and kindergartens in Nanking [Nanjing] in 1928. He founded an Experimental Early Childhood Education Normal School in Chiangsi [Jiangxi] in 1940. This became a national early childhood normal school in 1943 (Hwang, 1976). Here teacher training was practiced within the context of "education through life." In 1945 the Chiangsi [Jiangxi] school was merged with the Nanchang Women's Normal School and was moved to Shanghai (Chung, 1979, 1981). During this period, Chang Hsueh-men [Zhang Xue-men], another famous kindergarten educator, was principal of the Peking [Beijing] Preschool Education Normal School, which was founded in 1930. The curriculum included Chinese language, Dr. Sun Yat-sen's Three People's Principles (nationalism, democracy, and livelihood), philosophy, early childhood education, kindergarten administration, children's literature, child psychology, play, children's hygiene, practice, music, fine arts, and physical education. The school stressed the relation of theory to practice, the importance of teaching skills, independent thinking for kindergarten teachers, and their involvement in the social life of the community. There seemed to be less stress here on "learning by living" (Ching, 1983).

Early childhood teacher education in Taiwan

The first early childhood education department in Taiwan was founded in Taipei Girls' Normal School in 1946. That department enrolled junior-high school graduates and provided a three-year training program (Hwang, 1976). Tainai Normal School and Kaohsiung Girls' Normal School followed that example. After the Kuomintang government moved to Taiwan in 1950, the Taipei Day Care Center established an apprenticeship program — a teacher training program attached to a children's kindergarten program. This type of apprenticeship teacher training continued until 1961. Although the Ministry of Education revised the standard teacher training curriculum in 1952, the preparation of early childhood teachers was not given much attention during this period.

In 1955, the Department of Education of the Taiwan Provincial Government ordered the Tainan Provincial Normal School to close down their early childhood education department in order to train more elementary school teachers. Kaohsiung Girls' Normal School followed this example in the next year. In 1960, owing to the change from normal schools to normal junior colleges and the improvement of primary education, the government proclaimed that the normal junior colleges do away with early childhood education departments. By 1965, early childhood education departments no longer existed in Taiwan (Ko, 1974). From then until

1983, early childhood teachers were prepared through in-service education, offered in evening and summer classes for kindergarten teachers who lacked certification. The quality of early childhood education declined during these years because of the absence of professional preparation and commitment in kindergarten teachers.

Owing to the high proportion of working women in Taiwan, and the social changes that had occurred, the need for kindergartens increased. With the increase in kindergartens the Government found it necessary to again establish programs to prepare kindergarten teachers. In 1983, the Ministry of Education approved two-year early childhood education programs in four normal junior colleges — Taipei Municipal Normal Junior College, Taipei Provincial Normal Junior College, Taichung Provincial Normal Junior College and Chiai Provincial Normal Junior College. High school or vocational school graduates were recruited for these programs. Two years later, the other four normal junior colleges in Taiwan also established early childhood education departments. Since then, the preparation of early childhood teachers has formally been a part of the teacher education system, and pre-service education has been emphasized.

In 1981, the government passed the *Early Childhood Education Act* (Ministry of Education, 1981), the most important law for early childhood education in Taiwan. For the first time early childhood education was given a legitimate place in the educational system. Two years after the passage of that law, the *Guidelines for the Selection and Certification of Early Childhood Teachers and Directors* (Ministry of Education, 1983) were issued. As a way to upgrade the quality of early childhood teachers, the government established criteria for qualified kindergarten teachers. It also did away with the role of assistant teacher in kindergarten. Evening and summer session teacher training programs ceased in 1985. The normal junior colleges became teachers colleges in 1987, and recruited senior high school graduates. Prior to this time, they had recruited junior high school graduates, and provided four year teacher training programs. The graduates of these programs now earn bachelor's degree and can become elementary school or kindergarten teachers. Early childhood education departments however, only offered two-year training programs. These programs consist of at least 90 credits of study. Students who were graduated from these departments were qualified only as kindergarten teachers. In order to improve the quality of childhood teachers, the government established four-year kindergarten teachers training programs in 1990. Taipei Municipal Teacher College was the first college to establish such a program. The other eight teachers colleges may soon follow these examples.

In summary, during the past 45 years, early childhood teachers in Taiwan were originally prepared in pre-service training programs. This preparation changed as only in-service programs became available. More recently, pre-service training program has again been established. Originally, pre-service teacher preparation was limited to three-year training programs in normal schools. Later, kindergarten teachers were prepared in two-year programs in normal junior colleges and teachers colleges. Now, four-year teachers college programs are being established.

While these changes have occurred to meet the current need for kindergarten teachers and to improve their preparation, there are still problems in these training programs. In the following section, the current status and pressing problems in the preparation of early childhood teachers in Taiwan will be discussed.

The Current Scene

Children between the ages of four and six are educated in kindergartens in Taiwan. These kindergartens are primarily private establishments, although increasingly kindergartens are being established as part of county or city elementary schools. According to the Bureau of Statistics of the Ministry of Education (1989), three times as many children are enrolled in private kindergartens and preschools as in public school kindergartens. Ninety percent of the private kindergartens are independent of any elementary school affiliation, while 97% of the public school kindergartens are affiliated with elementary schools.

There are nine teachers colleges in Taiwan that prepare kindergarten teachers. There are two types of early childhood teacher training programs in Taiwan; their content and requirements differ. The typical two-year normal teachers college program consists of at least 90 credits of study. This is divided into 33 credits[2] of general education, including history, language, philosophy; and 57 credits of professional course, including 19 credits of educational foundation, 20 credits of curriculum and methods, 10 credits of practice, and 8 credits of elective courses. The total hours in this program is 124. Presently, eight of the nine teachers colleges offer this two-year training program.

The typical four-year normal teachers college program consists of at least 148 credits. This is divided into 52 credits of general education, including history, language, philosophy, science; and 96 credits of professional courses. The professional courses include 26 credits of educational foundations, 18 credits of curriculum and methods, 10 credits of practice, and 42 credits of elective courses. The total hours for this four-year program is 196. This program is presently offered in only one teachers college in Taiwan.

While the four year program requires 58 more credits for graduation, the ratio of general education to professional education courses remains the same. However, fewer credits are required in language courses in the four-year program, while more credits are required in the natural science. There is also a greater proportion of elective courses in the four year program. Students in the four-year program also take fewer credits each semester than do students in the two-year program. Although the number of total credits is significantly greater in the four year program, the number of credits in student teaching is exactly the same in both programs.

Field experiences play an important role in all teacher education programs. Field experiences allow teachers-in-training to relate what they have learned in their college classes to actual classroom practice. Both observation and participation are important parts of field experience.

---

[2]The term credit here is used similarly to credit allocations in American universities. It is generally related to the number of course contact hours per week per semester. In some cases, however, the contact hours differ from the credit allocation. Thus the two are given here.

In the two-year training program, first year field experiences, which emphasize observation, are designed to help the students become aware of the many elements of the classroom setting. The role of the teacher, the behaviors and interactions of students, the use of materials and equipment, and the importance of scheduling and room arrangement are all observed. While students are required to take seven credits in pre-student teaching field experiences, no specific number of contact hours are required in the *Standards for Teacher Preparation Curriculum*. Student teaching is offered in the second semester of the last year, with students assuming full responsibility for the kindergarten class and for the decisions related to teaching.

The student teaching experience is designed to enable students to integrate their professional knowledge and create their own core of personal practical knowledge to guide their teaching. While the students are required to enroll for three credits of student teaching, again no mention is made in the *Standard of Teacher Preparation Curriculum* of the number of hours required. Student teaching is generally a four-week experience, always in a kindergarten, not a nursery school. Because the four-year program only started in 1990, the details about the content of field experience and student teaching experience are not known. Student teachings in the four-year program are still 10 credits.

General standards

According to the *Early Childhood Education Act* (1981) and the *Guidelines for the Selection and Certification of Early Childhood Teachers and Directors* (1983), graduates of early childhood education programs in teacher colleges, of programs related to early childhood education in other colleges or universities, of senior high schools who have taken twenty credits of early childhood education courses in government-designated school, or persons who had a kindergarten certificate prior to the *Early Childhood Education Act* can all be kindergarten teachers. There is debate about the second and third options.

Although several universities and colleges have programs related to early child-hood education, such as home economics, social work, or child welfare, the *Guidelines for Selection and Certification of Early Childhood Teachers and Directors* do not allow graduates of these programs to become kindergarten teachers. The Ministry of Education has stated that "those departments which are related to the early childhood education in colleges and universities" noted in the guidelines refers to other programs in normal teachers college and in education departments in normal universities, rather than in departments with programs related to early childhood education in other institutions of higher education. Thus, graduates of general colleges or universities cannot become kindergarten teachers. In recent years, many graduates of such universities who have wished to become kindergarten teachers have petitioned for a new interpretation of this rule. Until now, however, the government has not been willing to revise its interpretation.

As noted earlier, the teachers colleges began to offer two-year pre-service early childhood teacher preparation programs in 1983. At that time, summer and evening in-service training programs were cancelled. Since no college presently provides in-service programs, the third option is meaningless. There are thirty-one vocational schools and senior high schools with child care departments in Taiwan which offer three-year training programs. Graduates of these programs are qualified to become caregivers in nursery school, but are not qualified to become kindergarten teachers. In 1990, the Department of Education allowed eight provincial normal teachers colleges to recruit forty-five graduates of these programs annually into their early childhood programs. The program requirements for these students are different from those of regular students, even though the number of credits are the same — at least ninety credits.

Public kindergartens in Taiwan are currently affiliated with elementary schools. The teachers in these public school kindergartens receive higher salaries, higher employment benefits, and better working conditions than do teachers in private kindergartens. Increasingly, qualified kindergarten teachers are becoming public kindergarten teachers. A public kindergarten teacher must pass a written examination and demonstrate teaching ability in a simulated situation. Skill at playing the piano or organ and in telling children's stories are also required.

Most kindergarten teachers in Taiwan are women. Although the government allowed men to enter early childhood education programs in 1985, only fourteen have been enrolled. Unfortunately none of them became a kindergarten teacher upon graduation. Instead, they sought employment in other fields instead.

Current Issues

Currently there are a number of issues related to the preparation of kindergarten teachers in Taiwan that need to be resolved. Among the most pressing are the following:

A limiting certification system

As noted above, there is a continuing debate regarding qualifications for kindergarten teachers. Presently, graduates of general college and university cannot become kindergarten teachers even if they have taken appropriate early childhood education courses. Yet they have strong backgrounds in early childhood education and could be expected to become highly competent early childhood teachers.

There is some flexibility in the system. The *Guidelines for Selection and Certification of Early Childhood Teachers and Directors* allows local education authorities to conduct certification examinations for kindergarten teachers when needed. After passing the examination, limited course work is required of these teachers. Although allowed, such examinations have not been given. Recruiting university graduates as kindergarten teachers through these examinations might be one way to increase the number and upgrade the quality of kindergarten teachers.

The other issue related to the certification system is that certified elementary school teachers are considered qualified to be kindergarten teachers, even though they have not taken any early childhood education courses. There is a widespread misconception that one can work effectively with young children without the benefit of specialized knowledge. In fact, the younger the children taught, the more critical the need for knowledgeable, qualified, competent early childhood teachers.

Inadequate student teaching in teacher preparation

Student teaching is always done in the last semester of the last year of a teacher preparation program in Taiwan. Although pre-student teaching field experiences are provided, student teaching provides the first opportunity for students to apply the knowledge they have gained from courses into practice, actually planning and teaching, and experimenting with discipline and teaching techniques. It is also the time for novices to construct and modify their knowledge and skills, and explore teaching as a career. Because student teaching occurs so late, prospective teachers do not have time to remedy any deficiencies in their preparation that might become evident in student teaching. It is also too late for them to change their career orientation if they find that teaching does not suit them.

All student teaching in the early childhood programs is done in kindergarten. However, not all the graduates of these programs teach in kindergarten; some work in nursery schools or day care centers. Providing diverse student teaching settings would allow the students to know more about different early childhood education programs, so they can make an appropriate career choice for their future.

The shortage of kindergarten teachers

There are a number of factors which contribute to the current shortage of early childhood teachers in Taiwan. Many early childhood teachers do not remain in teaching. High teacher turnover and short tenure are characteristics of the early childhood field. Low salaries, few employment benefits, poor working conditions, heavy workloads, and no opportunity for career enhancement are some of the reasons for this high turnover. According to a recent survey, of the 20,549 qualified kindergarten teachers in Taiwan, only about 8,700 are currently teaching. The annual turnover rate is 57.7% (Tsai, 1989).

A second factor contributing to the shortage of kindergarten teachers is the rapid increase in the number of programs for young children. The number of early childhood programs, including kindergarten, nursery school, day care center, family day care for young children doubles every year in Taiwan (Taipei Provincial Teachers College, 1989). However, only 450 qualified teachers are graduated each year. With the establishment of new children's programs, the need for professionally trained teachers increases.

The number of early childhood teachers prepared each year is not sufficient to staff these expanding programs. As a result, the need for kindergarten teachers is outstripping the supply. The issue of how to provide qualified kindergarten teachers for the existing and evolving programs remains unresolved.

Lack of professional, experienced teacher educators

Early childhood education is not compulsory in Taiwan nor has it been considered important. Until recently, few educators in Taiwan have paid much attention to the field and few pursue advanced study in the field. Although nine teachers colleges have early childhood education departments, few professors in these departments are experts in this field. Many professors who teach early childhood teacher education courses do not have a background in early childhood education. For example, only

Table 1

Subjects	2-year program credits[a]	2-year program hours	4-year program credits	4-year program hours
General Education	33	33	52	90
Chinese	8	8	6	6
Mandarin	3	6	2	4
English	4	4	8	8
History	2	2	2	2
The Thoughts of Dr. Sun Yat-sen	2	2	2	2
Physical Education	4	8	0	16
Music	2 (vocal)	2	2	4
Instruments	6 (piano)	12	6	12
Fine Arts	2	2	2	4
Introduction of Social Sciene			4	4
Ethics or Laws or philosophy			2	2
Mathematics			2	2
Computer Science			4	4
Introduction of Arts			2	2
Manual Arts			2	4
Introduction to Natural Science			6	6
Professional Courses	57	68	96	106
Education Foundation	19	19	26	26
Introduction of Early Childhood education	4	4	2	2
Kindergarten Administration	2	2	2	2
Family Education	2	2	2	2
Children's hygiene	2	2	2	2
Psychology	2	2	2	2
Child Development and Guidance	3	3	2	2
Introduction to Kindergarten Curriculum	2	2	2	2
Special Education	2	2	2	2
Counselling			2	2
Guidelines of Instruction			2	2
Design of Learning environments			2	2
Observation of Child Behavior			2	2
Children's Literature			2	2
Curriculum and Methods	20	21	18	18
Nursery Rhymes			2	2
Children's Play & Physical Activities	2	2	2	2

Table (*continued*)

Subjects	2-year program credits[a]	hours	4-year program credits	hours
Audio-Visual Education	2	2	2	2
Teaching Methods of Language Arts	2	2	2	2
Teaching Methods of General Knowledge	4	4	6	6
Teaching Method of Arts	2	2	2	2
Teaching Methods of Music	2	3	2	2
Teaching Methods of Health Education	2	2	2	2
Design of teaching Material			2	2
Practice	10	20	10	20
Field Experience	7	14	7	14
Student Teaching	3	6	3	6
Elective	8	8	42	42
TOTAL	90	124	148	196

[a] The term credit here is used similarly to credit allocations in American universities. It is generally related to the number of course contact hours per week per semester. In some cases, however, the contact hours differ from the credit allocation. Thus the two are given here.

three of the professors in Taipei Provincial Teachers College majored in this field. The others majored in other fields of education. To some extent this issue reflects the lack of advanced programs in early childhood education in Taiwan. Educators wishing to pursue graduate degrees in early childhood education must seek education in other countries.

Inadequate supervision

In order to maintain kindergartens standards, many local education authorities bureaus supervise and evaluate both public and private kindergartens in their districts. Assessing kindergarten facilities, administration, teachers, instruction, and child care are important components of this supervision. In principle, this evaluation is designed to help kindergartens meet regulations and to improve the quality of kindergarten education. In fact, the process does not work effectively. Few kindergarten supervisors are prepared and experienced in early childhood education. Supervisors may not be able to provide the help kindergarten teachers need to improve their skills. Supervisors may also overlook important regulations. For example, according to the *Early Childhood Education Act*, each kindergarten class should have two qualified teachers for a maximum of thirty children. In fact, few kindergartens meet this requirement, with fewer teachers and more children in many kindergarten classes.

Difference in standard for kindergarten teachers and nursery school caregivers

Kindergartens and nursery schools are both popular in Taiwan. The former serves children from ages four to six, while the latter serves children from one month to six years of age. The two programs are regulated by different agencies — kindergartens by the local educational authority, nursery schools by a social welfare agency — and their staff requirements are different. A caregiver must have a high school or vocational school diploma with at least three months of child care training. In contrast, only graduates of teachers colleges can become kindergarten teachers.

Individuals who are qualified to teach in kindergarten are also qualified to teach in nursery school; the reverse is not true. These two programs follow different regulations and use different standards to recruit staff. Whether nursery schools and kindergartens, which both serve children from age 4 to six, should be supervised by the same agency or should have the same staff requirements is an issue that needs to be debated.

DISCUSSION

The history of early childhood education in China is relatively short and its history in Taiwan is even shorter. The development of Kindergartens has been impressive as has been the development of early childhood teacher education. As the Republic of China moved to Taiwan in 1949 there began a forty year period of development when the island went from a rural province to an urbanized, industrialized country. Modern educational institutions, including kindergartens, which had a short history in China, had to be reestablished all over again as Taiwan went from a developing area to a developed one.

The problems that are found in the field are not unlike that found in other developed nations. The preparation of early childhood and elementary teachers in the United States moved from normal schools to normal colleges to multipurpose colleges and universities some time ago. England, Australia and Israel has more recently moved the preparation of early childhood and primary school teachers to universities. All such developments involve some degree of dislocation that will probably be experienced as teacher preparation in Taiwan continues the process.

In the United States and in other countries a similar distinction is made in the standards established for nursery schools and child care centers and kindergartens, especially when kindergartens are part of the public school system. Higher salaries, greater benefits and better working conditions for teachers in the public school systems as compared with teachers in private schools also seem to exist in other countries. These differences parallel differences in the preparation of teachers in these two types of institutions and in the requirements for their employment. The problems of early childhood teacher preparation in Taiwan can be better understood when seen in the context of international developments in the field. Out of the experience of early childhood teacher education, and an understanding of current conditions, a number of suggestions can be made for improving the preparation of early childhood teacher education in Taiwan.

There are some clear cut signs that such improvement will be forthcoming. During the past few years, the Ministry of Education has begun to pay increasing attention to the preparation of the early childhood teacher. For example, four-year training programs have been established for kindergarten teachers, and there is increasing recruitment for these programs. In order to improve the quality of kindergarten teachers quickly, other reforms are necessary. These reforms should include the following:

Establishing suitable and flexible certification system

At present, all graduates of normal teachers colleges in Taiwan are qualified to teach kindergarten, regardless of their preparation. In contrast, graduates of general universities or colleges cannot qualify as kindergarten teacher even though they may have taken early childhood education courses and have strong commitments to early childhood education. The system needs to be modified to allow qualified college and university graduates to become certified kindergarten teachers. At the same time, only those qualified in early childhood education should be eligible to become kindergarten teachers. This would strengthen kindergarten education at the same time that it opens up alternative preparation, a move that could help relieve the kindergarten teacher shortage.

Alternative certification programs may need to be established in order to solve the current kindergarten teacher shortage. These alternative certification programs could admit persons with at least a bachelor degree and with a commitment to kindergarten education. These potential kindergarten teachers would already have completed their general education requirements. Summer programs could be offered prior to their beginning teaching to provide about at least 20 credits of early childhood education courses. Additional preparation could be provided in summer or evening time to allow these individuals to receive the standard kindergarten certificate. Such a program should not be considered a shortcut to becoming certified to teach kindergarten, but another route to certification. In order for that to be the case, admission to such programs should be done with care and the courses that are offered to individuals in such a program should be comparable to those in regular teacher education programs.

Extending student teaching period

At present, only four weeks of student teaching is required in both two-year and four-year early childhood education programs in Taiwan. Student teaching is always done in the last semester of the last year. Although students have opportunities to observe or participate in classroom setting before student teaching, they do not have any direct experience in teaching except for that four week period. Extending the student teaching period and putting at least part of it earlier in the program would improve students' competence and provide the opportunity for them to make up what they lack. In addition, providing student teaching experiences in different early childhood education settings would allow students to make a more informed choice for future placement.

Improving the salaries and benefits for kindergarten teacher

Because of low salaries, poor working conditions, and heavy workload, the turnover among kindergarten teachers is very high. Many prospective teachers do not consider early childhood education as a career choice, and teachers leave their jobs. Increasing salaries and benefits, creating a career ladder, providing good working condition benefits, and reasonable workload, offering further in-service training or advanced education, and benefits are needed. The idea of establishing a career ladder system is allowing kindergarten teachers to move through stages to higher levels of professionalism. Classroom teachers should be able to qualify for positions as supervisors and teacher educators. This will only be possible when opportunities for advanced study in the field of early childhood education are available in Taiwan and when the quality of the teacher education programs is of a high enough caliber to allow its graduates who have become classroom teachers to qualify for advanced degree programs.

Improving supervision system

In order to upgrade the quality kindergarten teaching, there needs to also be an improvement in the quality of specialists in education bureaus who are responsible for early childhood education. These specialists could supervise kindergartens and help kindergarten teachers modify and improve their practice. They can also ensure that kindergarten regulations are uniformly met.

In addition, qualified teacher educators (professors in teachers colleges) in early childhood education programs should be recruited and those teaching in these programs should be helped to improve their knowledge of early childhood education. Revising the related regulation about the standard of kindergarten teachers and nursery school caregivers for the children from age 4 to six is needed. This would require that the education and social welfare institutions compromise and create a common standard for early childhood practitioners who serve children of the same age. This is not a simple matter and depends on economic as well as pedagogic issues. Nursery school caregivers, who have lower qualifications, also receive lower salaries. It would not be reasonable to have kindergarten teachers meet the lower qualifications of the nursery school. If they are to be expected to meet the same qualification as kindergarten teachers, then they ought to be paid the same, with salaries comparable to those in public school kindergartens. This has not happened in other countries. It is questionable whether it could happen in Taiwan.

CONCLUSION

This chapter presented the history of early childhood teacher preparation in Taiwan, described its current status and discussed contemporary problems in the field. Suggestions for improvements were also suggested.

Early childhood teacher preparation is a relatively new field in Taiwan; its history is relatively short. Although there are some problems in the current situation, we believe these problems can be solved. Solutions, however, will require the cooperation of government officials and educators. It will also require increased economic resources. As Taiwan moves into greater parity with western developed countries, we believe that the education establishment will realize the importance of early childhood education as the foundation of children's educational development and will work to create the necessary improvements.

References

Chang, Hsueh-Men (1933) *New Early Childhood Education.* Peking [Beijing]: Children Books

Ching, Hen-Chiang [Jing Hen-qiang] (1983) Peking [Beijing] Preschool Education Normal School. *You Er Jiao Yo* [Preschool education]

Chung, Tsao-Hua [Zhong Zeo-hua] (1979) Chen He-qin and the Nanjing Gulou kindergarten. *Nanking Shih Fan Hsuan Pao* [Journal of the Nanjing Normal University]. Issue 4

Chung, Tsao-Hua [Zhong Zao-hua] (1981) Chen Heo-qin's Educational Ideas and the Jiangsi Experimental Early Childhood Education Normal School. *Nanking Shih Fan Hsusn Pao* [Journal of the Nanjing Normal University]. Issue 2

Hwang, Pao-Chu (1976) *The Collection of Early Childhood Education.* Taipei: Taipei Municipal Normal Junior College

Ko, Wei-Chun (1974) Preparation of Early Childhood Teachers. *Journal of Taiwan Education,* **277–278**, 13–15

Ministry of Education (1981) *The Early Childhood Education Act.* Taipei: Ministry of Education

Ministry of Education (1983) *Guidelines for The Selection and Certification of Early Childhood Teachers and Directors.* Taipei: Ministry of Education

Ministry of Education (1989) *Educational Statistics in Republic of China.* Taipei: Ministry of Education

Ministry of Education (1988) *Study on the Preparation of Early Childhood Teachers in Taiwan.* Taipei: Ministry of Education

Spence, J.D. (1990) The Search for Modern China. New York: W.W. Norton

Spodek, B. & Saracho, O.N. (1990) Early Childhood Teachers Preparation in Cross-Cultural Perspective. In B. Spodek and O.N. Saracho (eds.), *Early Childhood Teacher Preparation* (pp. 102–117). New York: Teachers College Press

Taipei Provincial Teachers College (1989) *Inferential Study to Predict the Amount of Kindergarten Teachers needed in the Coming Years, 1990–1995.* Taipei: Taipei Provincial Teachers College

Tsai, Chun-Mei (1981) *Improvement of Teacher Preparation System in Early Childhood Education.* Taipei: Hsin-I Foundation, Institution of Preschool Education

Tsai, Chun-Mei (1989) *Investigation of Early Childhood Teachers' Turnover in Taiwan.* Taipei: Tapei Provincial Teachers College

Wang, Feng-Chieh (1977) *The History of Chinese Education* (15th ed.). Taipei: Chen-Chon Books

Wang, Ching-Chu (1980) Early Childhood Education (8th ed.). Taichung: Provincial Taichung Normal Junior College

Yuan, Ang (1948) Perspective of Early Childhood Education in China. *Journal of Education,* **33**(1), 24

The preparation of Early Childhood Teachers in Japan. PART I

What is the goal of early childhood care and education in Japan?

In connection with revisions of the new guidelines for kindergarten education and the new syllabus for the care and education at the day-nursery in Japan

EMIKO HANNAH ISHIGAKI

Seiwa College, Okadayama, Nishinomiya, Japan

(Received August 1991)

This paper considers the current goals and priorities of early childhood provision in Japan in the context of a changed social order and consequent modifications to the National Guidelines on curriculum at kindergarten and day nurseries.

Key Words Early Childhood Education, Japan

INTRODUCTION

Whether we take an international point of view or not, we may not ignore the importance of the education of teachers and care-takers when we think about early childhood care and education, ECCE. Why do we bring up children? Is it because we love them? Because they are cute? Because it is necessary for the future of humanity?

Almost all the students, who take the training course for kindergarten teachers or care-takers, will say, "We choose this course because we love children". At least, most of the Japanese students will. This is an important quality of the students who are going to be teachers and care-takers, but needless to say, it is not enough. They must get professional knowledge about the development of children and consider why they take part in ECCE and what their purpose is. In this chapter, I would like to describe what is the goal of ECCE and how we achieve it.

In 1989 and 1990, big changes were made in Japanese early childhood care and education. The Guidelines for Kindergarten Education and the Syllabus for the Care and Education at the Day-Nursery were revised, and the Ministry of Education and the Ministry of Health and Welfare published them. Before the revisions, officials of the Ministry of Education, officials of the Ministry of Health and Welfare, professors concerned, teachers and care-takers had heated discussions. And now, its interpretation is being discussed.

In this chapter, I will introduce the outline of the New Guideline for Kindergarten Education and the New Syllabus for the Care and Education at the Day-Nursery and consider what is the goal of early childhood care and education. Before that, there is a convenient word *hoiku* in Japanese, and, in addition the *kyoiku*. I will explain the difference between *kyoiku* and *hoiku* and make it easier for the reader to understand the situation in Japanese education.

The Meaning of Kyoiku and Hoiku

The meaning of Kyoiku

Japanese word for education is *kyoiku*. *Kyo* means teaching, and *iku* means bring up. The word is used to mean "education" in English, "e<a>ducation" in French and "Erziehung" in German. The origin of these words is *educare* in Latin, which means "bring out". Therefore, education is an action which brings out hidden abilities of children and adults and helps it work by itself. To bring out hidden abilities, it must be prepared by useful stimulations and good environments.

Thus, the origin of the word "education" shows it is an action that brings out hidden abilities of children and adults, provides a suitable environment where they get new abilities, gives them good cultural stimulations, and helps them grow up healthy in mind and body.

This education started with the origin of human beings. Without education, human culture, such as language, would not have succeeded from generation to generation, and the cultural development based on it would not have occurred.

However, school systems do not have a long history. The first school might have been established in Greece in 600 BC.

Until the 19th century, most of the schools were for children of the elite, such as the nobility. Most citizens did not go to school.

School is a place where people are educated, but those who did not go to school still lived as human beings, which shows school is not the only place for education.

Education can be divided into two categories according to place. One is at school, whose purpose is formal education. The other is at other places without schools, whose purpose is not only education. The former aims to give education efficiently. We might say the education at school is intentional and systematic. Teachers educate children in accordance with the developmental stage of children. They carefully consider what is their goal and what kind of development is their aim, and set up suitable conditions and environments. In all points, schools aim at more desirable growth and progress of children.

However, children are greatly influenced at other places. First of all, almost all children learn at home from their birth through the relationships with their parents, especially their mothers. Parents often teach their children with clear intention. But children are also influenced by the daily activities of their family. We should say the latter influence is stronger.

In addition, children see and hear what adults and other children do on roads, in parks, at shops, and in conveyances,and are greatly influenced. It is impossible to know these influences in advance. It is very accidental.

The influence over children at the other places is as great as that at school. But it does not always have good influences. Its effect is neither intentional nor systematic. We should try to make this effect as positive as possible. For this, adults around children must be good models in their daily life: they must be educated and make good human environments.

Like the Compulsory Education Level Schools, kindergartens and day-nurseries are organized as the places to intentionally and systematically educate pre-schoolers. Teachers and care-takers, who finished the specialized course, try to achieve the developmental tasks, prepare suitable institutions, facilities and educational contents. Kindergartens and day-nurseries are ideal, harmonious and efficient places to promote desirable growth and development. However, it is not only intentional and systematic educational effects in a narrow sense, but a great deal of unintentional and unsystematic ones in a broad sense that influence children because teachers and care-takers make daily contact with children. Therefore, teachers and care-takers must act as educated people not only when they teach and care for children but also in daily life.

The meaning of Hoiku

Hoiku in Japanese means early childhood care and education. In Japan, the word has been used in books and records since 1879. "Ho" means care and protection, "iku" means bringing up and education. The word *hoiku* was legally used for the first time in the School Education Law in 1947. The law says the aim of kindergarten is to "*hoiku*" children. This "*hoiku*" is a contraction of "*hogo-kyoiku*". The outside protection and the inside promotion of the growth are regarded as one thing, the nature of early childhood education.

In 1947 and 1948, the Japanese government also enacted the Child Welfare Law and the Minimum Standards for Child Welfare Institutions. There is little difference between *hoiku* at *hoikusho*, day-nursery, and that at kindergarten. According to the Ministry of Health and Welfare, it is not necessary that *hoiku* means the instruction at kindergarten that is regulated in the School Education Law. It is the word for *hogo-kyoiku*, protection and education, in general. The support for working mothers is established in the law.

But gradually, people expect little difference between the content of *hoiku* at kindergarten and that at day-nursery.

In connection with this, many arguments were made over the words *kyoiku* and *hoiku*. It seems proper to define the words as giving children protection and instruction in order to promote their growth in mind and body.

Like *kyoiku*, *hoiku* can be classified into three groups:(1) intentional and systematic, (2) intentional and unsystematic, (3) unintentional and unsystematic.

The first type develops as intentional instruction at kindergarten and day-nursery. However children do not concentrate their attention for long periods. The length of hours of care at day-nursery is eight hours a day and four hours at kindergarten, on average. Therefore, the rate of type (2) is high especially at day-nursery. The type (3) works on and has great influence over children at kindergarten and day-nursery as well as at home. Teachers and care-takers at kindergarten and day-nurseries, who take part in (2) and (3) as well as (1), must be educated and make all their speech and behavior useful for better growth and development of children.

The Aim and Content of Hoiku

The aim and methods

It is necessary for teachers and care-takers at kindergartens and day-nurseries to have an image of an ideal infant in their mind. The image of an ideal child comes from each educator's philosophy of life, sometimes from God. This image is supported by teachers' and care-takers' idea of infants and their development and actualizes through a long-range outlook for full life of children at kindergartens and day-nurseries and moulding desirable human beings, that is, daily *hoiku* aims at the actualization of self-fulfilment of children. The goal of *hoiku* is to build up children's character based on the image of ideal children.

To achieve this goal we need concrete manipulation. Without it, we will not be able to achieve the goal. It is said that method is an intentional manipulation to attain an aim. An intentional manipulation has three facets: the object, the content, and the method to manipulate. Needless to say, the object of *hoiku* is infants, the content is curriculum, and the way is a technique of operating the care and education. These are the methods of *hoiku* in a narrow sense.

In this point of view, we might say the content and curriculum are a way to achieve the goal. If ideal character building is the goal of *hoiku* in a long-range outlook, the *hoiku*-content is a method of ideal human character building. We cannot think about the problems of *hoiku* if we cut off the content from the goal of *hoiku*. Therefore, to achieve the goal we should indeed choose suitable *hoiku*-content.

In Japan, *hoiku*-content at kindergarten and day-nursery has undergone many changes. The reflection tells not only the changing times but also of the idea of *hoiku* and infants.

The hoiku-content at the kindergarten

Changes in *hoiku*-content at the kindergarten level can be divided into six stages:

(1) The beginning stage (1876–1899)

The first national kindergarten, a kindergarten attached to the Tokyo Women's Normal School (founded in 1876), introduced Froebel's ideas of kindergarten into its education.

Until 1897, the educational methods prevalent in foreign countries were introduced by the national kindergarten and women missionaries who established Christian kindergartens in Japan. In this period, "Gabe" Play, room meeting, song, play, exercise, drawing, reading, writing, and playing with shells, a traditional game in

Japan, were practiced in the kindergartens, but most of the time was spent in Gabe Play.

(2) The stage of four forms of education (1899–1926)
In 1899, the Act of the Content and Facilities of Kindergarten Education was proclaimed.

It was the first time for the content of early childhood education to be prescribed by the government. According to this law, there were four educational forms: play, song, speech and handicrafts.

Gabe, which had been emphasized before, was included with handicrafts. Within these four forms, so-called educational elements were prescribed in detail.

Since kindergartens were not strictly forced to use these four forms, each one freely planned its own curriculum. For example, meeting, gardening, instruction outside of the room, reading and counting were included. Gabe which had been regarded as a very important tool hitherto, was now included together with handicrafts.

In 1911, all of these educational prescriptions were discontinued, and the content of kindergarten education could freely be decided.

(3) The stage of five forms (1926–1947)
In 1926, an Imperial ordinance on kindergarten education, the Kindergarten Act, was proclaimed. According to this act, the various forms of kindergarten education included play, song, observation, speech, handicrafts, and so on.

In a new act, "and so on" was added in the sentence on forms. Since the content of education had been decided freely by each kindergarten, the government thought that the system should be changed to be more flexible than before in order to fit what was actually happening. Because of this change, the content of education became much freer than before. Besides the five forms, meeting, gardening, excursions, drawing, reading, counting, life training, discipline, health education, physical training, and special events were introduced as various aspects of education.

From 1937 to 1945 Japan was involved in wars. Due to the influence of war, worship of the Imperial family, emphasis on national morality, hoisting of the national flag, worship of tutelary deities, and the playing of war games were introduced into the content of kindergarten education. Listening training in order to distinguish enemy planes from Japanese planes was also given. As the war spread, training of evacuation to air—raid shelters was often given.

(4) The stage of multiple forms (1948–1956)
In 1947, the School Education Law was passed, and a new form of education started. In 1948, the Standard of Early Childhood Education, a Guide to EarlyChildhood Education was published, and twelve forms such as field trip, rhythm, rest, free play, music, story telling, drawing, handicraft, observation of nature, playing house, drama, playing dolls, health education, and annual events were decided as the content of education. This stage is called the stage of multiple forms.

Though technical terms of education such as "form" were used in kindergarten education, the actual contents were fairly flexibly taught through daily life in which these forms were blended. The government tried to reduce regulations to a minimum.

(5) The stage of six areas (1956–1989)
In 1956, the Guidelines for Kindergarten Education was passed to take the place of the Standard of Early Childhood. The content of education was divided into six areas: (1) health, (2) society, (3) nature, (4) language, (5) music and rhythm, and (6) art and craft.

In 1965, the Guidelines for Kindergarten Education were enforced by the Ministry of Education. The contents of these six areas were prescribed in detail, and kindergarten education became more curriculum-oriented like that of elementary education.

The detailed contents of the six areas were as follows:

(1) Health: habits and behavior promoting health, various kinds of exercise, habit and behavior promoting safety.
(2) Society: proper habit and behavior contributing to individual and social life, interest and concern for social phenomena familiar to children.
(3) Nature: human attitudes towards animals and plants familiar to children, simple skills needed for daily life, interest and concern for the concepts of number and quantity.
(4) Language: comprehension and expression of spoken language, the use of Japanese needed in daily life, interest and concern about creative ability in connection with picture books and picture play shows.
(5) Music and rhythm: singing songs and playing simple musical instruments, rhythm in body movement and group play, familiarity with music and expression of personal feeling through songs body movement.
(6) Art and craft: expression through drawing and handicrafts, interest and concern for design and decoration, awareness of materials and tools, interest in art. For each of these items several detailed points were concretely explained.

These areas were different from subjects in elementary schools. These six areas were not the premises which regulated children's activities. They were only operational notions which were used by teachers when they educated children: in other words, these areas were the tools for teachers when they considered and developed balanced curricula.

The content of education was understood by looking at the aims of each area. For example, we found "Do whatever we can by ourselves", "Following the rules of play", and so on. In order to achieve these aims, teachers creatively planned what to make children do. Detailed plans should be made according to the level of development of the children as well as their experience and the condition of the society which they belong to.

(6) The stage of the New Guidelines (1989–   )
The New Guidelines for Kindergarten Education was passed in November 1989.

This revision was done under the consideration of social changes and those of children's lives and their consciousness and the desire to build a foundation of life-long education. The aim is to bring up generous people who can cope with changes in the 21st century.

The Guidelines consist of three chapters: (1) general provisions, (2) the aim and the content, (3) points of considerations to plan for instruction. The six areas of content in the past were done away with, and five new areas were made: (1) health, (2) human relationship, (3) environment, (4)language, (5) expression. I will write about the details in Paragraph 3.

The hoiku-content at day-nursery

We have two kinds of institutions for the care and education of preschool children, that is, the kindergarten and the day-nursery. Efforts are being made to treat the children equally regardless of which institution they are entrusted to. However, due to the differences in the administration system they belong to, there are naturally some differences found in the content of the care. The following are what distinguishes the day-nursery from the kindergarten

(1) Care of infants below 3 years.
(2) In the day-nursery the length of hours of care is longer (8–11 hours) than that of kindergarten.
(3) As a result, the day-nurseries have the following features: (a) It is possible to have consistent policy of care from 0-year-old babies to 6-year-old children. (b) As the nursing hours are long, the content of care should and could include both educational and physical aspects, making it integrated care, which (c) will ensure the all-round development of children, guaranteeing their mothers freedom to work.

In the 1890s, day-nurseries for poor children were established in big cities. The industrial revolution had just started and a proletariat that moved from the farm to the cities created slums. Children in the slum created considerable social problems, and day-nurseries called "slum kindergarten" were built by the people. The Ministry of Home Affairs organized them and gave them national grants. This was the origin of day-nurseries which were different from kindergartens.

The aim of the day-nursery was to take care of infants in the day time, replacing working mothers. Thus the nurseries opened early in the morning and closed in the evening. The content of education was similar to that of kindergartens, since kindergartens had again been the models for the day-nurseries. But it changed gradually and soon developed its own characteristics. According to the Standard of Content for Day-Nursery in Tokyo (1934), the three areas of Training for Daily Life, Human Development, and Health Development were mainly emphasized in day-nursery in the 1930s. The content was strongly influenced by the Ministry of Home Affairs' efforts to "maintain public peace and order". Thus, as a reaction to that, the Proletarian Day-Nursery Movement began in 1931, although it came to an end shortly.

In 1937, the Japanese-Chinese War began, and in its wake came the Second World War. During the war women were sent to factories and the demand for day-nurseries increased. By the end of the war, day-nurseries had been established at temples, shrines, libraries, schools and in many other places in Japan.

After the war, day-nurseries were organized for the first time by the Child Welfare Law (1947), which brought about their remarkable spread. The Child Welfare Law prescribes that the day-nursery is a facility where infants are to be taken care of with the consent of parents according to the principles of child welfare. In 1951, the law was revised and the day-nursery became the facility where infants, who were lacking in familial care, were taken care of. In 1965, the Ministry of Health and Welfare set up the statutes of day-nursery education in day-nurseries. Although they were not binding regulations, it is intimated that, (1) care of infants under 2-years-olds should consist of living plus play, (2) care of 2-year-olds: health, society, and play, (3) with 3-year-olds: language should be added, (4) with 4 to 6-year-olds: nature observation, music and handicrafts should be added. These areas roughly correspond, it should be noted, to the six areas of the content of kindergarten education.

With the revision of the Guidelines of Kindergarten Education, the Syllabus for the Care of Children at the Day-Nursery was revised and proclaimed in March, 1990, as the New Syllabus for Care and Education (hoiku) at the Day-Nursery.

THE NEW GUIDELINES FOR KINDERGARTEN EDUCATION AND THE NEW SYLLABUS FOR CARE AND EDUCATION AT THE DAY-NURSERY

The New Guidelines for Kindergarten Education

The Guidelines of Kindergarten Education had not been revised for more than 30 years. During the period, the social structure, environment and the idea of hoiku were greatly changed. The Ministry of Education set forth the basis of kindergarten education which is given through the environments making indirect education. The guidelines say, "It is important that preschool children are stimulated by every environment around them, go into various actions with interest, and find satisfaction". Therefore, kindergarten education must create suitable circumstances for the educational content and promote the desirable development of infants through life in which they can act independently.

Early childhood is the time when children spontaneously and independently concern themselves with the environment and develop feelings, wills, and attitudes which are the basis for living through direct and concrete experiences. We must take notice of the features of preschool children and aim at cultivating their feelings, wills, and attitudes. The following five areas were established by putting the goal and the content of instruction in the context of the development of preschool children:

(1) Health: the area concerned with the health of mind and body.
(2) Human Relationship: the area concerned with the human relationship.
(3) Environment: the area concerned with environments around infants.

(4) Language: the area concerned with the acquistition of language.
(5) Expression: the area concerned with sensitivity and expression.

In addition, the guidelines say every kindergarten must decide the goal and organize the concrete contents which meet the needs of preschool children and local situations.

The new syllabus for care and education (hoiku) at the day-nursery

The establishment of the New Guidelines for Kindergarten Education followed that of the New Syllabus for Care and Education (*hoiku*) at the Day-Nursery in March, 1990. This is the first revision in 25 years, since the old Syllabus was settled in 1965. While the New Guidelines for Kindergarten Education consists of three chapters, the New Syllabus for the Care and Education (*hoiku*) at the Day-Nursery consists of twelve chapters:

Chapter 1: general provisions;
Chapter 2: the development of children;
Chapter 3: *hoiku*-content for babies under six months;
Chapter 4: *hoiku*-content for babies from six months to infants under one year and three months;
Chapter 5: *hoiku*-content from one-year-and-three-months to under two years;
Chapter 6: *hoiku*-content for children of two years old;
Chapter 7: *hoiku*-content for children of three years old;
Chapter 8: *hoiku*-content for children of four years old;
Chapter 9: *hoiku*-content for children of five years old;
Chapter 10: *hoiku*-content for children of six years old;
Chapter 11: points of consideration to plan *hoiku*;
Chapter 12: points of consideration concerned with health and safety.

Regarding the principles of *hoiku*, the Syllabus attaches importance to three points: (1) the goal of *hoiku*, (2) the methods of *hoiku*, (3) the environments of *hoiku*. The content is mainly shaped in accordance with the New Guidelines for Kindergarten Education and follows the five areas. From Chapter 3 to Chapter 10, it shows "the features of development" and "matters to consider". In Chapter 12, it details concretely the features of day-nursery, health activities, medical examination, vaccination, illness, accident prevention, cooperation with homes and communities.

THE SIGNIFICANCE OF THE REVISIONS TODAY

It is more than 25 years since the old Guidelines and the Syllabus were established. Why did the Ministry of Education and the Ministry of Health and Welfare make amendments at the same time? The background is as follows:

(1) The social structure has changed in 25 years. The number of large families is decreasing, and that of nuclear families is increasing.

E.C.D.—E

(2) The average family consists of a couple and one or two dependent children. It is rare that three generations live together.

(3) In the age of high growth of the economy, young fathers, "soldiers of industry", work at their office for many hours.

(4) In big cities, the sudden rise of land prices makes it difficult for young couples to live near offices. It takes hours to go to the office because they live in the suburbs, where they can get houses at lower prices.

(5) Young husbands rarely stay at home. Children are often sleeping before their fathers go to work and when they come home.

(6) Young fathers are so tired that they have little time to play with their children.

(7) Because of economical reasons, young couples live in apartment houses where they have little space to play with their children. There are few parks and play grounds in the neighborhood.

(8) Recently, mothers have received more education and they seek public life and professions. Because their husbands' incomes are not enough, they keep working after childbirth.

(9) Recently, the birthrate has fallen, and the average number of children at one home is 1.57.

(10) The main reasons for the fall of the birthrate are as follows.

Women seek independence: they are independent economically and socially. It is difficult to bring up children in the social system. For example, school expenses are very high.

(11) The housing conditions are another cause. Japanese houses, as they are called, "rabbit hutches", are narrow and expensive. There are many difficulties to bringing up children in high rise apartment houses.

(12) People are indifferent to their neighbors. Because the interdependent community based on bloodline is lost and there are few other facilities to help mothers bring up children.

(13) In cities, young parents have little contact with their own parents. In childcare, young mothers are isolated and feel uneasy.

(14) In spite of the increase of working mothers, facilities such as day-nursery for babies are not completed. The number of working mothers has increased, but the system of nurseries is not completed.

These facts create the following situations:

(1) Children, who are pressured by high expectations from parents and grandparents, are overprotected, weak in mind and body, and depend too much on their parents.

(2) Because they have no or few brothers and sisters, they are less sociable.

(3) They cannot acquire the techniques of human relationships because they seldom quarrel* with their siblings and friends.

(4) Because they seldom quarrel*, their physical ability, especially the capacity for locomotion and regulation which they should acquire in their infancy does not develop. They will act clumsily and often become injured.

---

* Note· read perhaps: squabble; rough and tumble play; learn to give and take.

(5) Because parents always pay careful attention, children have a good environment for study, but at the same time, they are forced to study too hard.

Thus, the social condition in Japan has changed greatly in the past quarter century and made childcare difficult. With a wish for better growth of children who live in the 21st century, the guidelines and the syllabus were revised through much discussion and analysis.

To avoid the evil of too much intellectual training from infancy, in a society which lays stress on school careers, the Guidelines for Kindergarten Education was divided into five areas. As I wrote earlier, the emphasis on education through environment is a result of the intention to avoid the intentional instruction of knowledge and makes great account of the unintentional and unsystematic influence of education. At the same time, the guidelines insist on the respect for the independence and spontaneity of children and wishes the promotion of free thought and expression of children.

As I wrote in the previous paragraphs, there is a word *hoiku* in Japanese, which means preschool care and education, besides a word kyoiku which means education. The purpose of the revision this time is to go back to the original meaning of *hoiku*. It is doubtless that the goal of "Early Child Care and Education" is returning to the original meaning of hoiku in Japanese.

OMEP (Organisation Mondiale pour l'Education Prescolaire, World Organization for Early Childhood Education) started the project of "care and education" and international research a few years ago. The word "education" in English is not enough to meet the needs of young children. OMEP aims to add the meaning of "care" and unite care and education into one.

The New Syllabus for the Care and Education at the Day-Nursery clearly shows the union between care and education. Baby nursery and long hours of nursery from eight hours to ten hours have required the union between care and education, this time the union is emphasized. The Syllabus requires a closer connection between day-nursery and homes or communities. The Ministry of Health and Welfare makes an estimate for the grant-in-aid for the home and community-centered programs at the day-nursery.

Secondly, the significant revision contributes to the improvement of the social rank of women. Japan has been, typically, a society where men stand at advantage over women. Though the number of working women is increasing and the feminist movement is active in some cities, society has not yet changed. Some conventional people still hold to the idea of the division of labor between men and women and think it proper for women to devote themselves only to housework and childcare. Husbands and their families may allow wives to work but think wives should take the responsibility for housework and childcare. The consciousness of the family has not changed.

Under these conditions, the revisions, especially that of the New Syllabus at Day-Nursery, and the amendments of systems will improve the social position of women and make it easier for them to work outside the home.

Thirdly, we must value the revisions in relation to the present condition in which Japan receives international attention in various fields. Even though a country of high technology and of great economic power, Japan is not always rated highly. Without

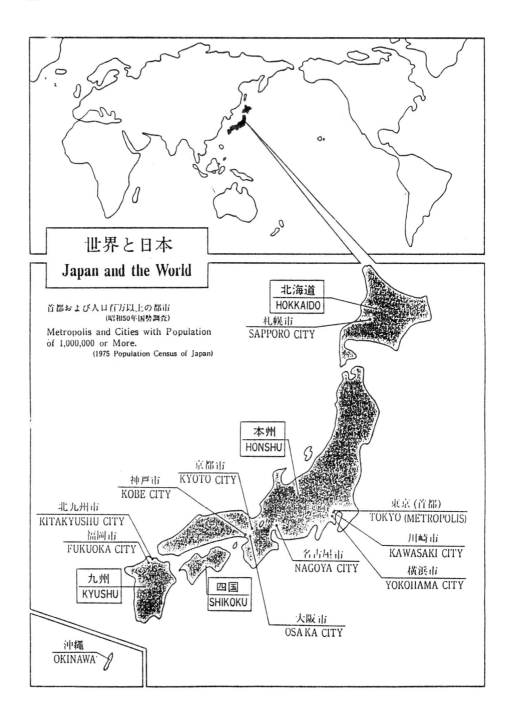

学校組織/Schooling System of Japan

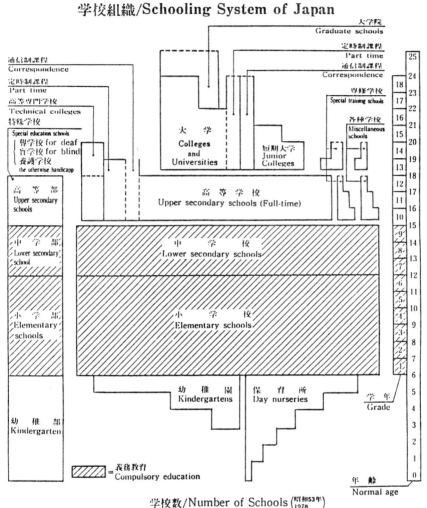

学校数/Number of Schools (昭和53年/1978)

種　類　Kind of schools	学校数 Schools				教師数 Teachers	生徒数 Students	
	国立 National	公立 Public	私立 Private	計 Total		男 Male	女 Female
幼稚園：保育所　Kindergartens：Day nurseries	47	18,688	16,096	34,831	259,706	2,275,639	2,135,231
小　　学　　校　Elementary schools	71	24,589	166	24,826	445,719	5,715,019	5,431,840
中　　学　　校　Lower secondary schools	76	10,150	551	10,777	247,732	2,581,526	2,466,767
高　等　学　校　Upper secondary schools	17	3,846	1,235	5,098	233,936	2,230,590	2,184,484
高等専門学校　Technical colleges	54	4	6	64	3,734	45,810	826
短　期　大　学　Junior colleges	34	49	436	519	16,027	45,252	335,047
大　　　学　Colleges and universities	87	33	313	433	98,173	1,451,720	410,542

(厚生省昭和53年10月1日社会福祉施設設調査及び昭和53年5月1日文部省全国学校基本調査による)
(From the data of the Ministry of Health and Welfare and the Ministry of Education, 1978.)

doubt, however, all the countries of the world pay attention to Japan and wonder why Japan has developed in such a short time. Some people seem to find the key in the system and method of Japanese education. Especially, they think the efficient intellectual training in infancy has brought prosperity to Japan.

It is true that some kindergartens willingly promote academic teaching and have achieved a commercial success in the age when the number of children is small. However, the Ministry of Education found that such teaching makes children look clever for some time but does not promote desirable growth and thus revised the guideline. Care and education that results in healthy and generous men and women must start in infancy.

Thus, the revision, which was done with the changing times and the consciousness of the people, is very meaningful for children and working mothers in society and for the future position of Japan in the world.

Lastly, the revised guidelines and the syllabus point out the importance of teachers and care-takers. As I wrote in Paragraph 1, they have the greatest influence on infants and take the most important part in human environments. I hope they love children, are educated, and are instrumental in the better growth and development of children.

CONCLUSION

I have described the ECCE in connection with two laws concerned with it. There is a word *hoiku* which expresses ECCE in a brief and clear manner. Paragraph 1 shows today's definition of *hoiku*: to protect and instruct so that children are brought up healthy in mind and body. As I wrote earlier it is important for us to go back to the meaning of the word *hoiku* and aim at the goal, bringing up healthy and generous men and women.

Then, what are healthy men and women? We must have a clear image of an ideal child who is brought up properly. The image of an ideal child comes from educators' philosophy of life, sometimes from God. This image is supported by the idea of humanity and human development and actualizes through a long range outlook of life from birth to death in the daily life infants are faced with. The goal of ECCE is to build children's character based on this image. To reach the goal, various concrete *hoiku*-contents and methods have been devoloped.

The readers in other countries, not being familiar with the Japanese educational system, training system of teachers and care-takers, and the educational methods, may neither be interested in nor fully understand what I have described. If you want to know the background of Japanese education, other books such as *Education in Japan* will be helpful. This chapter mainly deals with the latest news of ECCE in Japan, the revisions of the two Laws. Every country has educational problems. It will be a great pleasure if readers learn something from the knowledge of Japanese problems of preschool children and actual circumstances of ECCE.

SUMMARY

There is a Japanese word *kyoiku*, which means education. At the same time, there is a word *hoiku*, which is convenient and proper for ECCE. Its meaning is "to protect and instruct pre-school children so that they are brought up in mind and body". The Guidelines for Kindergarten Education and the Syllabus for Care and Education at the Day-Nursery were recently revised. When we study the revisions, our goal can be nothing but going back to the original meaning of *hoiku* in Japanese. The main theme of the revisions is "education through environments" and the most important people who organize the environments are teachers and care-givers. Therefore, we must train them to be educated people who love children and contribute to the growth and development of children.

References

Ministry of Education, Science and Culture, Government of Japan (edited) (1978) *Education in Japan*, Gyosei Pub. Japan

Early Childhood Education Association of Japan (edited) (1979) *Early Childhood Education and Care in Japan*, Child Honsha Co.

Ishigaki, Emiko H. (1980) *How Do We Educate Teachers for Early Childhood Education: Early Childhood Educators in Japan*, Vol. 8, Bulletin of Seiwa College

Ministry of Education, Science and Culture, Government of Japan (edited) (1986) *Education in Japan: A Brief Outline*, Monbusho, Japan

OMEP Japanese Committee (edited) (1989) *Fact Sheets No. 3. Working Mothers and Their Children's Care*

Ministry of Education (edited) (1989) *The Guidelines for Kindergarten Education*, Fröbel-Kan, Japan (in Japanese)

Ministry of Health and Welfare (edited) (1990) *The Syllabus for Care and Education at the Day-Nursery*, Hoihu-kyokai, Japan (in Japanese)

SUPPLEMENTARY MATERIAL

Japan and the World.
Chronology of Childhood Education and Care in Japan.
Schooling System of Japan.
School Education Law 1947 (Summary).
The Minimum Standards for Child Welfare Institutions 198 (Summary).
Guidelines for Kindergarten Education 1964 (Summary).
Syllabus for the Care of Children at the Day-Nursery 1965 (Summary).
The New Guidelines for Kindergarten Education 1989 (Summary).
The New Syllabus for the Care and Education at the Day-Nursery 1990 (Summary).

Chronology of Childhood Education and Care in Japan

1773   A retired old man by the name of Genshin gathered infants and cared for them.

1849   Shin-en Sato, a classical scholar, made a proposal for establishing child care institutions.

1871   A training school of child care for American women was opened in Yokohama by a Christian missionary woman.

1872   The first modern educational system, including a school for infants was promulgated, but it was never put into effect.

1876   The first national kindergarten, attached to the Tokyo Women's Normal School, was founded.

1880   The first Christian kindergarten attached to the Sakurai Girl's School, was founded.

1884   The Ministry of Education issued an order for prohibiting entry of infants into the elementary school and recommended establishment of kindergartens to take care of infants.

1899   The first national standard with regulations on child care and facilities and equipment was promulgated.

1926   An Imperial decree on Regulations of Kindergartens was prescribed.

1947   "The Fundamental Law of Education" was promulgated and set in detail the aims and principles of education in accordance with the spirit of the Constitution.

1947   "The School Education Law" was promulgated, whereby kindergartens were made part of the school system.

1947   "The Child Welfare Law", among others, stipulating the regulations of day nurseries, was promulgated.

1948   "The Minimum Standards for Child Welfare Institutions" was promulgated as the Ordinance by the Ministry of Health and Welfare.

1948   The course of study for preschool education, a syllabus for kindergarten education, was published by the Ministry of Education.

1948   The Early Childhood Education Association of Japan was organized.

1956   "Guidelines for Kindergarten Education" was published by the Ministry of Education, which indicates the content of early childhood education.

1964   "Guidelines for Kindergarten Education" was revised to conform to the standard prescribed by the government.

1965   "The Syllabus for the Care of Children at the Day-Nursery" which conforms to the standard prescribed by the government, was published by the Ministry of Health and Welfare.

1974   "Kindergarten Accreditation Standards" was promulgated.

1989   The new "Guidelines for Kindergarten Education" was prescribed.

1990   The new "Syllabus for the Care and Education at the Day-Nursery" was revised.

School Education Law (Summary)

(Law No. 26, March 31, 1947)

Chapter I. General Regulations

Article 1. The schools provided for in this law shall be primary schools, secondary schools, high schools, universities, higher professional schools, schools for the blind, schools for the deaf, schools for the handicapped and the kindergartens.

Article 2. The State, prefectural and local public entities and school juridical persons provided for in Article 3 of the Private School Law (hereinafter to be referred to as school juridical persons) alone can establish schools.

(2) The "Government schools" in this law means the schools established by the State, the "public schools," the schools established by prefectural and local public entities, and the "private schools", the schools established by school juridical persons.

Article 3. Those who want to establish schools shall do that in compliance with the school establishment standard of equipment, organization and others set up by the competent authorities according to the types of schools.

Article 6. Schools may collect tuition fees. As to compulsory education, however, in government and public primary schools and secondary schools, or schools for the blind, schools for the deaf and schools for the handicapped, which are equivalent to the above, no tuition fees shall be collected.

Article 12. Schools shall, as otherwise prescribed by law, conduct health examinations in order to increase the health of students, pupils and children as well as teachers, and shall take necessary measures for the preservation of health.

Chapter II. Primary School

Article 17. The primary school shall aim at giving children elementary general education according to the development of their minds and bodies.

Article 19. The course of the primary school shall cover six years.

Chapter VII. Kindergarten

Article 77. The kindergarten shall aim at bringing up young children and developing their minds and bodies, providing suitable environment for them.

Article 78. In order to realize the aim in the foregoing Article the kindergarten shall endeavor to attain the objective in each of the following items:

(1) To cultivate everyday habits necessary for a sound, safe and happly life and to effect a harmonious development of happly life and to effect a harmonious development of bodily functions;

(2) To make children experience in the kindergarten a group life and to cultivate willingness to take part in it as well as the germ of the spirit of co-operation and independence;

(3) To cultivate the germ of the right understanding of and the right attitude towards the surrounding social life and happenings;

(4) To guide the right usage of the language and foster an interest in fairy tales and picture books;

(5) To cultivate an interest in expression of their own through music, dances, pictures and other means.

Article 79. Matters concerning the content of education in the kindergarten shall be decided by the competent authorities according to the provisions of the foregoing two Articles.

Article 80. Those who can enter the kindergarten shall be children from the age of full 3 years up to the age at which they are sent to the primary school.

Article 81. The kindergarten shall have a chief, head teacher and teachers. Provided that, if there exist special circumstances, it may not have the head teacher.

(2) The kindergarten may, in addition to those of the preceding paragraph, nurse-teachers, nurse-assistant-teachers and other necessary staff.

(3) The chief shall manage the affairs of the kindergarten and supervise teachers and other staff.

(4) The head teacher shall assist the chief, arrange the affairs of the kindergarten, and if necessary manage the bringing up of young children.

(5) If there exist special circumstances, regardless of the provision of paragraph 1, assistant teachers or lecturers may be assigned instead of teachers.

(6) Teachers shall take charge of nursing of children.

Article 82. The provisions of Article 28 paragraphs 5, 7, and 9 through 11, and Article 34 shall also apply to the kindergarten.

(Article 28.

(5) The head teacher shall act the functions of the principal as his proxy in the case of any accident thereof, and perform his functions in the case of vacancy thereof. In these cases, if there exist two or more head teachers, the functions shall be acted or performed in the order as previously determined by the principal.

(7) The nurse-teachers shall take charge of nursing and protection of children.

(9) The assistant teachers shall assist the teachers in their duties.

(10) The lecturers shall engage in similar functions to those of teachers or assistant teachers.

(11) The assistant nurse-teachers shall assist the functions of the nurse-teachers.)

(By courtesy of the Eibun-Horei-Sha, inc.)

The Minimum Standards for Child Welfare Institutions (Summary)
(Ministry of Health and Welfare Ordinance No. 63 of 1948)

Chapter I. General Provisions

Article 2. The minimum standards shall ensure that inmates of a child welfare institution are to be brought up sound in minds and bodies so that they can adapt themselves to society, in a bright and hygienic environment under the guidance of educated and competent personnel who have received proper training (hereinafter to include the superintendent of a child welfare institution).

Article 6. In the construction and equipments of a child welfare institution, due consideration shall be given to lighting, ventilation and other facilities to preserve the health of inmates and to the prevention of injury to them.

Article 8. The personnel engaged in the care of children in a child welfare institution shall be persons sound in mind and body and having enthusiasm for child welfare service, and shall be persons who are trained as much as possible in theory and practice of child welfare work; and the personnel other than those whose requirements are stipulated by this Ministerial Ordinance or other laws and ordinances, shall be persons having proper qualifications.

2. The superintendent of a child welfare institution established by the State, prefecture, city, town or village, shall be a person having more than two years' experience in child welfare service and ability to properly manage a child welfare institution.

3. A person who seeks to engage in child welfare service for the first time and who seeks to become personnel of a child welfare institution, as prescribed in the preceding paragraph, shall, as a general rule, be a person under forty-five years of age.

4. The retirement age for personnel engaged in the care of children in a child welfare institution, as prescribed in paragraph 2, shall be sixty-five.

Chapter V. Day Nursery

(Equipments)

Article 49. The day nursery shall be provided with equipments necessary for the care of babies and infants and for the conduct of clerical work.

(Standards for equipments)

Article 50. The standards for the equipments to be provided in a day nursery admitting more than thirty babies and infants shall be as follows:

(1) A day nursery for babies or for infants under two years of age shall have baby rooms or crawling-rooms, medical room, kitchen and lavatories.

(2) The area of a baby room shall be 1.69 square meters or more per baby or infant mentioned in the preceding item.

(3) The area of a crawling-room shall be 3.3 square meters or more per baby or infant mentioned in item (1).

(4) An indoor slide, chair-swing, wheeled-walker and pushcart shall be provided in baby rooms or crawling-rooms.

(5) A day nursery for infant over two years of age shall have nursery-rooms or play-rooms, outdoor playground, (including ground located near the day nursery which may be used as an outdoor playground), kitchen and lavatories.

(6) The area of a nursery-room or play-room shall be 1.98 square meters or more, and that of an outdoor playground shall be 3.3 square meters or more, per infant mentioned in the preceding item.

(7) Musical instruments, black boards, tables, chairs, building blocks and picture books shall be provided in the nursery-room or play-room.

(Personnel)

Article 53. The day nursery shall have nursery teachers and a non-regular physician.

2. The number of nursery teachers shall be, as a general rule, one or more for every six babies or infants under two years of age, and one or more for every thirty infants over two years of age. However, the number shall not be less than two in any single day nursery.

(Nursing hours)

Article 54. The nursing hours in a day nursery shall be, as a general rule, eight hours a day and shall be decided by the superintendent of the day nursery after taking into consideration the working hours of the guardians of babies and infants in its surrounding area and their family conditions.

(Nursery care)

Article 55. In addition to observation of health conditions, personal examinations, free play periods and naps, the care provided at a day nursery shall include the health examination prescribed in Article 13, paragraph 1.

2. The observation of health condition shall be conducted daily at the time of arrival with regard to complexion, temperature, skin troubles and state of cleanliness.

3. The personal examination shall be held daily at the time of departure with regard to cleanliness, cuts or wounds, state of clothing.

5. The free play shall include music, rhythm, drawing or painting, manual arts, story-telling, nature and social studies, and group games.

Guidelines for Kindergarten Education (Summary)

(Prescribed March 23, 1964   The Ministry of Education Ordinance No. 69)

Section I.   General Provisions

1. Fundamental Principles

Education of children in kindergartens should be conducted in accordance with the provisions of the Fundamental Law of Education and in order to achieve the objects and aims shown in the School Education Law, based on the following fundamental principles:

(1) To assist the harmonious psychological and physical development of the child and to nurture the foundations for a healthy mind and body.

(2) To build basic living habits and correct social attitudes, to nurture artistic sentiments, and to cultivate the child's developing morality

(3) To foster interest in nature and society, and to cultivate the seeds of a capacity for rational thought.

(4) To develop in the child correct attitudes in listening to others, and a willingness to express himself understandably to others, and to assist him in acquiring correct use of language.

(5) To enrich creativity through free expression.

(6) To offer such nursing and care as the child requires, to promote autonomous and spontaneous activities, and to nurture independent attitudes.

(7) To fully understand the actual state of mental and physical development of the individual child and to offer appropriate guidance, in accordance with his individual needs.

(8) To offer comprehensive guidance to the child, according to his experiences in life, and based on his interests and desires.

Organization of Curricula

(1) In each kindergarten appropriate curricula should be organized, conforming with the provisions of the Fundamental Law of Education, the School Education Law with its enforcement regulations, and the Guidelines for Kindergarten Education, as well as the rules and regulations of local education committees, and also being adapted to the actual state of mental and physical development of the children, as well as the circumstances of the kindergarten and the community it serves. In doing this, consideration should be given to securing effective guidance by organising items in each of the areas of health, social development, nature, language, music and rhythm, and art and crafts as shown in Section II and by selecting and arranging appropriate and desirable experiences and activities for children in the kindergarten.

(2) It is prescribed that the number of days of attendance in each year in the kindergarten shall be no less than two hundred and twenty days.

(3) The standard number of hours for education each day in the kindergarten is prescribed as 4 hours.

1. Health

1) The acquiring of habits and attitudes necessary for a healthy life.

2) Interest and willing participation in movement.

3) The acquisition of habits and attitudes necessary for a safe life.

2. Society

1) The acquiring of desirable habits and attitudes in personal life.

2) The acquiring of desirable habits and attitudes in social life.

3) The development of interest in the phenomena of the surrounding society.

3. Nature

1) To kindness to animals and appreciation of nature.

2) Interest in natural phenomena and learning to deal with them.

3) Acquiring simple skills indispensable for everyday life.

4) Interest in quantity and geometrical shapes.

4. Language

1) Understanding what others say.

2) Communication experiences and thoughts.

3) Saying correctly the necessary expressions for daily life.

4) The development of imagination and creativity through enjoyment of picture books and picture-card shows, etc.

5. Music and Rhythm

1) Experiencing the joy of expression through singing and playing instruments.

2) Experiencing the joy of expression through free and rhythmical movements.

3) Interest in and enjoyment of music.

4) Expression of feeling and thoughts by sound or movement.

6. Art and Crafts

1) Experience of the joy of expression through drawing and painting.

2) Expression of feelings and ideas in work.

3) Learning to use materials and tools.

4) Interest in beautiful objects.

[By courtesy of Japan Private Kindergarten Federation (Nihon Shiritsu Yochien Rengokai)]

The Syllabus for the Care of Children at the Day Nursery (Summary)

(The Ministry of Health and Welfare, The Child and the Family Bureau Ordinance No. 622, August 6, 1965)

1. Principles

(1) Aims of Child Care

The child has latent possibility for growing up with vigor. It is the aim of child care to have the child live the present as best as he can, and to lay the foundation of bringing about his desirable future.

For the purpose, efforts must be made in the child care to realize the following:

1) To enable the child to cultivate his emotional stability, in relaxed atmosphere, and to achieve balanced development of mind and body.

2) Have the child cultivate the habit of health and safety, basic to the daily routine behavior, in an environment carefully arranged.

3) Stimulate the child to play spontaneously and do work of his own accord, and cultivate in him the social attitude of independency and co-operation, etc.

4) Have the child take an interest in natural and social phenomena.

5) Have the child acquire rich and correct language necessary for daily life.

6) Cultivate in the child creativity through various means of expressions.

7) Cultivate in the child, by means of different aspects of life, rich sentiments, and lay the foundation of thinking power and moral sentiments.

(2) Method of Child Care

1) Nurse the child, on the basis of understanding of child development.

2) Nurse the child, on the basis of understanding of his individual differences, his family and his regional environment.

3) Assure the balanced pose of the child and make the most of his autonomous activity.

4) Make the most of the initiativeness, interests and nature of the child, and give to the child an integrated guidance based on his experiences of daily life.

5) With due consideration of his individual activity, have the child participate in group activity interacting with other children.

(3) Environment of Child Care

To reap full benefits from child care, it is necessary to have environment arranged in good shape.

Efforts must be made to provide the facilities with sufficient lighting, device for ventilation, and keeping the temperature of the room in good condition, and keeping the place in sanitary condition. It is also necessary to have facilities for the children to take a nap and a rest. Due consideration must be paid for prevention of accident and for safety of the children.

Also efforts must be made to the keep the nursery room in family-like atmosphere where children can move about at ease.

2. Fundamental Principles for Construction of the Content of Day Care

For that purpose, the program must be constructed on the basis of the above-mentioned principles of day care as well as with considerations for the following:

(1) Areas of the Content of Child Care

It is possible to divide the activities of the child into several areas and to consider the questions of the content of child care. However, in view of the fact that the activities of the child are of synthetic nature, it is not proper to take and consider one segment apart from the others.

Take for instance the case of a child who is engaged in drawing pictures. He is engaged in plastic art activity; but at the same time, he is, conversing with his friend, also engaged in linguistic activity as well as social activity. Therefore, when you look at the following areas of the child activities, it is always necessary to pay attention to the relatedness of the areas to one another with respect to the child's experience.

Age	Areas
under 1-yr-3-mos	Life, Play
1-yr-3-mos to 2-yr-olds	
2-yr-olds	Health, Society, Play
3-yr-olds	Health, Society, Language, Play
4-yr-olds	Health, Society, Language, Nature, Music, Plastic art
5-yr-olds	
6-yr-olds	

Infants, up to the age of 2 years, engage in life-preserving activities which we call *living*, and activities which they direct against themselves which we call *play*. Thus their activities are divided into two areas.

As they grow older, their activities become differentiated. Thus, about the 2-year-olds, those activities which have to do with human interactions have been taken out of the two areas of life and play, and have been named society. About the 3-year-olds, the linguistic area has been added. From the 4-year-olds on, the areas of the child activities thus determined roughly correspond to the six areas as depicted in the Course of Study for Preschool Education.

The six areas of the child's activities have been determined with respect to the development of the child of each age group, and different aspects of the child's abilities have been selected in an adequate manner so that the child's abilities may attain balanced development.

THE NEW GUIDELINES FOR KINDERGARTEN EDUCATION (Summary)

(Revised March 15, 1989)

Chapter I. General Provision

1. The Principles of Kindergarten Education

The basis for kindergarten education are the understanding of the features of infancy and education given through the environment. Teachers must cultivate trust between themselves and children, and create the better educational environment for children. Efforts must be made in child education to realize the following:

(1) Understand that children with emotional stability show their individualities and they must have experiences necessary for their growth, promote spontaneous actions of children, and help them to lead a suitable life for the early childhood.
(2) Understand play as children's spontaneous activity is an important study which fosters harmonious psychological and physical development, and attain the aim stated in chapter II through play.
(3) Understand that the development of children is attained through the interaction between mind and body and the various processes, and that each child has its own experience in life, offer appropriate guidance for a child's individual needs and the development tasks.

2. The Goals of Kindergarten Education

Early childhood is the time to build the foundation of the formation of character. Teachers must attain the goals of kindergarten education through life in kindergarten based on the fundamental principles.
(1) Build basic living habits and attitudes for a healthy, safe and happy life, and nurture the foundation for a healthy mind and body.
(2) Cultivate in the child love and trust in others, independent and cooperative attitudes and seeds of morality.
(3) Foster interest in nature, and cultivate the seeds of a capacity for sensibility and a capacity for rational thought.
(4) Foster interest in the language in daily life, and cultivate the atitude to speak and listen to others willingly, and assist the child in acquiring correct use of language.
(5) Enrich sensitivity and creativity through various experiences.

3. Organization of Curricula

In each kindergarten appropriate curricula should be organized, conforming with the law and the Guidelines for Kindergarten Education, and also adapted to the actual state of mental and physical development of children, as well as the circumstances of the kindergarten and the community it serves.

(1) In order to totally achieve the aims shown in chapter II, consideration should be given to the period of time of education, children's experiences in life and their development, and the concrete aim and content must be organized. In this case, teachers must have a long-range view from entrance into the kindergarten through graduation and help each child lead a full life.

(2) It is prescribed that the number of weeks of attendance in each year in the kindergarten shall be no less than 39 weeks except in unavoidable circumstances.

(3) The standard of hours for education each day in kindergarten is prescribed as 4 hours. Proper consideration should be given to the development of children and the changes of the seasons.

Chapter II. Aims and Contents

Health

This area aims to develop a healthy mind and body, and cultivate the ability to lead a healthy and safe life.

1. Aims
(1) Cheerful and free action and sense of satisfaction.
(2) Full exercise and willing participation in movement.
(3) The acquisition of habits and attitudes necessary for a healthy and safe life.

2. Contents
(1) Activities with teachers and friends with a sense of security.
(2) Full movement in various play.
(3) Willing play outside.
(4) Willing participation in various activities.
(5) The acquiring of the healthy rhythm of life.
(6) The acquiring of the habit of keeping oneself clean and tidy and the activities necessary for life such as putting on and taking off clothes, eating, and excretion.
(7) Learning the way of life in kindergarten and arranging the place to live.
(8) Interest in health and willing participation in necessary action such as inoculation.
(9) Understanding dangerous places and play, what to do in accidents, and behavior promoting safety.

Human Relationships

To live on friendly terms with the others; this area aims to bring up independence and the ability to associate with others.

1. Aims
(1) Enjoying life in kindergarten and acquiring the sense of satisfaction from acting by oneself.

(2) Willing association with people around and developing love and trust.
(3) The acquiring of desirable habits and attitudes in social life.

2. Contents
(1) Going to kindergarten willingly and getting on well with teachers and friends.
(2) Thinking and acting by oneself.
(3) Doing what they can do.
(4) Playing with friends actively and sharing pleasure and sorrow.
(5) Communication with each other.
(6) Enjoying playing and working with friends.
(7) Recognition of what they should not do or say in relationships with friends.
(8) Recognition of the importance of rules in the happy life with friends.
(9) Using common toys and tools carefully with friends.
(10) Interest in various people who are deeply connected with their life.

Environment

This area aims to develop the ability to be concerned with nature and social phenomena positively and the right to adapt to life.
1. Aims
(1) The development of interest in the environment and various phenomena through the contact with nature.
(2) Dealing with the surrounding environment willingly, adapting it to life, and appreciation of it.
(3) Enrichment of the sensitivities toward the nature of things and numbers, measures and weights.

2. Contents
(1) Keeping in touch with nature, and getting recognition of its size, beauty, and mystery.
(2) Recognition of the changes of nature and human life in each season.
(3) Interest in the surrounding phenomena, such as nature.
(4) Kindness to animals and appreciation of nature.
(5) Appreciation of surrounding things.
(6) Play by using and thinking of the surrounding things.
(7) Interest in the construction of toys and tools.
(8) Interest in numbers, measures, weights and geometric shapes.
(9) Interest in information and facilities which are deeply connected with life.
(10) Affection toward the national flag in ceremonies at the kindergarten and at other places.

Language

This area aims to express experiences and thoughts through spoken language and develop the correct attitudes and a willingness to listen to what others say, and acquire correct use of language.

1. Aims

(1) Expressions for what one feels and enjoyment of communication.

(2) Listening to what others say carefully, and telling experiences and thoughts.

(3) Enjoyment of picture books and stories and enrichment of imagination as well as understanding the necessary words for daily life.

2. Contents

(1) Interest in what teachers and friends say and listening to it willingly.

(2) Expression of what one did, saw, heard and felt through language in one's own way.

(3) Expression of what one wants to do and what one wants others to do through words and questioning of what one does not understand.

(4) Listening carefully to what others say and speaking correctly enough for others to understand.

(5) Understanding the necessary words for daily life.

(6) Daily greeting with affection.

(7) Recognition of the joy and beauty of language in life.

(8) Enrichment of image and language through various experiences.

(9) Enjoyment of listening to stories with interest and of imagination through picture books and stories.

(10) Interest in signs and letters necessary for daily life.

Expression

This area aims to bring up sensitivities, the will to express feelings and thoughts, and enrichment of imagination.

1. Aims

(1) Sensitivity toward various natural, human, and beauties.

(2) Expression of feelings and thoughts in various ways.

(3) Enrichment of images in life and enjoyment of various expressions.

2. Contents

(1) Recognition and enjoyment of sound, colors, shapes, feelings, and movement in life.

(2) To come in touch with beauties and events which move the mind, and to enrich images.

(3) Enjoyment of communicating excitement in many events.

(4) Expression of feelings and thoughts by sound, movement, writing, and creating freely.

(5) Familiarity with various materials and play with toys or materials inventively.

(6) Familiarity with music and enjoyment of singing and using simple rhythm instruments.

(7) Enjoyment of writing, creating, playing and decorating with what one creates.

(8) Expression of images by movement and language, and enjoyment of performing.

(translated by E.H. Ishigaki)

THE NEW SYLLABUS FOR CARE AND EDUCATION AT THE DAY-NURSERY (Summary)

(Revised March 15, 1990)

Chapter I. General Provisions

The day-nursery is a child welfare institution whose aim is to care for and educate babies and infants in accordance with Child Welfare Institutions. Therefore, the care and education at day-nursery must be the most suitable to promote the welfare of babies and infants.

The day-nursery is a place where babies and infants spend much time in an important period to cultivate the foundation of character building. The bases for care and education at the day-nursery are making up for the nurture at home, but with a close connection with home and community, arranging for the suitable environment for children to lead a healthy, safe life with emotional stability; enabling them to express themselves and act freely; and achieving healthy development of mind and body.

The primary feature of care and education at the day-nursery is to bring up warmhearted children through protection and education.

1. Principles of Care and Education

(1) Goals of Child Care and Education

The child has a latent possibility for growing up with vigor. It is the goal of child care to have the child live the present as best as he or she can, and to lay the foundation of bringing about a desirable future.

For this purpose, care and education aim to achieve the following:

(a) To preserve the children from danger, to enable the child to cultivate his or her emotional stability in an environment carefully arranged and in a relaxed atmosphere to satisfy various needs.

(b) Have the child cultivate the habit of health and safety, basic to the healthy mind and body.

(c) Cultivate in the child love, trust, respect for human rights, an attitude of independence and co-operation, and moral sentiments.

(d) Have the child take an interset in nature and social phenomena, and lay the foundation of rich sentiments and mental development.

(e) Have the child take an interest in language and acquire rich language and the attitudes to speak and listen to others willingly.

(f) Cultivate in the child, by means of different aspects of life, rich sentiments and imagination.

(2) Method of Child Care and Education

In child care and education, care-takers' speech and behavior greatly influence children. Therefore, care-takers' love, intelligence, and technique must be given to each child.

For this purpose, efforts must be made in child care and education to realize the following:

(a) Accept the child warmly, give him or her proper protection and care on the basis of understanding of his or her statement, his or her family and regional environment, and have him or her act with emotional stability and sense of trust.

(b) Nurse the child, on the basis of understanding of child development, his or her individual character, and developmental tasks.

(c) Value the child's rhythm of life and make the most of his or her autonomous activity, and assure the balanced life of the child.

Have the child acquire the sense of stability by dealing with each child especially when he or she enters the day-nursery. Have him or her participate in group activities interacting with other children.

(d) Arrange a good environment where children act spontaneously and willingly. Make the most of the initiatives of the child, and give him or her integrated guidance and suitable experience for infants through play.

(e) Make the most of the individual activity, and have the child participate in group activity with other children.

(3) Environment of Child Care and Education

Environment of child care and education consists of human environment, such as care-takers and children, material environment, such as facilities and toys, and natural and social phenomena. Human beings, materials, and places relate to each other and give children an environment. It is important to make the child's life stable and enrich his or her activity in this environment.

Facilities and outdoor playground of the day-nursery must be big enough for children's actions. Toys and tools must be supplied and used fully.

Efforts must be made to provide the facilities with sufficient lighting, device for ventilation, a proper temperature control, and cleanliness. Due consideration must be paid for prevention of accidents and for safety of the children. It is also necessary to have facilities for the children to take a nap and a rest.

Efforts must be made to keep nursery-rooms in a family-like atmosphere where children can move about at ease.

Efforts must be made to introduce natural and social phenomena so that children will be interested in them.

2. Fundamental Principles for Construction of the Content of Care and Education

(1) Aims and Contents

The meaning of care and education consists of "aim" and "content". "Aims" are the embodiment of the goals of care and education. This article which shows "what care-takers should do" to have the child lead a stable life and move about freely, and "the desirable feelings, wills, and attitudes of children" as a result of care-takers' assistance to children's spontaneous and willing activities.

"Contents" are the fundamental article which shows what care-takers should do according to children's situations and what care-takers should help to achieve the aim from the aspect of children.

The fundamental article in the content, which is necessary to the stable life of children, that is, the maintenance of life and emotional stability, deals with children of all ages. Especially, the content of each age over two is put together and shown as "the fundamental article".

From the aspect of children's development, five areas are set forth: "health" the area concerned with the health of mind and body; "Human Relationships" the area concerned with the human relationship; "Environment" the area concerned with environment around infants; "Language" the area concerned with the acquisition of language; and " Expression" the area concerned with sensitivity and expression. It is difficult to divide the care of children under three into five areas; therefore, they are summed up with fundamental principles.

Given through children's activity, care and education are not limited in one area but develop totally among all the areas.

Chapter II Development of Children

1. Relationship between Children and Adults

Children are born with immature bodies and minds, protected and nurtured by adults. They grow up desirably and acquire necessary abilities for human life through the full interaction with adults. The most important thing is to foster in children the trust of others and independence, which are cultivated in the interaction between adults and children through the protection and care of affectionate and thoughtful parents.

Children come to love and trust through protection, love, and trust of adults toward them. Through the interaction with adults, children develop emotional stability and the will to respond to adults' expectations, begin to act spontaneously, have interest in and relations with siblings and the other people around, and acquire self-consciousness.

2. Development of Children

Development of children is achieved through the interaction with people around, nature, materials, and events.

It is important to recognize children's power, which is subjectively concerned with development. Development is the process. This is accomplished through which children get new attitudes, knowledge, and ability with the natural growth of mind and body by approaching the things in the surroundings and the interaction with them on the basis of the spontaneous interest, curiosity, and previous knowledge and ability.

The most important thing is the interaction with people. Children want the association with adults, conversation, their understanding. They also try to understand adults and have social interaction with other children. The social interaction with other children, who have the same point of view, is an essential experience for their intellectual development as well as emotional, social, and moral development.

3. Life of Children and Assistance to their Development

Children develop through the interaction with each other and their surroundings. In order to quicken this development, not only adults approach to children but also children's spontaneous and active approach is necessary. Therefore, the day-nursery must arrange a good environment where each child lives safely, is given proper stimulation and help, and movesabout actively and willingly.

Care-takers must see children as they are, understand, accept them, and have confidence in the stable life of the child concerning his or her region and home.

Children's activities are divided into two groups: these concerned with life: meals, excretion, rest, and clothes, and those concerned with play. The latter is primary.

Children's play is strongly concerned with children's development and quicked it. Because play is the total actions associated with necessary experiences for the children's development, comprehensive care through play is necessary. Care-takers, living and playing with children, understand the physical and psychological situation of each child and assist their development.

(translated by E.H. Ishigaki)

The preparation of early childhood teachers in Japan. PART II

ISAAKI NOGUCHI

Faculty of Education, Hirosaki University, Aomori, Japan

(Received August 1991)

This paper looks at the structure and context of training programmes for early childhood education in the light of recent revisions to the laws controlling curriculum and certification. The routes to professional status are described.

Key words: Early Childhood Education: Japan; certification

1. THE EDUCATION OF CHILDREN IN THE 3 TO 8 AGE RANGE IN JAPAN: RANGE OF PROVISION

In Japan, the education of children in the 0 to 8 years age range is being carried out as follows:

Early childhood education and care between 0 to 6 years is undertaken at Day Care Centres within the jurisdiction of the Ministry of Health and Welfare; early childhood and/or infant education which may start as young as 3 years and which ends at the age of 6 years is carried out in kindergartens. Children's education between the ages of 6 years and 12 years is carried out at the elementary school. Both kindergartens and elementary schools are within the jurisdiction of the Ministry of Education, Science and Culture.

Pre-school education (or early childhood education) in the 0 to 6 range in Japan includes both day care centres which take care of babies and infants needing nursery care, thus functioning as welfare institutions, and kindergartens, which educate children beyond 3 years and which increasingly acquire the character of "school". All children in Japan over 6 years of age are required to attend a six-year elementary school as compulsory education. The elementary school aims to provide children with the common and general education necessary for their mental and physical development.

139

A. Day Care Centres

Day Care Centres, which lie within the jurisdiction of the Ministry of Health and Welfare are essentially Child Welfare Facilities providing day care for babies, infants and pre-school children. Day care centres serve purposes common to many countries and are for children whose parents or guardians are unable to provide family care for their own children because of the demands of work or by reason of illness, etc.

The nursing content of day care centres includes both education and day care for children needing nursery care, but the areas of experience perceived as appropriate to children of 3 years and older consist of the five fields of health, human relationships, environment, language, and self-expression. These harmonise with the curriculum of "kindergarten" education and thus facilitate transference.

B. Kindergartens

Kindergartens have been established for pre-school children who enter between the ages of 3 to 5 years, the main emphasis being on education until entrance to the elementary school at the age of 6. Kindergartens aim to promote the mental and physical development of children by providing them with stimulating experiences within a safe, caring environment. In essence kindergarten education emphasises five areas of experience: Health, Human Relationships, Environment, Language, Expression.

C. Elementary School Education in the 6 to 12 Years Range

In Japan, all parents or guardians have to send their children to an elementary school for six years, as required by Article 4 of the Fundamental Law of Education.

Taking a reasonably common definition of the age span of "early childhood education" as extending to about 8 years of age, the "lower grades" of elementary schools in Japan provide a common general education for 6 and 7 year olds with due consideration for their infant nature. The curriculum is not differentiated by subject to the extent that occurs in later years and focusses on children's experiences through themes in areas such as Life Studies and Environmental Studies.

D. Japanese "Teachers" in Early Childhood and Elementary Education

In Japan, personnel at Day Care Centres are called "Hobo" (Nursery teachers) and achieve qualifications through the requirements of the "Nursery Teacher Certificate". Training facilities for nursery teachers exist at university and/or junior college institutions and are authorised by the Minister of Health and Welfare. On the other hand, personnel at kindergartens and teachers at elementary schools are called "kyo-yu" (teachers): work in kindergartens requires the "Kindergarten Teacher Certificate" as provided for by the Educational Certification Law. Elementary school teachers must possess the "Elementary School Teacher Certificate".

There is a clear distinction in the training requirements for nursery teachers serving Day Care Centres, teachers at kindergarten and elementary school teachers.

In considering the preparation of early childhood teachers in Japan, this paper will focus on the nature of the training programmes relevant to: nursery teachers at day care centres, teachers at kindergartens, and elementary school teachers with particular regard to the "lower grades".

2. TRAINING PROGRAMMES OF EARLY CHILDHOOD AND ELEMENTARY TEACHERS IN JAPAN

As seen in the previous section (1), children in the 6 to 8 age range are educated at elementary school in Japan. Hence the lower grades of elementary schools serve the upper range of "early childhood education" programmes. It is necessary therefore to include aspects of elementary teacher preparation in the description of training arrangement for early childhood personnel.

A. Characteristics of Japanese Nursery Teachers and Teachers

First, Tables 1 and 2 show the number of nursery teachers, teachers working at day care centres, kindergartens and elementary schools, as of 1987.

Male nursery teachers are only rarely evident in day care centres; most nursery teachers are female. Women account for 93.8% of all kindergarten teachers and 56.0% of all elementary school teachers.

In the kindergarten, the number of young teachers, i.e. below 25 years is markedly evident, and accounts for 40.5% of the total. The main reason is that the women teachers in kindergartens account for 93.8% of the whole and many of these resign their post as teachers because of marriage, to bear children, and to raise their family. The same may be said of nursery teachers in day care centres.

Tables 4 and 5 show the percentage distribution of nursery teacher, kindergarten and elementary school teachers (full-time) by educational attainment.

The completion of training facilities for nursery teachers in this table include universities and colleges, junior colleges, special vocational schools, miscellaneous schools and training centres for nursery teacher graduates. About 80% of the nursery teachers have graduated from an Institute of higher education including junior college (or the equivalent). This shows a nursery teachers tendency to higher educational attainment.

The proportion of kindergarten teachers completing Junior College is high (78.3%). A minority, (9.1%) are drawn from the ranks of college graduates. At the elementary school level, university or college graduates account for 58.8% of the total work force of school teachers, while junior college graduates are relatively less evident (32.4% as of 1983).

It may be added that 0.4% of the teachers at kindergarten have graduated from the graduate course.

Table 1   Number of Nursery Teachers (full-time) etc. (As of October 1987)

Number of Nursery teachers (full-time) at day care centres.		
Total	Qualified	Unqualified
178,072	176,796	1,278

Table 2   Number of Teachers (full-time), etc. (As of May 1987)

Type of Institution	No. of Teachers	% who are female teachers
Kindergarten	99,170	93.8
Elementary school	468,672	56.0

Table 3   Composition of Teachers Classified by Age (As of October 1983)

Age	'School' Type Kindergarten	Elementary school
less than 25	40.5(%)	7.5(%)
25–29	20.8	21.8
30–34	11.4	16.9
35–39	7.1	10.8
40–44	4.5	7.0
45–49	4.9	10.2
50–54	3.6	15.1
55–59	2.6	10.4
more than 60	4.7	0.4

Table 4   Percentage Distribution of Nursery Teachers (full-time) by Educational Attainment (as of 1988)

Total No.	Completion of Training Certificate for nursery teachers	Completion of Upper Secondary Course etc.
176,796	141,353 (80%)	35,443 (20%)

Table 5   Percentage Distribution of Kindergarten and Elementary School Tenders

	Completion of University Course (4 years)	Completion of Junior College Course (2 years)	Completion of Upper Secondary Course
Kindergarten	9.1%	78.3%	5.2%
Elementary School	58.8%	32.4%	7.8%

B. Training and Certification of Nursery Teachers

In Japan, nursery teachers at day care centres are trained in facilities approved by the Minister of Health and Welfare. The training facilities for teachers described here include universities and colleges, junior colleges, special vocational schools, miscellaneous schools within the jurisdiction of the Ministry of Education, Science and Culture, and training centres for nursery teachers within the jurisdiction of the Ministry of Health and Welfare respectively, and which are authorised by the Minister of Health and Welfare.

As shown in Table 6, the number of training facilities for nursery teachers has remained relatively stable in recent years. Only the staff directly engaged in day care centres that provide day care for infants and pre-school children are discussed here. In addition to nursery teachers, there are of course personnel engaged in Maternity Homes that provide medical care for pregnant women with both medical and financial problems, Baby Homes that care for babies without guardians and Mother-&-Child Homes that care for mothers with dependent children in fatherless families. These may all be regarded as Child Welfare Institutions.

Table 6   Trends in number of training facilities for nursery teachers (as of 1988)

	1981	1982	1983	1984	1985	1986	1987	1988
Number	330	331	337	339	339	338	335	339

In order to become a nursery teacher at a Day Care Centre or other facility, personnel are required to obtain a Nursery Teacher's Licence approved by the Minister of Health and Welfare according to their certification of universities, junior colleges, special vocational schools, miscellaneous school and training centres for nursery teachers.

A Nursery Teacher's Licence is also given to upper secondary school graduates (or the equivalent) who have passed the Nursery Teachers' Qualifying Examination set under the supervision of the Urban and Rural prefectures concerned. All people, regardless of sex, can obtain a Nursery Teacher's Licence under certain conditions, in accordance with more favourable criteria introduced in March 1977. At present a number of male nursery teachers have cut conspicuous figures in some child welfare facilities.

C. Training and Certification of Kindergarten Teachers and Elementary Teachers

Kindergarten and elementary school teachers in Japan are trained in the Universities or Junior College approved approved by the Minister of Education, Science and Culture.

Table 7 presents the major posts within the profession such as principal, vice-principal, teacher, etc. and their job specification in kindergarten and elementary schools as regulated by the School Education Law and subsequent Enforcement Regulations.

Table 7 Major Types of posts and Their Job Specifications in Kindergartens and Elementary Schools

Grade within Profession	Job Specification
Principal	To administer the affairs of the school and direct the personnel
Vice-principal Kindergarten	To help the principal, arrange the affairs of the school, and be involved as appropriate with the care and education process.
Vice-principal Elementary school	To help the principal, arrange the affairs of the school, and be involved as appropriate with the educational process.
Teacher Kindergarten	To foster the development of the whole child
Teacher Elementary school	To educate the whole child

Although job specifications of teachers may vary, the large majority of kindergarten and elementary school teachers take charge of a single class, and are responsible for children's education within the class.

To become a teacher at kindergarten or elementary school, individuals are required to obtain a Teacher's Certificate granted by the Prefectural Boards of Education in accordance with their certification of relevent universities and colleges (faculties, graduate school and junior colleges).

Teacher Certificates are classified into three major categories; regular certificates, special certificates. and temporary certificates. The regular certificates are subdivided into three classes: Major certification; first class certification, second class certification. These may be acquired in respect of either kindergarten or elementary school.

First class certification for kindergarten and elementary school teachers are granted to university graduates (or the equivalent) having a Bachelor's degree. Second class certification for kindergarten and elementary school teachers are granted to those who have studied for at least two years in a university or junior college (or the equivalent) and acquired a specified number of course credits. For the major certificate the requirement is to have a Master's degree or its equivalent.

The special certificates for elementary school teachers, are given only in respect of each of four subjects; Music, Art and Handicraft, Homemaking, and Physical Education. They are valid for a period stated by the Prefectural Board of Education which may be from three years up to ten years.

The temporary certificates for kindergarten and elementary school teachers are given only when a person holding the regular certificate cannot be appointed. Temporary Certificates may be granted to graduates (or the equivalent) who have been successful in the Teacher Certificate Examination held under the supervision of the Prefectural Board of Education, and is valid for three years only in the prefecture concerned.

A regular Teacher Certificate is valid in all prefectures and for life. There is no great economic or legal distinction between teachers holding major, first class or second class certificates.

3. TYPE AND CURRICULUM OF TEACHER TRAINING IN JAPAN

A. Type and Curriculum of Nursery Teacher Training

The preparation of Nursery Teachers generally carries the following requirements — either: (a) to study in a training facility for nursery teachers authorised by the Minister of Health and Welfare, or (b) to pass the Nursery Teacher Certificate examinations conducted under prefectural auspices. This test is defined in the law: The National Nursery Teacher Qualification Test.

(a) The curriculum of training facilities for nursery teachers

This is organised according to Notification No. 352 of the Ministry of Health and Welfare that stipulates all the subjects to be studied, the minimum units of credit, and the ways to acquire credits. The facilities that train nursery teachers include universities and colleges, junior colleges, special vocational schools, miscellaneous schools, and training centres for nursery teachers.

The curriculum is generally classified as general education subjects and specialised subjects.

As for general education subjects the above Notification requires at least a total of 14 credits from among the following three fields: Humanities, Social Science, and Natural Science. The health and physical education to be included in the "general education" subjects requires 2 credits.

As for elective subjects, nursery teachers at day care centres are required to study from among "Principles of Childhood 2 (2 credits)", "Psychology of infants (2 credits), Health (1 credit)", "Language (1 credit)", "Art and Craft (1 credit)", "Bringing up of babies 2 (2 credits)", "Music 2 (2 credits)", and "Upbringing practice 2 (2 credits)".

The prescribed minimum units of credits in specialised subjects requires at least a total of 54 credits from among these eight fields: Welfare (6 credits), Nurture and Education (12 credits), Psychology (12 credits), Health education (10 credits), Nursery education (16 credits), Fundamental Level of Skills (8 credits), Teaching Practice (8 credits), Domestic Science (2 credits).

Japan is now at a turning-point in Nursery Teacher Training for two main reasons: a decrease in the population of infants; and a recognition that provision for education and care must adapt to the various needs of people of a new age. To respond to these

Table 8 Standard Credit Requirements for General Education Subjects

	General Education Subjects	
		Credits
Requirements	required	elective
2 Subjects or more from Humanities	4 (L)	
2 Subjects or more from Social Science	4 (L)	
2 Subjects or more from Natural Sciences	4 (L)	
Foreign Language		2 (S)
Health Education	1 (L)	
Physical Education	1 (P)	
(Note)		
(L) = Lecture (S) = Seminar (P) = Practice		

challenges a new curriculum for Nursery Teacher Training is undergoing investigation and development at the Ministry of Health and Welfare.

A new curriculum for kindergarten teachers, has been in force since April 1990, with an associated revision to the Educational Personnel Certification Law, 1989.

(b) Nursery teacher certificate examination: the National test

Besides the nursery teachers training system through the approved facilities mentioned above, there also exists a purely vocational route to certification through a recognised education pathway, eligibility for which is granted to upper secondary school graduates (or the equivalent) through the School Education Law. The different administrative divisions within Japan have a legal obligation to ensure that candidates have an opportunity to present themselves for examination on at least one occasion in the year and to subsequently certificate any person who has passed the examination covering the prescribed 8 subjects: social welfare in general; an introduction to child welfare work; child psychology and mental hygiene; sanitation and physiology; nursing science and practice; nutrition and nutritious practice; the theory of upbringing; nursery teaching practice. The percentage of nursery teachers who qualify through the vocational route associated with the Nursery Teachers' Certificate Examination is now declining from 27.4% of all Nursery Teachers in 1973 to 20% in 1987. The decrease in this percentage is received favourably on the grounds that it indicates a tendency for nursery teachers to be increasingly drawn from "college" graduates. Recently four year university students in the kindergarten teachers course are taking the test to become day nursery teachers.

B. Type and Curriculum of Kindergarten and Elementary School Teacher Training

(1) Training and certification of teachers in Japan

In Japan, the curriculum of teacher training in the universities and colleges

Table 9 Standard Credit Requirement for Special Subjects for Nursery Teacher Training

Subject	Credits required	elective
Professional Subjects for Nursery Teacher Training		
Welfare		
Social Welfare 1	2 (L)	
Child Welfare	2 (L)	
Social Welfare 2	2 (S)	
Nurture & Education		
Childcare principles 1	4 (L)	
Childcare principles 2		2 (L)
Nursing principles 1	4 (L)	
Nursing principles 2		2 (L)
Educational principles	2 (L)	
Psychology		
Child psychology	2 (L)	
Mental hygiene	2 (L)	
Educational psychology	2 (L)	
Psychology of adolescence		2 (L)
Clinical psychology		2 (S)
Psychology of infants		2 (S)
Health		
Chidren's nutrition	2 (L)	
Practice at nutrition	1 (P)	
Chldren's Health 1	4 (L)	
Children's Health 2		2 (L)
Practice at Health	1 (P)	
Contents of early Childhood Education and Care		
Health	1 (S)	1 (S)
Human Relations	1 (S)	
Environment	1 (S)	
Language	1 (S)	1 (S)
Music and Rhythm (Expression I)	1 (S)	1 (S)
Art and Craft (Expression II)	1 (S)	1 (S)
Briging up of babies 1	2 (L)	
Bringing up of babies 2		2 (S)
Contents of Nursing		2 (S)
Basic Skills		
Physical education	2 (S)	
Music 1	2 (S)	
Music 2		2 (S)
Art & Handicraft	2 (S)	
Upbringing Practice		
Upbringing practice 1	4 (P)	
Upbringing practice 2		2 (P)
Upbringing practice 3		2 (P)
Domestic Science		
Household administration		2 (L)

* As for elective subjects, nursery teachers at day care centres are reqruied to study from among "principles of childhood 2 (2 credits)", "Psychology of infants (2 credits), Health (1 credit)", Language (1 credit)", "Art and Craft (1 credit)", "Bringing up of babies 2 (2 credits)", Music 2 (2 credits)", and "Upbringing practice 2 (2 credits)".

(including graduate school) and/or junior colleges is organised according to the Regulations of The Ministry of Education, Science and Culture as defined in the Standards for the Establishment of Universities, the Standards for the Establishment of Junior Colleges, and the Standards for the Establishment of Graduate Schools which prescribes the requirements for graduation. It is also organised according to the Educational Personnel Certification Law and the Regulation for the Enforcement of the Educational Personal Certification Law which stipulates the minimum criterion required for certification.

The curriculum is generally classified as general education subjects, foreign language subjects, health and physical education subjects, and professional education subjects for teacher training, as shown in Table 10.

Table 10

Subject Areas	Graduate school	University & college	Junior college
Length of course	2 yrs	4 yrs	2 yrs
* General Education	—	36	8
(Humanities, Social Science, Natural Sciences			
Foreign Languages	—	8	—
Health & physical Education	—	4	2
* Professional Education	30	76	28
Additional credits	—	—	24
TOTAL	30	124	62

* Since 1990 these distincvtions are less sharply defined.

For general education subjects, Standards for the Establishment of a University requires at least a total of 36 credits (in Junior Colleges 8 credits or more) from among these three fields: Humanities, Social Science, and Natural Sciences. Moreover 8 credits (in Junior Colleges there are usually no rules) in one foreign language and credits (in Junior Colleges 2 credits or more) in health and physical education must be acquired by students. The prescribed minimum units of credits in Professional Education subjects are 76 credits (in Junior Colleges 28 credits or more). But these vary with school level and according to types of certificates as stated in the next section.

(2) Curriculum of major certificates and first class certificates for kindergarten and elementary school teachers

Profession Education subjects are in two fields: Teaching subjects and Professional subjects (Article 5 of the Educational Personnel Certification Law). (Revised 1990)

The Educational Personnel Certification Law and the Regulation for the Enforcement of the Educational Personal Certification Law say that at least 16 credits for Professional subjects are required in the case of regular certificate of kindergarten teachers; and the regular certificates of elementary school teachers requires at least 18 credits of Professional subjects. The minimum units of credits in Teaching subjects are 35 in respect of regular certificates of kindergarten teachers, and a minimum of 41 in respect of regular certificates for elementary school teachers.

First class certificates are granted to Bachelor's degree holders, whilst 2nd class regular certificates require the acquisition of at least 62 credits after 2 years' study at university or junior college.

Major certificates for kindergarten and elementary school teachers are granted to Master's degree holders and those who have acquired a total of 24 credits in Professional and Teaching subjects.

As illustrated in Table 12, Regulation for the enforcement of the Educational Personnel Certification Law prescribes in full the minimum units of credits in Teaching subjects as set out in Section 2 to 6 according to the kinds of certificate.

The student teacher in order to deepen further the lectures and seminars in the universities and faculties of teacher training, is required to practice lessons and extracurricular activities under the instruction of the teacher in the training school, laying stress on either kindergartens or elementary schools. Teaching practice is usually carried out for four weeks.

For Professional subjects, as they relate to Major certificates and First class certificates for elementary school teachers, the second of the Regulations for the Enforcement of the Educational Personnel Certification Law requires at least 2 credits of Professional subjects in each of: Japanese Language (including Copying), Social Studies, Arithmetic, Science, Life, Music, Art & Handicraft, Homemaking and

Table 11 Minimum Requirements for Teacher Certificates

Types of Certificate	Teaching subjects	Minimum number of credits to be earned at University (or Junior College) in: Professional subjects	
Kindergarten teacher	1st class regular certificate	16	35
	2nd class regular certificate	8	23
Elementary school teacher	1st class regular certificate	14	41
	2nd class regular certificate	10	27

Table 12   Minimum Number of Credits Required for Teacher Certificate

1st sec.	Teaching subject	Kindergarten Teacher		Elementary School Teacher	
		1st	2nd	1st	2nd
2nd sec	Essentials and aim of education related Subjects				
	Mental and physical development and process of learning of children realted subjects	12	6	12	6
	Social side, system and management of education related subjects				
	Educational methods and skill (including) the practical use of instruments and teaching materials on information) related subjects.				
3rd sec. (only in elementary school	Methods of teaching related subects				
	Moral education related subjects			22	14
	Special activities related subjects				
4th sec. (only in kindergarten	Curriculum in general related subjects				
	Contents of kindergarten education related subjects	18	12		
	Teaching Methods related subjects				
5th sec. (only in in elementary school	Schoolchild guidance and educational consultation related subjects			2	2
6th sec.	Teaching practice	5	5	5	5

* Minimum number of credits for Major certificate is the same with 1st class certificates.

Physical Education. The regular certificate for kindergarten teachers requires 4 credits or more of Professional subjects in each of Music, Art & Handicraft and Physical Education as well as 2 or more credits in each of 2 subjects from among: Japanese Language, Arithmetic and Life from the Curriculum of the Elementary School Certificate Professional Subjects requirements (Article 5 of the Regulation for the Enforcement of the Educational Personnel Certification Law).

(3)   Curriculum of second class certificates for kindergarten and elementary school teachers

In order to obtain a second class regular certificate, the students are required to study at the university (including junior college or teacher's training schools approved by the Minister of Education, Science and Culture) for at least 2 years and acquire 62 or more credits, as shown in Tables 10–12. For elementary school teachers, teaching subjects must account for at least 27 credits (23 credits for kindergarten teachers).

The Professional Subjects requirement specifies a minimum of 2 credits in at least 5 subjects, from among: Japanese Language (including Copying), Social Studies, Arithmetic, Science, Life, Music, Art & Handicraft, Homemaking and Physical Education in regular certificates for elementary school teachers. In the case of kindergarten teachers, the Professional Subjects requirements specifies at least 2 credits or more in Music, Art & Handicraft and Physical Education, with additional credits being sought in basic skill areas relevant to older age groups.

4.   ISSUES OF TEACHER TRAINING FOR YOUNG CHILDREN IN JAPAN

A.   Location of Training Institutes for Teachers of Young Children

In Japan, colleges and universities (faculties, graduate schools; hereafter universities) and junior colleges play an important role in preparing teachers for work in the nursery, kindergarten and elementary school, context. Based on statistics published in 1988, the universities and junior colleges account for about 71% of all training facilities for nursery teachers. These facilities collectively account for about 80% of all nursery teachers in training. On the evidence of the number of students, the same may be said of kindergarten and elementary school. That is, as for nursery teachers the university and junior colleges graduates comprise 97.8% of all kindergarten teachers in 1983. Teachers who are university and junior college graduates also account for 94% of the elementary school teachers.

In 1988 the total number of training institutions for nursery teachers was 339, distributed between the universities (20) junior colleges (221), special training schools (58), miscellaneous schools (1), training centres for nursery teachers (39).

Kindergarten and elementary school teachers in Japan are trained mainly in the universities and colleges (including graduate schools) and junior colleges approved by the Minister of Education, Science and Culture.

Most elementary school teachers and some kindergarten teachers are trained at 4-year kindergarten and elementary teacher training courses at national universities which are established in each prefecture.

E.C.D.- F

Table 13   Percentage Distribution of Teachers by Completed Education

Educational attainment	Nursery Teachers	Kindergarten Teachers	Elementary School Teachers
Completion of University course (including Junior college)	79.4% (as of 1988)	97.8% (as of 1988)	94.0% (as of 1988)

Some are trained at local public and private universities and junior colleges authorised by the Minister of Education, Science and Culture under the important principle of open system.

The total number of training institutions for kindergarten teachers authorised by the Minister of Education, Science and Culture, is 350 since 1 April 1974. The breakdown of this figure between different institutions is; universities (87), junior colleges (198), training facilities for nursery teachers (65).

B. The Problem Before Us

As seen in the discussion above, there are several problems to be solved regarding the preparation of early childhood teachers in Japan.

First, it was pointed out that two-year junior colleges, etc. not four-year universities and colleges, take the lead in the work of training personnel (Nursery teachers at day care centres, teachers at kindergartens). Personnel at day care centres and kindergartens are required to possess specialist and expert knowledge and a high level of technique. To achieve this level of competence it is important that training of early childhood teachers should be pursued through a complete course of study at a four-year institution, whether university or college.

Secondly, it has also been pointed out that the standards of professionalism are different at day care centres and kindergartens, Nursery teachers at day care centres must possess a nursery teacher certificate as provided through certain training facilities for nursery teachers authorised by the Ministry of Health and Welfare or as granted to upper secondary school graduates (or the equivalent) who have passed the examinations for nursery teacher certificate conducted under prefectural auspices. On the other hand, teacher certificates for kindergarten are granted by prefectural boards of education. To achieve the latter, one is required to possess the prescribed number of credits through studying for two years in a college, university or a junior college (or the equivalent) recognised by the Ministry of Education, Science and Culture. Certification requirements vary with school level: nursery teacher certificates are granted to upper secondary school graduates, who have to pass the test, while certificates for kindergartens are granted to those who have studied for two years in a university (or the equivalent).

Thirdly, it is also important that the unification of training facilities for day care and kindergarten personnel should be provided through an appropriate and coherent system. Students are required to acquire prescribed credits in the curriculum of training for nursery teachers *and* for kindergarten teachers respectively on account of the dual system of training. In order to obtain both teacher certificates, the student is forced to acquire a lot of professional subjects in two training courses: training course for nursery teachers and for kindergarten teachers.

It is necessary to established unitary teacher education, not only through rationalisation of the system but also by articulating a programme of professional progression with clear specification of required knowledge, attitudes and skills along the route.

5. BIBLIOGRAPHY SPECIFICALLY CITED IN THIS PAPER

Books in Japanese

Ministry of Education, Science and Culture.
Author: Gakko-Kihon-Chosa-Hokokusho
Title: *A Report of Fundamental Investigation on Educational Institutions in Japan.* Tokyo: Minister's Secretariat, 1989.

Ministry of Education, Science and Culture.
Author: Gakko-Kyoin-Tokei-Chosa-Hokokusho
Title: *A Report of Statistical Research on Japanese School Teachers.* Tokyo: Minister's Secretariat, 1983.

The Principles of Early Childhood Education and Care.
Authors/Editors: Teshima Nobumasa, Noguchi Isaake, Hosoi Fusaaki, Hoiku-Genri. Tokyo: Kenpaku-sha, 1983.

The Principles of Early Childhood Education and Care for Beginners.
Authors/Editors: Hosoi Fusaaki, Noguchi Issaki, Fukushi Tadao, Shoshin-sha no tameno Hoikiu Genri. Tokyo: Gakujutsu-tosho, 1985.

New Publication The Principles of Early Childhood Education and Care.
Authors/Editors: Teshima Nobumasa, Noguchi Isaaki, Sekiguchi Hatsue, Oyama Nozomi, Shinpan Hoiku Genri. Tokyo: Kenpaku-sha, 1990.

Books in English and Japanese

Education in Japan (Nihon no kyo-iku)
Authors/Editors: Takakura Sho, Murata Yokuo Tsukuba: Tsukuba Association of International Education, 1989.

Ministry of Education, Science and Culture
Author: Outline of Education in Japan 1989 (Nohon no Kyo-Ku 1989) Tokyo: The Asian Cultural Centre of UNESCO, 1989.

Children and Families Bureau Ministry of Health and Welfare
Editor: Me de miru Jido-Fukushi (Graphs and Charts on Japan's Child Welfare Services) Tokyo: The Japan Research Institute on Child Welfare, 1988 & 1989.

Books in English

Ministry of Education, Science and Culture
Author: Education in Japan (Nihon no Kyoiku) Tokyo: Gyosei Pub. 1979 & 1989.

Japanese University Accreditation Association
Author: Japanese Universities and Colleges 1975 (Nihon no Daigaku) Tokyo: Japanese University Accreditation Association, 1975.

The Assocation and International Education, Japan
Editor: Japanese Colleges and Universities 1985 (Nihon no Daigaku 1985) Tokyo: Maruzen, 1985.

Training early childhood educators in India

MIRA CHOUDHRY

*Department of Preschool and Elementary Education, N.C.E.R.T.
New Delhi - 110016, India*

(Received August 1991)

The National Policy on Education (1986) has given a great deal of importance to early childhood care and education (ECCE). It views ECCE as an important input in the strategy of human resource development, as a feeder and support programme for primary education and as a support service for working women of the disadvantaged sections of society. It has also taken into account the *Holistic* nature of ECCE and has pointed out the need for organising programmes for the all round development of the child. The significance of play and activity approach and the need for child-centredness in the programme of ECCE as well as in primary school education have been spelled out. The importance of community involvement has also been high-lighted. The need to establish a linkage between ICDS and ECCE programmes has been pointed out. Keeping in view the above mentioned necessities, all the teacher training programmes are reviewed and reconstructed. A strong component of field placement under supervision has been included. Media support is provided to convey the messages of ECCE to the parents and community; child care practice and play-way methods have taken the place of early introduction to basic skills.

The origin of pre-school education in India can be traced to kindergartens established by European missionaries towards the end of the nineteenth century. Initially kindergarten teachers were brought from foreign countries, but in course of time a kindergarten teachers' training institute was established in Saidapet, Madra (Tamilnadu) in 1888 by the missionaries.

In India, a pioneer of pre-school education was Gijubhai Badhaka who started a training institute "Dakshine Murti" in Bhavnagar (Gujarat) in 1924.

In 1939, Madam Maria Montessori visited India and conducted several short term courses in different parts of the country. The Montessori method caught the attention of Indian educators and in 1945 Smt. Tarabai Modak started a pre-school training institute at Bordi (Maharashtra) from where she moved it to Kosbad hills to work for the tribal children. This model has now been accepted as the most adequate and suitable model for working with vulnerable groups of children and has been incorporated in the *Integrated Child Development Services* (ICDS) Scheme of the Government of India.

In 1947, the Arundale Montessori Training Centre was set up in Adyar, Madras (Tamilnadu). At present the Association Montessori International runs Montessori teacher training programmes in different regions of India.

Gandhiji's philosphy of Basic Education also gathered momentum around the same time. The Aryanayakam and their colleagues in the Wardha Ashram (erstwhile central provinces) Madarashtra, extended it into the pre-school stage and termed it *Pre-Basic Education*. Under the auspices of Kasturba Gandhi National Memorial Trust many centres were established for training women to work in rural Balwadis.

Prior to independence, programmes for the development of pre-school children had been mostly conducted by voluntary organisations. These programmes were primarily in big cities for the children of upper socio-economic groups. The first breakthrough in Early Childhood Education came after independence when there had been an increasing awareness of the significance of early childhood and the need to provide care and education to children from the poorer sections of Indian society. The Central Social Welfare Board (CSWB) planned programmes for training multi-purpose workers, whose duties had been to look after the welfare of needy women, children from low SES, the handicapped and the destitute.

Subsequently, a number of teacher training institutes were established by either the Central Government or State Governments, the oldest of these institutes being the Central Institute of Education (CIE), University of Delhi, set up in 1947. An experimental nursery and a basic school was attached to it for teaching practice. University Departments of Child Development in the Colleges of Home Science are also involved in such programmes.

In 1961, the Indian Council of Child Welfare (ICCW) with the assistance of the Central Social Welfare Board (CSWB) set up the first Bal Sevika Training Programmes in Delhi. Gradually training centres were started in different states; at present 22 States are running Bal Sevika training programmes.

The success of a programme entirely depends on the competencies and experiences of those who are responsible for planning and implementing the programme. In order to get the best results from ECCE programmes it is necessary that the objectives of pre-school education are properly understood by workers in this field and that they have received training appropriate to their responsibilities in the programme setting.

Table 1 indicates the existing pre-school programme and types of training programmes available in India.

MAJOR TEACHER TRAINING PROGRAMMES
INTEGRATED CHILD DEVELOPMENT SERVICES

The Integrated Child Development Services (ICDS) Scheme was launched by the State Council for Child Welfare, erstwhile Ministry of Social Welfare, in 1975. ICDS currently represents the biggest programme of early childhood development in India. It aims at providing a package of early childhood services to children of 0-6 years and expectant and nursing mothers. The package consists of:-

(i) Supplementary nutrition
(ii) Immunization
(iii) Health checkup

Table 1

Existing Programmes for pre-primary and primary school children	Existing Teacher Training Programmes	Organising Agencies
1. Nursery and Kindergarten	Unrecognised Nursery Teacher Training	run by Private (voluntary) organisations such as, convents and Christian Missions.
2. Montessori Schools	Montessori Teacher Training	The Association Montessori International voluntary organisations
3. Pre-Basic and primary basic schools	Pre-Basic and Basic Teacher Training	Kasturba National Memorial Trust
4. a. Balwadis in urban slums	a. Balsevika training programme for urban slums	a. Indian Council for Child Welfare
b. Balwadis in rural and tribal areas	b. Balsevika training programmes for rural and tribal areas	b. Central Social Welfare Board
5. Anganwadis	Anganwadis workers Training Programme	State Council for Child Welfare under Min. of Social Welfare.
6. Government/Municipal Corporation pre-school/ nurseries	Government pre-primary teacher Training Institutes	State Departments of Education
7. Laboratory Nursery Schools	Post-Graduate/Graduate Diploma in Child Development	State Institutes of Education and Colleges of Home Economics

(iv) Referral services
(v) Nutrition and health education
(vi) Non-formal pre-school education.

Studies have indicated that at present less than 10% of the child population of the country receives all the essential services from conception to the age of 6 years. Although *every* child *should* in principle be assured access to the fulfilment of all basic needs. The 1986 National Policy on Education proposed that 70% of the child population would be serviced under ICDS programmes by 2000 AD. It has also been felt that the organisational and functional responsibility for the delivery of services and monitoring their effectiveness has not been appropriately focused on the key workers. Anganwadi workers (AWW) being the key persons in this scheme have to be fully acquainted with the job responsibilities. These include:

1. Survey of the Community
2. Service delivery which includes:
    (1) (a) Organising non-formal pre-school education
        (b) Preparing and using aids for pre-school activities
        (c) Replenishing aids
        (d) Planning the pre-school programme
        (e) Educating parents about the importance of pre-school education for the overall development of the child
        (f) Helping in the admission of older children in the primary school
    (2) Growth Monitoring
    (3) Organisation of Supplementary Nutrition
    (4) Providing support to primary Health Centres
3. Community Contact and Education
    (1) Community participation
    (2) Community education
    (3) Communication
4. Management and Administration
    (1) Maintenance of Records
    (2) Reporting to CDPO, Supervisor, Medical Officer
5. Utilisation of the Services of the Helpers

Training of Anganwadi Workers (AWW)

Duration of the course   3 months
Minimum Qualification   Matriculate or 8th grade Standard Certificate
Age Limit   18–44 years, preference is given to a local village woman

Training Syllabus

In-service training courses have been designed to equip workers with the knowledge and skills needed to discharge their job responsibilities effectively. The various components of training are given in Table 2 and subsequently elaborated in the following texts.

I. General Orientation

The main objective of the general orientation is to familiarise the AWW with the existing status of women and children in the country/region and the need for organising programmes, particularly in the ICDS, for their development. It also introduces the worker to the objectives, services, scope, benificiaries and staffing pattern of the ICDS programme, as well as their own roles and responsibilities *vis-a-vis* that of the supervisor, Child Development Project Officer, Health Officer, Lady Health Visitor and the Auxiliary Nurse/Midwife.

Table 2

Subject	Classroom instruct-tions (hrs)	Field work (hrs)	Library and Audio visual (hrs)	Total Hours
1. General Orientation	$13\frac{1}{2}$	$19\frac{1}{2}$	3	36
2. Pre-school Education	15	$66\frac{1}{2}$	$1\frac{1}{2}$	83
3. Nutrition and Health Education	34	54	$5\frac{1}{2}$	$93\frac{1}{2}$
4. Community Participation, community education and communication	56	$67\frac{1}{2}$	4	$127\frac{1}{2}$
5. Population Eucation	9	3	—	12
6. Management	$23\frac{1}{2}$	$35\frac{1}{2}$	—	59
7. Holistic approach to child. Review	12	—	—	12
8. Evaluation	9	—	—	9
	172	246	14	432

Fieldwork includes: Classroom practicums (137 hrs); visits (13 hrs) and Placement in ICDS project (96 hrs).

Curriculum content

Generally this refers to:

(i) Status of children and women in India from health, nutrition and educational perspectives.

(ii) Need for child development programmes.

(iii) ICDS, its philopsophy, scope, objectives, package, beneficiaries, coverage and staffing pattern.

(iv) Roles and responsibilities of an Anganwadi worker.

(v) Need for conducting a Community survey.

(vi Community participation; concept and importance.

Pre-school education

One of the services of ICDS is to cater to the developmental needs of children between three and six years of age and to prepare them for formal schooling. The AWW is expected to promote the all-round development of children through non-formal play activities. She must organise a variety of activities and utilise the natural resources in her environment to structure learning at the Anganwadi.

Curriculum content

(i) Need and importance of organising non-formal pre-school activities.

(ii) Development of children from birth to six-years; milestones in development and needs of children.

(iii) Activities for physical-motor, language, cognitive, personal social and emotional development, preparation and use of aids and play materials for organising these activities.

(iv) Use of environmental resources in organising pre-school activities.

(v) Thematic approach to organising pre-school activities.

(vi) Nature walk as an activity to promote overall development in children.

(vii) Planning the pre-school programme.

(viii) Problems faced in the field in organising pre-school education.

(ix) Common behavioural problems in children.

(x) Use of library and other visual aids in a pre-school situation.

Nutrition and Health

The nutrition and health components of the ICDS scheme aim at reduction in mortality, morbidity and malnutrition among children and to bring about an improvement in the health and nutrition status of mothers and children.

Curriculum contents

(i) Nutrition and health service in the Anganwadi

(ii) Good nutrition for children and mothers

(iii) Feeding and weaning practices

(iv) Personal and environmental hygiene

(v) Safe water supply

(vi) Immunization of children

(vii) Malnutrition, the major problem among children

(viii) Diarrhoea

(ix) Nutritional deficiency diseases

(x) Common ailments and other diseases in children and how to handle these

(xi) Growth monitoring

(xii) Organisation of supplementary nutrition, methods of cooking, preparation of simple recipes

(xiii) Nutrition and health education of mothers

(xiv) Ante and post natal care

(xv) Early detection of disabilities

(xvi) Health infrastructure in the area

(xvii) Treatment of minor accidents and injuries

Community Participation and Education

The ICDS Scheme has been conceived as a people's programme. The AWW therefore, need to develop skills in contacting the community, mobilising community participation and educating the community about the needs of children, the objectives and services of the ICDS programme and proper childcare practices.

Curriculum contents

(i) Community Participation — Role of AWW, areas of community participation, recognising community participation, methods of mobilising community participation, ways of utilising individuals, groups and agencies in the programme, coordinating and working with other professionals and para professionals.

(ii) Communication — Forms of communication, principles, methods and barriers; conducting a home visit, forming and activating a mahila mandal, arranging and conducting a meeting of mahila mandal, organisation of bal melas, exhibitions, sports meetings, competitions, festivals and baby shows to create community awareness and mobilise participation and interest.

(iii) Parent and community education — settings in which community education may take place; planning and organising parent education programmes, — Health and nutrition education, role of the community and fathers in creating healthy environments for children; management of the home, cleanliness and sanitation of the environment and home. — Education of mothers to promote overall development of children under three years; socio-economic programmes for women, e.g. operating a savings bank account. — Population education — Preparation land use of aids for community education.

(iv) Need for and methods of conducting a survey.

Management

As part of her responsibilities, the AWW has to maintain records, fill progress reports, plan the AW programme and maintain links with other professionals. It is therefore necessary to develop her skills in this area.

Curriculum contents

(i) Location of the Anganwadi in terms of its adequacy for delivery of services
(ii) Procurement and storage of stocks and supplies for the Anganwadi
(iii) Maintaining correspondence with other professionals, voluntary organisations, individuals and agencies
(iv) Maintenance of registers and records; returning monthly and quarterly progress reports
(v) Facilities available to the Anganwadi worker and helper
(vi) Planning the AW programme
(vii) Maintaining good relationships with Helper, Supervisor and Child Development Project Officer
(viii) Problems in "field" situations; problem solving

Review

At the end of three month training the AWW will spend two days in viewing the child in a holistic manner, recalling all that has been done during the training and her roles and responsibilities in this regard.

Evaluation and award of certificate

Evaluation is the responsibility of the supervisory staff and of agencies at the district, state and national levels.

At the end of three months training, the trainees (AWWs) are assessed on the basis of their performance during the training course; the evaluation in one in the following areas:

(i) Assignment during the course
(ii) Classroom practicums
(iii) Field work
(iv) Written test
(v) Preparation/maintenance of records/diary work done during training
(vi) Preparation of kit material
(vii) Viva Voce.

At the end of the course the Training Centre awards Certificates to all AWWs who have satisfactorily completed the course and met the requirements of Assessment.

INTEGRATED TWO-YEAR COURSE IN PRE-SCHOOL AND EARLY PRIMARY TEACHER EDUCATION

In 1973, the National Council for Teacher Education (NCTE) was set up by the Ministry of Education, Government of India. The NCTE appointed a Pre-school Teacher Education Committee, which recommended "An Integrated Two-year Course in Pre-school and Primary Teacher Education for teachers of children in the age group 3–8 years. It is one of the basic training programmes for pre-school and primary school teachers.

Objectives of the Course

The student teacher on completion of this course should have:

1. developed an understanding of the principles and processes of the various aspects of children's growth and development and the ability to plan educational activities in accordance with them;
2. developed acquaintance with the basic principles of early childhood care and education keeping in view the national goals of education;
3. acquired an appropriate historical perspective on early childhood care and education;
4. familiarise herself with the methods, equipment and materials of early childhood care and education and their effective use in practice;
5. developed the ability to utilize the physical and social environment effectively for nurturing physical and motor, cognitive and social emotional development of pre-school and early primary school children;

6. developed acquaintance with the various media of creative expression and acquired essential skills for fostering creative expression in children;
7. developed an understanding of the importance of health, nutrition and welfare services for the child and the ability to nurture healthy habits, prepare nutritive and inexpensive meals and render first aid in case of minor injuries and accidents;
8. developed awareness of the role of parents and community in the education of pre-school and early primary school children and be able to plan ways of enlisting their active help and co-operation in various ECCE programmes;
9. developed an understanding of the various tools and techniques of child study;
10. acquired the skill to organise, plan and administer the school programmes.

I. Course Content of First Year Child Development and Educational Activities

Objectives
— To help the student teacher understand the principle and processes of children's growth and development.
— To acquaint the student teacher with the different stages and aspects of child development, with special reference to early childhood, and the factors that influence it.
— To develop in the student teacher an understanding of the psychological needs of children and the competence to conduct activities for fulfilment of these needs.
— To develop in the student teacher a concern for children and an understanding of individual differences.
— To help the student teacher acquire knowledge of various tools and techniques of child study, including maintenance of records and skills in using them.
— To create in the student teacher an insight into the role of parents home and society in child development.

Course Content

1. Introduction to Child Development
2. Growth and Development
3. Principles of Child Development
4. Simple methods and techniques of child study
5. Major Aspects and Child Development; physical motor emotional, personal social language and cognitive development of the child

II. Early Childhood Education in Emerging India

Objectives
— The student teacher should be able to list aims and objectives of Early Childhood

Table 3 Distribution of Marks for Theory and Practical

	First Year Courses	Elements in:	Marks Ext.	Int.	Total
A.	I	Child Development & Educational Activities	75	25	100
	II	Early Childhood Education in Emerging India	35	15	50
	III	Programme Planning for pre-school	35	15	50
	IV	Health and Nutrition	75	25	100
B.	Practice Teaching	(36 working days)	200	100	300
C.	Practical	(See Table C)	175	50	225
			G. TOTAL		825
	Second Year				
A.	Paper I	Child Development	75	25	100
	Paper II	Working with Parents & Community	35	15	50
	Paper III	Programme Planning for class 1 and 2	75	25	100
	Paper IV	School Organisation	35	15	50
B.	Practice Teaching:				
	i) 36 Working days		200	100	300
	ii) Summer Vacation assignment (15 days)			100	100
C.	Practical Actvities (See Table C)		175	50	225
			G. TOTAL		925

Care and Education
— The student teacher should be familiar with the contribution of individuals and institutions to the pre-school movement
— The student teacher should be aware of the major policy changes and innovations in early childhood education.

Course content

1. Introduction
2. Nature, aims and objectives of early childhood care and education.
3. Development of pre-school education with a brief mention of the contribution of Rousseau, Pestalozzi, Froebel, Montessori and Dewey.
4. Pre-school movement in India — pre-independence and post independence movement.
5. Policy Recommendations in ECCE.

Table 4 Analysis of Evaluation of Practical Activities

S. No.	Activity	Internal Assessment	External Assessment	Total
1.	Preparation of teaching material	—	50	50
2.	a) Skill development music, drama, pupperty, creative abilities	25	—	25
	b) Art and craft	—	25	25
	c) Skills in communication	—	25	25
3.	Observation of children maintenance of cumulative record cards	15	—	15
4.	Health and Nutrition			
	a) First Aid	—	20	20
	b) Cooking	—	30	30
5.	Field visits (Reports)	10	—	10
	G. TOTAL	50	150	200

Table 5 Second Year

1.	Preparation of teaching learning material	—	50	50
2.	a) Art and Craft	—	25	25
	b) Skill in communication	—	25	25
3.	Project work based on environmental studies	—	50	50
4.	Case study	—	25	25
5.	Parents and community Activities			
	a) Home Visits	15	—	15
b) Organisation of parents programmes – health, hygiene and nutrition	20		20	20
	c) Organisation of children's programmes for parents	15	—	15
	G. TOTAL	50	175	225

Practical activities

1. Visit to the following institutions and preparation of report:
    a. Essential — (i) Montessori School, (ii) Anganwadi/Balwadi, (iii) Mobile Creche Centre, (iv) Sos Village,
    (b) Enrichment (i) Balbhavan, (ii) Natural History Museum (Pre-school wing)

III.   Programme Planning for Pre-school

Objectives
— To develop in the student teacher knowledge and understanding of the basic methods, practices, equipment and materials oearly childhood education.
— To develop in the student teacher an understanding of the basic principles of programme planning.
— To develop in the student teacher an understanding of the inter-relationships between the environment and teacher — learning materials and the skills in development and use of these in the day to day work.

Course content

1.   Curriculum Development
2.   Planning and Evaluation of the Programme
3.   Principles of programme planning
4.   Observation, recording and reporting
5.   Maintenance of reports and records

Practical activities
1.   Plan programme for 3 year olds, 4 year olds and 5 year olds, grading the activities.
2.   Observe a child in different activities in the school using observation schedule, and report on it.

IV.   Health and Nutrition

Objectives

— To develop in the student teacher an understanding of health hygiene and nutrition in relation to personal development.
— To develop in the student teacher an alertness to the signs of common ailments and a disposition to promote preventative health measures in the community.
— To develop in the student teacher an understanding of their own role and the role of others in developing the school health programme.

Course content

1.   Concept of health and its importance in child development.
2.   Health and Hygiene Programmes.
3.   Concept of balance diet and nutritional needs of pre-school children.
4.   Identification prevention and remedial measures for common ailments and disease.

5. First-aid and Home Nursing.
6. Nutrition programmes.
7. Organisations and Agencies working in the area of Health and Nutrition.

Practical work

1. Maintenance of Health Records.
2. Meal Planning and Preparation.

Practical activities

1. Preparation of teaching learning materials.

Units
(a) Flash cards for number and language activities.
(b) A collection of twenty children's stories with their objectives.
(c) A collection of at least twenty children's games with their objectives.
(d) Puppet-making — specimen of each of the three types
    (i) rod and stick (ii) glove (iii) finger
(e) Two charts for picture reading and conversation with specific objectives.
(f) One specimen plan for outing/excursion and field trip with the evaluation schedule and following work.
(g) A record file containing the specimen of each of the following pro forma duly filled in from actual classroom.
    (i) observation schedule
    (ii) anecdotal record
    (iii) health record
    (iv) cumulative record — folder
    (v) growth chart
    (vi) a specimen of one duly filled in progress report from classroom situation
    (vii) one specimen each of communication with parents about child's progress, irregular attendance, parent-teacher association meeting and annual function or any competition in school.
(h) Recipe book containing twenty recipes of maximum nutrition value.
(i) Album of creative art. A specimen of all the activities mentioned in Paper 1 under cognitive development and aesthetics.
(j) Album of nature study, a specimen of all the activities related to environmental concepts included in Paper 1.
2. (a) *Skill Development*
    Music, dance, drama, puppetry and creative abilities.
    This activity has two parts (a) participation of student teacher during training programme (b) capability of organising such activities.
    (b) *Art and Craft*
    There would be an external examination of three hours duration in Art and

Craft in which the teacher student shall be required to prepare any item/ items from a given list.

(c) *Use of teaching learning material/Montessori apparatus*
There would be an external examination of three hours duration to evaluate the student teacher mastery over the skill of presenting an equipment/ apparatus with clear simple instruction and using it in different teaching learning situations so as to achieve the desired objectives.

3. Observation of children, maintenance of cumulative record, progress records etc.
4. Health and Nutrition
5. Field visits reports

Practice of Teaching
Internal assessment   100 marks
External assessment   200 marks

The practice of teaching shall consist of the following three phases.

		Marks
Phase I	Training in skills: Simulatory approach	20
Phase II	Observing lesson in actual class room situation	20
Phase III	Independent charge of the class for two weeks	30
	One week gap for problems discussion, then again independent two weeks charge	30

This phase of four weeks, i.e. twenty four working days will carry a weightage of sixty percent marks.

Second Year

I. Child Development

Objectives: The same as given for Child Development and Educational Activities.

Course content

1. Personality Development
2. Intelligence and learning
3. Exceptional children
4. Play
5. Role of home in the development of the child.
6. Role of school in the development of the child.

7. Role of neighbourhood, community and the mass media in the development of the child.

Practical activities

Preparation of at least two detailed case studies on the basis of observations and interviews with parents, children and teachers, welfare workers, administrators, etc. connected with children. These should be one each of a boy and a girl, one of which may be an exceptional child, if available.

II. Working with Parents and Community

Objectives

— To help the student teacher know the value of cooperation between school — parent — community.
— To help the student teacher to understand ways of enlisting the help and cooperation of parents.
— To help the student teacher to plan a programme for the education of parents and community.

Course content

1. Rationale for the study of community for the teacher of the pre-school child.
2. Developing an understanding of the community and its characteristics.
3. Methods of making contact with parents and community.
4. Communication in community work.
5. Programme planning in community work.

Practical activities

This unit consists of three parts:
  (a) Home visits.
  (b) Organisation of parent programme on Health, Hygiene and Nutrition.
  (c) Organisation of children's programme for parents. Each student teacher will be maintaining a complete record in the form of a report under this unit. This report has to be submitted to external examiner at the time of Viva-Voce for case study.

III. Programme Planning for Classes 1 and 2

Objectives

— To develop in the student teacher knowledge and understanding of principles of programme planning, for education of children of classes 1 and 2.

— To develop in the student teacher knowledge and understanding of the methods and practices suitable for education of children in classes 1 and 2 with particular emphasis on playway and activity approach.

— To develop in the student teacher knowledge and understanding of equipment and material suitable for education of children in classes 1 and 2.

— To develop skills in the student teacher to foster in children necessary cognitive and social skills, values and attitudes to cope with the demands of the outside world.

Course content

1.   National curriculum framework.
2.   Importance of playway method, activity method, project method and integrated approach for classes 1 and 2.
3.   Incidental learning and learning from the environment.
4.   Planning of the programme of different subjects unit-wise for classes 1 and 2.
5.   Teaching of language, objectives and methodology of teaching mother tongue. Development of language skills.

Teaching of Mathematics.   Aims and objectives of teaching mathematics methods and materials for developing number concept, simple addition, subtraction, multiplication and division knowledge of geometrical figures and lines. Concept of weight, length, volume, time and money. Common number problems in children.

Teaching of Environmental Studies.   Methods of developing environmental awareness through field trips, collections, observation experimentation, discussion, games, audio visual aids, celebration of cultural and National Festivals.

Creative Art Experiences.   Its importance and objectives. Techniques of use of different material, planning activities.

Evaluation of Children.   Criterion reference and diagnostic evaluation, using playway method to evaluate children. Using evaluation results for remedial teaching.

Practical activities

I   Activities and learning material based on playway method and activity approach for the following:
   (a) Development of the four language skills.
   (b) Teaching of Mathematics.
   (c) Teaching of Environmental Studies.
II Planning programme for classes 1 and 2.
   (a) Yearly planning.
   (b) Term planning.
   (c) Monthly planning.
   (d) Daily planning.

III   Filling and maintenance of records and preparation of records.
IV   Development of a project by each student teacher on one or two themes.
V   Demonstrating integrated approach by taking up any topic.
VI   Activities for development of creative arts and aesthetics.
VII   Activities for work experience for classes 1 and 2.
VIII   Evaluating children in each of the subjects by assessing their performance in activities and oral questioning.

IV. School Organisation

Objectives

— To enable the student teacher to understand the role of local authorities in Educational Administration.
— To acquaint the student teacher with the service rules and code of conduct and methods of team work in school.
— To enable the student teacher to select, use and maintenance of toys, books and other equipment for pre-school and classes 1 and 2.
— To enable the student teacher to understand procedure of maintaining school accounts, preparing bills, maintaining necessary records and registers and using them.

Course content

1.   Concept of organisation and administration of school and its needs.
2.   School premises — its maintenence beautification of school premises by planting trees and plants.
3.   Play grounds — different types of play ground and play equipment for indoor and outdoor play.
4.   Criteria for selection of furniture and other essential equipment, e.g. books, toys, display boards, vessels for storing water, etc. maintenance and storage facilities.
5.   Rules and regulations for school education act.
6.   Maintenance of school records and their importance.

Practical activities

I.   Practice in maintaining school registers and records. Contact agencies for repairing different types of equipment and materials.

BALSEVIKA TRAINING PROGRAMME

The Balsevika Training Programme (BST) was initiated by the Indian Council for Child Welfare in 1961. The first centre was opened in Delhi under the direct supervision of the council. For the successful implementation of the programme on a country wide scale it was decided to have a training centre in each state where the field level worker can easily identify herself with the children, their families and community with the understanding of subcultural patterns and language in their respective state.

Objectives of the Training

Programmes are to train Balsevika to:
— Co-ordinate the services in the area of health, nutrition, education and social welfare at the field level, for the total development of the pre-school child.
— Maintain contact with parents, especially with mothers and give them fundamental knowledge on health, nutrition and child development.
— Involve the community in the programme so as to have maximum possible community participation.

Duration of the Course: 11 months
Minimum Qualifications: Matriculation or equivalent
Total Enrolment per centre: 60 candidates (50 stipendary and 10 non stipendary)

Course Content

1. *ORIENTATION:* The trainees are acquainted with the basic rights and duties of citizens, conditions and need of an integrated approach to child welfare, i.e. preventative, developmental, curative and ameliorative services of children.
2. *CHILD DEVELOPMENT:* The objective is to provide basic information regarding the development of children from the pre-natal stage up to six years. Some of the subject areas covered are the influence of family background on the child's development, common behavioural problems and factors influencing growth and development.
3. *PRE-SCHOOL EDUCATION:* To develop knowledge and understanding of the practices, equipment and materials of pre-school education and to develop skills which are required in the day to day work.
    Planning developmental activities for social skills, language development, creativity and motor development, simple science experiences and development of concepts, play, recreation, the functional prerequisities for Balwadi, techniques of observing and recording, aspects of growth, programme planning and the involvement of parents.
4. *HEALTH AND NUTRITION:*
    (a) *Health:* The stages of physical develoment, ante-natal and post-natal care, infant care, care of children in the Balwadi, environmental sanitation, communicable and other common diseases, recognition of minor defects, prevention of accidents, elementary first-aid and home nursing, health education, family planning, infant and maternal mortality and causes, basic knowledge of health services available in the area and the maintenence of health records.

(b) *Nutrition:* Diet in the Balwadi (midday meal) nutrition deficiency diseases, food values, methods of weaning, methods of cooking, methods of food preparation, storage of food articles, food poisoning, helping children/mothers to acquire good dietary habits, introduction to other nutrition services available, maintenance of simple records, food budgeting, local food habits and parent education.

5. *SOCIAL WELFARE:* The important topics in social welfare are family patterns in rural, urban and tribal areas, child welfare, children in need of special care and the services available for them, communication and general administration. Practicals and field work are an integral part of this training. Each trainee must prepare a set of kit which she is expected to carry with her after completion of the training.

Table 6 The time allotted for the different subjects in the syllabus

Subject	Theory	Practical	Total Hours
1. Orientation	18	—	18 hrs.
2. Child Development	79	30	109 hrs.
3. Pre-school Education	108	88	196 hrs.
4. Health	117	96	213 hrs.
5. Nutrition	110	118	228 hrs.
6. Social Welfare	106	210	316 hrs.
	538	542	1080 hrs.

THE DISTRIBUTION OF THE TIME IN THE TRAINING PERIOD IS AS FOLLOWS

Duration of the course — 11 months   330 days

i.	Observation tours and visits to institutions	10 days
ii.	Examinations	15 days
iii.	Weekly holidays	40 days
iv.	Field work (8 days in a month — twice weekly)	40 days
v.	Block placement	15 days
vi.	Theory, oral and practical work (six hours each day — 6 hrs × 180 days = 1080 hrs)	180 days

Methodology

Training is important through classroom discussions, lectures, practicals, field visits and field work.

Monitoring and Supervision

The training centres are supervised by the Indian Council for Child Welfare (ICCW)

as well as the State Council for Child Welfare (SCCW). An advisory committee formed under a Chairperson at state level takes care of the day to day functioning of the training centre. Similar committees formed at national level make policy decisions and monitor the implementation of these decisions in the centres.

MOBILE PRE-SCHOOL TRAINING FOR RURAL WOMEN

The Aim and Objectives

— To promote pre-primary education in rural areas by starting Balwadi in as many villages as possible.
— To train rural girls and women at Taluka towns to run Balwadi in their own or nearby villages.
— To enable Balwadi teachers to function as multi-purpose workers, so that the value of education, family planning population education, nutrition, health and child care is also communicated to rural parents through home visits and/or monthly parents' meetings.
— To improve the quality and efficiency of rural Balwadi teachers by organising enrichment programmes through holiday camps.
— To publish a bi-monthly journal to furnish the rural women with the latest information and to provide to her an opportunity to write about her experiences and an outlet for her talents.
— To provide hostel facilities to rural school children who have to come long distances from the interior or attend secondary schools in the bigger villages, to help save their energies for studies.

Qualifications   S.S.C. to
    Minimum qualifications   8th or 9th std. School Certificate
    Duration   Six months
    Age   18 to 25 years

The course curriculum aims at preparing Balwadi teacher as well as a multi-purpose social worker in the village.
— Community worker to give information about nutrition, hygiene, child care population education, family planning and kitchen gardening.
— To impart training in tailoring.
— To acquaint them with new techniques and skills in pre-primary education.

The socio-economic background of the women
Most of these girls are from lower income groups facing financial difficulties, daughters or wives of small farmers, daily wage workers, construction workers on roads, milk men, family and traditional professions like shoe-maker, carpentry, earthenware, bidi maker or priesthood with low earnings.

TRAINING FOR INTEGRATED DAY CARE AT MOBILE CRECHES

Target group

0-3 age group	creche
3-6 age group	balwadi
6 + non formal	education
family of the child	adult education
migratory labour families	the day care worker has to act as substitute parent care taker
Training is pragmatic and multi disciplinary	pre-school and primary teacher, health worker, paramedic, nutritionist, adult education, social worker, community organiser.

Nature — Duration

On the job apprenticeship/internship type training:

Qualification	X or equivalent.
Duration	Minimum two year but can be extended up to three years at the discretion of the agencies.
Assessment	On the basis of competency of any care worker. No pass or fail standard.

Characteristics of Training Programme

Model	On the job training. The training is competency based, the objectives are the acquisition of skills for working with children. The worker is judged by standards of performance which reflect both skills/attitudes.

Methodology

It is pragmatic, inductive and participatory. It is based on the belief that skills are acquired by practice — the more skilled teach the less skilled at every level. Teaching is by demonstration, role modelling and personal guidance, while learning is by observation, imitation and practice.

Theory is well related to the practice, self study is through assignments which may include reading, survey, recording and finding out answers to questions.

Stage of Training

1. Orientation based on personal observation of field programme. During this period routine tasks are carried out by trainees and some theoretical orientation is also given.

2.   Demonstration of skills by experienced practitioners, followed by repeated practice under *close* supervision of experienced practitioner.
3.   Practical experiences — these include finding, making and using various material and aids.

Course content

1.   Infant care
2.   Pre-school education
3.   Non-formal education
4.   Health, hygiene and nutrition
5.   Administration and community work
6.   Adult education

Evaluation

The final evaluation is done by committee including both external specialist and supervisors/trainers. The rating is on a five point scale and consists of 50 marks for observation of work in the field, 20 marks for internal assessment (based on records of work done, assignments, and completion of skills on check list). 15 marks for a written examination and 15 marks for Viva Voce. Internal assessment includes self evaluation in course of year, informal evaluation by peers, children and parents and systematic evaluation by trainers and supervisors.

B.Ed. EARLY CHILDHOOD EDUCATION COURSE

The course is designed to develop knowledge, understanding, skills and attitudes which may be required by teacher educators and heads of pre-schools/early primary schools:-

The broad objectives are:

—   To acquire theoretical and practical knowledge about early childhood education based on principles of child development and to adapt this knowledge in the framework of Indian constitution.
—   To plan programmes for early, childhood education and work with children so as to facilitate their overall development.
—   To organise pre-schools and early primary schools and prepare equipment from indigenous material.
—   To learn the skill of supervising student teachers at work.
—   To master the many techniques of observing various aspects of children's growth and to be able to record this data, interpret it and use it in guiding children.
—   To acquire skill of working with people connected with early childhood education.

Qualification for Admission

Candidates seeking admission to this course should satisfy the following conditions:

Essential

A Batchelor's degree in Arts or Science of a recognised University or its equivalent.

Desirable

— Experience as head of a pre-school/primary school and/or teaching experience in a teachers' training college.
— Experience of actual work with children.
— Special ability in music, fine arts or in other field of performance art.
— The applicants should preferably be between the ages of 22 and 35 years.

Duration of the course: *One academic year*

Methodology of Teaching

Methods of teaching will involve lectures, group discussions, individual assignments, group assignments, individual consultations, project work, field trips, observations and practical work.

Course Content

1. Course in Early Childhood Education
2. Course in Child Development
3. Practical Work

The unit approach is used in the planning of this course.

Early Childhood Education Course Consists of units on

(a) Principles and philosophy of early childhood Education.
(b) Needs, objectives and goals of early childhood Education.
(c) Education for health and nutrition of the child.
(d) Education for:
   (i) motor development
   (ii) personal social development
   (iii) aesthetic development
   (iv) language development
   (v) development of number concepts
   (vi) cognitive development
(e) School organisation and administration including
   (i) organisation, administration, supervision and monitoring
   (ii) programme planning

   (iii) building and equipment
   (iv) records, reports
(f) Working with parents and community
(g) Staff preparation
(h) Evaluation

The course on Child Development Consists of units on

(a) Introduction of child development including meaning and significance of development, stage of development, factors affecting development and methods of studying development.
(b) Maturation and learning
(c) Motor development
(d) Social development
(e) Emotional development
(f) Language development
(g) Cognitive development
(h) Intelligence and concept of individual differences and children's learning
(i) Children's needs
(j) Family relationships
(k) Psychology of exceptional children
(m) Personality development

Practical Work

Practical work is divided into three parts:
   I. Practice teaching
   II. Development of skills
   III. Supervisory and administrative activities

Practice Teaching

Practice Teaching includes observation of teachers, participation in the classroom activities, teaching the class of young children.

Development of Skills

This will include the following assignments:
(a) Preparation of simple play equipment and teaching learning materials out of waste or inexpensive material.
(b) Selection of suitable story books and picture books for young children. Story telling with different techniques.
(c) Preparation of low cost play materials and games for children.
(d) Practice in materials and rhythmical theoretical exercises.
(e) Creative art activities.

(f) Techniques of Collecting Information, use of observation forms and Cumulative Record Folder for pre-school children.

(g) Celebration of Social Culture, National and Religious festivals in the school.

(h) Administration of first-aid.

(i) Preparation of nutrition, snacks and midday meals.

(j) Home Visits, parents' interview and preparation of case studies.

(k) organising parent teachers.

Supervisory and Administrative Activities

This includes developing skills in supervision and administration of school routine.

Evaluation

There will be external and internal evaluation. Equal weightage will be given to theory and practical work. Each unit of the theory will be separately evaluated, 50% weightage should be given for the classroom assignment.

Distribution of Teaching Time

For a 9 months training course 1000 hours of teaching time will be available. These 1000 hours will be distributed as follows:

1. Early Childhood Education   250 hours
2. Child Development   250 hours
3. Practical work   500 hours

ISSUES

Some of the important parameters for meeting the training requirements are:

I. Initiating a two year vocational course in ECCE at +2 level with the objective to create basic skills which can later be adopted through job training for specific situations;

II. Strengthening educational content of Integrated Child Development Services (ICDS) functionaries, training by providing appropriate training inputs resources, materials, etc. and extending it, where possible, to include a component of day care management;

III. Taking steps for setting up a higher course in ECCE for senior level functionaries of Integrated Child Development Services (ICDS), trainers in the various training institutions and the supervisory personnel;

IV. Creating a system of accreditation of training institutions dealing with ECCE and review of the existing training programmes;

V. Working out appropriate, task specific, flexible Models for day care training at field level in rural areas.

MONITORING AND EVALUATION

Under the National Policy on Education the system of monitoring and evaluation will
be strengthened on the following lines:

I. A Management Information System will be evolved for monitoring all ECCE
programmes. Information will be collected, compiled, analysed and acted upon at the
block/local authority level. The flow of information to different levels (District, State
and Centre) will be so planned that control functions at these levels can be performed
effectively without delay.

II. Assistance will be sought from professions institutions and expert bodies for
independent, objective evaluation that can identify gaps and problems and feasible
alternatives for remedial action. All types of programmes should be evaluated by
independent agencies once in five years and the reports of the evaluations followed up
in order to improve the quality of service.

III. In order to assess the contributions of ECCE from time to time an Index of
Human Development will be worked out which would include, among others, the
following elements
(a) infant mortality rate;
(b) incidence of malnutrition in the 2nd year of life;
(c) access to early stimulation and education;
(d) female literacy level.

Glossary of Abbreviations

1. AW   Anganwadi
2. AWC   Anganwadi Centre
3. AWW   Anganwadi Worker
4. ICDS   Integrated Child Development Services
5. ICCW   Indian Council for Child Development
6. SCCW   StateCouncil for Child Welfare
7. NPE   National Policy on Education
8. NCERT National Council of Educational Research and Training, Delhi.
9. CSWB   Central Social Welfare Board
10. SES   Socio-Economic Strata
11. CIE   Central Institute of Education
12. BST   Balsevika Training programme
13. CDPO   Child Development Project Officer
14. HO   Health Officer
15. LHV   Lady Health Visitor
16. ANM   Auxilary Nurse/Midwife

References

1. Indian Association for Pre-school Education (1972) *Proceedings of the Eighth Annual Conference on Pre-school Teacher Education*, Bangalore (Karnataka), October.

2. Indian Association of Pre-school Education (1976) *Proceedings of the Seminar on Integration of Pre-school and Primary Teacher Education*, Baroda (Gujarat), March.

3. Kaul, V. Working Paper, *National Study Group Meeting in Early Childhood Care and Education*.

4. Ministry of Education (1980) *Report on the Expert Group on Early Childhood Education*.

5. Ministry of Human Resource Development (1986) *National Policy on Education*.

6. Ministry of Human Resources Development (1986) *Manual on Integrated Management Information System for ICDS*.

7. Ministry of Human Resource Development, Department of Women and Child Development (1988) A Hand Book of Instructions regarding Integrated Child Development Services Programmes.

8. Ministry of Education and Social Welfare (1972) *Report of the Study Group on the Development of the Pre-school Child*.

9. *Muralidharan, R. and Banerhji, U. (1975) Effect of Pre-school Education on the school readiness of under-privileged children of Delhi. International Journal of Early Childhood, 7, 2.*

10. National Council of Educational Research and Training, Department of Pre-school and Elementary Education (1989) Integrated two-year Course in Pre-school and Early Primary Teacher Education, (revised).

11. National Council of Educational Research and Training, Department of Pre-school and Elementary Education (1986) Guidelines for Developing Curriculum at the lower primary stage, April.

12. National Council of Educational Research and Training (1981) Pre-primary Teacher Education. Third all India Educational Survey, July.

13. National Council for Teacher Education — NCERT (1976) B.Ed. Early Chldhood Education Course.

14. National Institute of Public Co-operation and Child Development: Training Requirements of Child Development Workers (1985).

15. National Institute of Public Co-operation and Child Development (1989) Syllabus for Job Training of Anganwadi Workers of ICDS Programme, February.

16. UNESCO (1983) Regional Training Workshop for Supervisors and Administrators of Early Childhood Care and Education, Bangkok.

17. UNESCO/NCERT (1983) Sponsored National Workshop in early Childhood Education.

18. UNESCO (1983) Study Group Meeting on New Forms of Pre-school Education. *NCERT*, Dehli, April.

19. UNICEF (1990) The State of the World's Children, Thomson Press, India.

Preparation of early childhood teachers in Sweden

BERTIL SUNDIN

Department of Education, University of Stockholm, Stockholm, Sweden

(Received August 1991)

This paper looks at the significant issues connected with early childhood teacher preparation in Sweden in the light of recent educational reforms. Training goals are discussed in the context of ECE ideology and the reform of higher education.

KEY WORDS: Early Childhood Teachers, Sweden

TWO EDUCATIONAL REFORMS

Two educational reforms have put a definite stamp on the preschool teacher training in Sweden.

The first one was initiated by a parliamentary committee appointed in 1968 (1968 Preschool Committee) which in a special report laid out the general principles of a common day care system. One result of its work was a law in 1973 which enjoined municipalities to provide preschools for all six-year-olds (school begins at seven) and for younger children with "special needs". In another report The Committee outlined a new training system for preschool teachers and a new law went into effect in 1975. The Committee also initiated many projects of an experimental type connected with teacher training and preschool work.

The second one was a far reaching reform of the higher education system in 1977, involving the creation of a single and coherent system for all types of post-secondary education. The system encompasses not only traditional university studies but various professional and semi-professional colleges as well, among them the preschool teacher training colleges.

Both these reforms, the new preschool system and the new higher education system, have brought about many changes in the preparation of early childhood teachers. As the teacher training system and the actual work in preschools are closely interrelated, both will be described in the following.

Present Status of the Preschool System

Preschool education comes under the Social Services Act (not the National Board of Education!) which came into force in 1982. Among other things the act lays down that municipalities must plan the preschool activities in such a way that child care amenities will be available to parents who need them.

As already mentioned, all six-year-olds are entitled to attend preschool. Younger children in need of special support are entitled to priority when the demand is bigger than the supply, which is usually the case. Especially in urban areas there is a shortage of qualified staff and available places for children. This jeopardizes the project decided by Parliament in 1985 that by 1991 public child care should be provided for all preschool children older than eighteen months.

The preschool population in January 1989 consisted ot 730,000 children (the population of Sweden is 8.5 millions). Of them

- 32% went to municipal day care centres or play schools,
- 17% went to family day care homes,
- 01% went to private or parent cooperative day care centres,
- 05% went to other private paid care,
- 03% went to private unpaid care.

As can be seen child-care outside the home is now provided for 58 per cent of the preschool population all together. The remaining 42 per cent are cared for solely by parents (the source for all statistical information is the official statistics of Sweden).

More than 98 per cent of the six-year-olds attend preschool (day care or play school) for at least three hours a day. More than 1,300 open preschools are visited regularly by children and parents or child minders. At those institutions a preschool teacher is employed to organize activities and to give parents and child minders advice.

In the age group 7-9, 45 per cent attend leisure centres (in connection with schools, the staff with similar training as preschool teachers), while the figure drops to 7 per cent for 10-12 year-olds.

The average annual cost per child in day care centres is around 6.000 British Pound, the state subsidies and the municipals contributing 44 per cent each. The remaining 12 per cent comes from parental fees.

Municipal authorities are responsible for the activities at the local level. During the eighties many "parent cooperatives" have come into being. In order to get public economical support they have to comply with the municipal rules. The National Board of Health and Welfare issues recommendations concerning objectives, content, working methods, in-service-training and so on but has no real executive power.

The staff comprise preschool teachers, child care attendants and catering staff. They have different training background and belong to different unions but are supposed to work closeby in teams with their tasks. Further in-service-training is provided by the municipalities. The availability and content of such further training varies much from one area to another.

Day care centres are usually open between 6.30 a.m. and 6 p.m., Monday to Friday, all year round. The children are in most cases divided into mixed age-groups (sibling groups). As an average, a child care centre has four groups or sections, each with some 15-18 children, two preschool teachers and one attendant (or vice versa).

Part-time groups (play schools) for children 4 to 6 years follow the school year and usually comprise one preschool teacher and one child care attendant. The groups meet for three hours, morning or afternoon.

History of Teacher Training

The pioneers in the Kindergarten movement in Sweden were themselves trained at the Froebel Seminar in Berlin, Germany. The first Swedish training colleges were founded around the turn of the century and were built close to the Kindergartens where the teachers were working. That made possible a smooth transmission of knowledge from generation to generation of teachers.

Right to the seventies it was possible to talk of a common basic view among the Kindergarten teachers, with emphasis on the child's self-activity and own initiative and much room for play and creative activities. That tradition was very different from the common teacher training with its strong central control and emphasis on method. The preschool seminaries were much freer than the teacher colleges. The differences between the two systems remained even after 1962, then the preschool teacher training was nationalized and the two systems got the same national authority, the National Board of Education, and sometimes also shared building facilities and teachers.

Another split, now within the preschool system, became evident during the sixties and seventies. The kindergartens or play schools had a pure education aim: to give as good opportunities as possible for growth from within. The difference from the compulsory school was emphasized. The children spent only a few hours in the institutions. Middle class parents were in a majority.

Day care homes evolved out of the creches in bigger towns from the last century. Their main function was social and economic, not educational: they were supposed to take care of the children while the parents (or the lonely mother) worked. The majority of the parents belonged to the working class and the staff had not the same training as those in play schools.

The different historical traditions of the two types of institutions were reflected in their kind of educational work, although the difference diminished after the Second World War, with public economical support to both kinds of institutions.

The 1968 Preschool Committee emphasized the children's day homes and part time preschools should have the same educational aims. The only difference should be the time spent at the institutions. The rhetoric was something like this: the preschool is a social political instrument but within this frame it primarily has an educational aim. Later research has shown, though, that the difference in hours spent in preschool has consequences for recruitment of staff and children and for cooperation for parents and for the kind of education provided. The different

functions of the day care centres (economical, social and educational) show in goal
conflicts, especially when the economy is drawn tight.

The 1970's became a very expansive decade because of the demand on the
municipalities to build new day care homes and a corresponding demand for more
preschool teachers and child care attendants. Before 1960 about 250 students a year
passed the final examinations at the training colleges. Ten years later the number had
grown to 1,200 and the years around 1980 more than 4,000 students finished their
training every year. Since then the number has gone down. During the school year
1988/89 around 2,500 student teachers passed their examination.

The big expansion during the seventies brought about a break with the transmission of tradition. Earlier there was much of a master-apprentice relationship in the
colleges and connected preschools, with teacher trainers and trainees working side by
side and with a predominantly oral transmission of skills and knowledge.

The expansion of the training system created a shortage of teachers. Many of the
newly hired teachers at the colleges had no previous experience of practical work in
preschools. Much more of the knowledge had to be transmitted through books than
before, the training became more theoretical than practical. The break in tradition
was especially noticeable in music, movement and similar subjects with craft
components.

1968 Preschool Committee: Ideological Aspects

The educational programme presented by the Preschool Committee was built in an
attempt to integrate the developmental theories of Jean Piaget and Erik H. Erikson.
The official goal was to provide the children with optimal conditions for a rich and
all-round development of their emotional and cognitive resources. The programme
was centred around three sub-goals: ego development, ability to communicate and
concept formation.

The activities in the preschool were structured around certain key concepts as team
work, sibling groups, activity stations, dialogue pedegogics, close cooperation with
the parents, etc. The ambitions were high and a vogue of enthusiasm and project
oriented teaching spread over the training colleges.

The committee saw the teacher training and the preschool as an instrument for
changing society in a democratic direction. Project studies became common and a
curriculum code which in Basil Bernstein's terms would be called integrated, with
weak classification and framing, was strongly promoted (Linné, 1979), and still is in
some colleges.

Teacher training in that way became an important arena for educational reform.
Today most researchers agree that the expectations on education as a means to
change society have not been fulfilled. The possibilities of training and changing of
pedagogic and personal attitudes were over-emphasized and the structural obstacles
in society were overlooked.

The attempt to build a public pedagogic programme on development psychological
theories has also been criticized: it gives upbringing a supposed value free and
unpolitical character and in that way it becomes a hidden ideology. It tends to

conceal social and structural conflicts in society, as much of the sociological research about the preschool tried to show.

Some of that critique is well founded but it overlooks the innovation in the attempt to apply psychological developmental theory on a national education programme. That attempt has made clearer the relationship between research and politics, between upbringing and values, between structural and cultural components of developmental stages. Today we know more about the range and limitations of development theories in preschool education than we knew before the work of the Committee.

As an answer to a sometimes hard critique against the ideas of the Preschool Committee a new educational programme was worked out for the preschools during the eighties. It was more group directed than the old one and emphasized structure and planning. The teacher training programmes were changed accordingly.

Teacher Training After the Reform of Higher Education

Recruitment and outline of training

In family day care the training background varies considerably. Most family child minders have taken an introductory course of 100 hours or a lengthier training. Some have also taken the special two-year study line in the upper secondary schools which leads to competence as a child care attendant.

In contrast the training of the preschool teachers is on a university level. Administratively some schools belong to universities, others to teacher training colleges. Teacher training takes place in twenty or so different institutions.

The general admission requirements for the training is completion of at least two years at upper secondary school or knowledge of the English and Swedish languages to at least two years at upper secondary school. Being at least 25 years old, having a record of at least four years of work experience and knowledge of English equivalent to two years at upper secondary school is an alternative admission requirement.

During the seventies there could be 20 applicants for every one who entered the training. Today some colleges have difficulty to fill their study places, a striking illustration to a declining popularity of the job.

The length of the training is either:

● two and a half years (100 points, every point equal to one week of full time study). This form is the usual one.
● two years (80 points), if the student has completed the two-year study line in the upper secondary school for child care attendants.
● one and a half years (50 points), if the student has the child care attendant training and has worked in preschools for at least four years.

There is a proposal that the present training courses for preschool teachers and recreation instructors should be substituted by a child- and youth-pedagogical study programme with a length of three years, divided into one course for work with

preschool children and one for work with school children. The courses were supposed
to begin in 1990/91 but the government has postponed the reform, mainly for
economic reasons.

Earlier the students had a fixed number of hours in every subject, similar in the
whole country. When the new training system started in 1975, the subjects were
divided into four groups or blocks which for the 80-point course is as follows:

- pedagogy-methodology (including psychology) 25 points,
- orientation in the surrounding world 10 points,
- practise 25 points and
- communication (language, literature, art, craft, music, educational drama,
movement) 20 points.

After the reform of higher education it became possible to go directly from the
secondary school to the training college without any intervening work experience with
children, which earlier was the claim. Another 20 points, consisting partly by
practical work in preschools, were than added. This alternative (100 points) is today
the dominating one.

Around 80 per cent of the students finish their studies before they are 24 years old
and more than 95 per cent of them are women (a somewhat higher proportion of
males existed in the seventies).

Training goals and the Decentralizing of Higher Education

As already mentioned, the reform of higher education encompasses not only
traditional university studies but also those at the various professional colleges and
some programmes previously taught within the upper secondary school system.

The old system was highly centralized which made the training formally homoge-
nous. The centrally issued directions for the different colleges were compromises
between different interests and opinions among the decision makers, but when the
directions had been formulated they gave clear directions to the local colleges what to
do. Through the reform the conflict arena between different interests moved down
one or several steps in the hierarchy.

The specified and centrally stated aims and objects for the training were
substituted by much more general frames and recommendations. New decision-
making bodies came into existence. The single training college got more decision
power and with that more conflicts between different interest groups within the
college. Take as an example the "communication block" (music, drama, movement,
language, arts & crafts) in a college. Before the reform the National Board of
Education decided the number of hours for every subject. Now the "block" got 20
points (equals 20 weeks of full time studies) but the distribution of those points among
the subjects and the money involved were left to the individual college to decide. It
had to "translate" the general central intentions to a local curriculum and to the
planning of lessons.

An example: The Teachers College in Stockholm

There are 15 different subjects at the preschool teacher courses at the Teachers College in Stockholm. In the local curriculum they are concealed behind different themes for every term. The theme for the first term in the 100-points course is THE CREATIVE HUMAN BEING, for term 2 CHILDREN'S DEVELOPMENT 0-12 YEARS, for term 3 INDIVIDUAL, GROUP AND SOCIAL INFLUENCE, for term 4 CHILDREN, CULTURE AND METHODS OF WORKING IN THE PRESCHOOL and for term 5 THE PROFESSIONAL ROLE OF THE PRESCHOOL TEACHER. The different subjects are requested to work closely together in order to help the students experience and understand the relationship theory/practise. Different problems of coordination are supposed to be handled at the local school.

In other colleges the education may be centred around the different subjects. This means that the content of the training today can be rather heterogenous in different colleges at the whole and between different subjects in a certain college. Relative importance of theoretical knowledge and practical vocational training, of general methods and concrete examples, craftmanship and personal development can vary greatly.

Teachers in the different subjects can be convinced that a solid discipline bound knowledge gives the best platform for teacher behavior. Teachers in psychology and pedagogics on the other hand tend to present generalizations and theoretical models as the best way to good teacher behavior while teachers in method and supervisors in the field offer practical suggestions and well-tried practical experience.

Conflicts such as those mentioned above will certainly be found in every higher educational system. There are other conflicts which more directly are the outcomes of the special features of Swedish preschool traditions.

Stronger links between higher education and research

The reform of higher education had two main purposes: to make possible for new categories of people to obtain higher education and to design a unified system, combining programmes and institutions which had previously been administered separately.

Another purpose was to strengthen the links between higher education and research. This made existing differences in epistemological traditions between different institutions and programmes visible and subject to substantial controversy.

The scientific tradition emphasizes systematic investigations, linear thinking, strivings for objectivity or intersubjectivity and empirical research methods. Some practically oriented professional training programmes have a long and natural residence in the academic world (medical doctors, lawyers, etc) and fit in with that epistemological tradition.

On the other hand you have a tradition of practical knowledge which has been the dominating tradition in the training of nurses, preschool teachers and similar jobs. The main part of their training consisted of transmission of practical and artistic knowledge. A similar epistemological tradition dominated the art, dance and music colleges.

When through the reform the preschool teachers were included in the academic system their training was supposed to be research oriented on a level equal to the universities. The student teachers should reflect upon their job in a research-oriented way and understand more of scientific methods and traditions. In practice that often came to mean more books and less vocational training, often with the addition of a lot of confusion.

The preschool teacher has in a way to pay respect to all three epistemological traditions, the scientific, the practical and the artistic. One of the main problems in preschool teacher training is how they could and should be combined. They all contribute to the acquisition of valuable knowledge. The scientific tradition cannot be applied to everything. Practical experience, intuition and non-verbal judgments which are difficult to verbalize have also an important place.

Theory and Practical Experience

The relationship between theoretical studies and practise can be used as an example. An earlier well defined vocational code, transmitted from master to apprentice has been substituted by a training where the two main components, theory and practise, no longer relate in a simple complementary way with the same clear-cut objectives. The training is often seen as an instrument for changing the society and to develop "the reflective practitioner" (Schön, 1983). Old patterns of training have given way for new professional codes. But not without protests and discussions about what type of teacher knowledge is most important.

One of the leading Swedish researchers in this area, Berit Askling (1987), has the impression that the function of the training as a tool for change tends to diminish the practical part of the training and create an exaggerated respect for the rhetoric in different curricula, commissional reports and so on. Different opinions of how the training should be are put against each other and it is with great difficulty one can find any clear criteria in the complex goal formulations.

In Sweden the 1968 Preschool Committee complicated the whole thing with a change in the practise system which was motivated more by ideological than by methodological reasons. In the existing order one of the teachers at the practise preschool was responsible for her student(s) and got some extra pay for that. Now everybody in the working team were considered competent for that and the responsibility of the supervision moved from individual teachers to work teams. That led to confusion about responsibility, pay and so on. A usual compromise is to give one teacher the responsibility but no money, a system which can hardly be described in positive terms. It will probably be changed in the centrally written directions which are supposed to be put into practice in the school year 1991/92.

Evaluation

The preschool reform initiated much research, most of it about the effects of preschools, less about teacher training. What exists in that latter respect was published in the years around 1980 (Johansson och Linné 1979; Johansson, 1981; Sundin, 1979, 1982, 1988). Johansson and Linné investigated the training as a whole, while the present authors' main interest was the role and possibilities of the arts in the curriculum.

The results from this research indicates that the training as a whole had succeeded in changing the students both in areas of personality development and in attitudes towards children and the profession. They saw themselves as more self-confident, open and tolerant and willing to show more what they thought and thought after the training. They had also got a clearer idea of the importance of the arts in the work with children and had high expectations for their future job in that respect.

The research also shows that high ambitions are not enough. There were great differences between the students in their ambitions of working with the arts in preschool. After a year as preschool teachers those differences had leveled out: the harsh reality of preschool life with its built in obstacles made the teachers work less with the arts than they had planned to.

Through the eighties there has been much discussion about the culture in preschools and the place the arts should have there and in the teacher training. Many projects have been carried out in that area, unfortunately without much scholarly documentation. There is some, though, and there are also some teachers in the training colleges and some preschool teachers who have been able to use the new possibilities for doing research being offered through the reform of the higher education. Sometimes this research works in other directions than older research traditions, sometimes it sticks close to them. In both cases there are reasons *for believing* it will in the long run raise the standard considerably, both on current working practices in the preschools and on the teacher training.

Hopefully it will also have something to say about the consequences for the children if the preschool shall continue to emphasize the care of children and the difference from the compulsory school *or* if the preschool shall be considered a school for small children. The arguments for the latter are both economical (getting the costs down) and neurological (using what we know about sensitive periods for speeding up the development). The steps being taken in the future will have consequences also for the training colleges.

References

Askling, B. (1987) Teori och praktik i lärarubildningen: kompletterande eller motsägelsefulla inslag (Theory and practise in teacher training : complementary or contradictory components). In Dahlgren, Gunnarsson, Kärrby (Eds) Barnets väg genom förskola, skola och in i vuxenlivet. Lund: Studentlitteratur

Johansson, J.-E. (1981) Att Utbilda sig till förskollärare (To train oneself to preschool teacher). Uppsala universitet: Pedagogiska institutionen

Johansson, J.-E. & Linné, A. (1975) Om Förskollärarutbildningen (On preschool teacher training). FOU-rapport 35. Stockholm: Skolöverstyrelsen/Liber

Kärrby, G. (1985) Utveckling i grupp (Development in the group). Om pedagogiskt arbete i förskolan. Stockholm: Liber/Utbildningsförlaget

Linné, AS. (1979) Teacher education in Sweden: A case study in curriculum evaluation. In Lundgren & Pettersson (Eds) Code, context and curriculum processes. Teachers' College, Stockholm

Schön, D. (1983) The reflective practitioner. New York
Sundin, B. (1979) Music in preschool treacher training. Council of Research in Music Education, Bull. No 59, 107–111
- Barnen och de sköna konsterna (Children and the fine arts). Stockholm: Statens kulturråd, Liber, 1982
- Musiken i människan (Music in man). Stockholm: Natur och Kultur, 1988
Statistics Sweden

Pre-service teachers' perceptions and their behavioral interactions with young children from international cultures

LINDA M. BURT and ALAN I. SUGAWARA

Oregon State University, Corvallis, Oregon, USA

(Received March 1992)

Theory and research suggest that preservice techers' personal teaching efficacy and their ethnic attributions contribute to their behavioral interactions with International children. Theoretical research contributions pertaining to personal teaching efficacy, causal attributions, and child-teacher interaction are reviewed and are included as conceptual components for a model of teacher-child interaction. Practical implications of this model are suggested for faculty and staff supervisors of teacher preparation programs.

Key words: Pre-service, teacher perceptions, diverse cultures

INTRODUCTION

Today, early childhood educators are faced with new challenges associated with upholding equity, acceptance, and respect in classrooms where multilingualism and multiculturalism exist. This is especially true among new and experienced teachers who are encountering increasing numbers of non-English speaking children from International cultures within their classrooms. As this trend continues, these teachers will likely begin to question their preparation for working with young children from culturally diverse backgrounds. Concerns have already been mounted among the teacher preparation faculty regarding the limited experiences preservice, new, and more experienced teachers have had in interacting with non-English speaking children from International cultures (Ramsey, 1987).

As a head teacher and instructor at Oregon State University's Child Development Center several years ago, I experienced increasing enrollments of children from International cultures in my preschool classroom. With many languages and cultures represented, I began to explore the reactions of pre-service teachers to children from these culturally diverse backgrounds. In my supervisory role as head teacher, I had the opportunity to become familiar with some of the concerns and anxieties experienced by pre-service teachers about their interactions with International children.

Address correspondence to: Linda M. Burt, Human Development & Family Sciences, Milam Hall 322 Oregon State University, Corvallis, OR. 97331, USA

Through their journals, staff conferences, and private consultations with me, they often disclosed many of their discomforts, seriously searching for solutions to their cross-cultural interaction dilemmas. Some examples of the more common statements made by preservice teachers about their experiences included:

"I don't feel comfortable working with Chu-Soo (Korean). He never looks at me!"

"Carlos (Mexican) seems so lazy. He won't participate in activities. He just sits and watches other children play!"

"Sophia (French) is so aggressive. She speaks French and hits my arm. I feel at loss for words!"

"Is Sung-chan (Chinese) delayed? He hardly ever speaks or plays with other children?"

Aside from reading and hearing of the concerns expressed by preservice teachers, I also had the opportunity to observe them interact with groups of three- to five-year-olds in an early childhood classroom. Frequently, the interactions which took place between them were more directed toward American rather than International children. Preservice teachers appeared to avoid International children, or to make brief statements and used closed-ended questions (yes/no) in conversing with them. Such observations were revealing, yet at the same time quite disappointing.

These informal experiences with preservice teachers prompted me to further explore the nature of their interactions with International children. Perhaps, the perceptions preservice teachers held about themselves, their teaching abilities, and the behaviors of International children played a role in influencing their interactions with these children. Furthermore, discovering how these factors might contribute to their interactions may provide us with important information about how preservice teachers can be helped to interact more effectively with children from a wide range of cultural backgrounds. Such competence in interactions may also help to ease the "cultural shock" often experienced by non-English speaking International children in American early childhood settings.

A Search for Answers

Although administrators, principals, and university faculty of teacher preparation programs have emphasized the need for preservice teachers to become more aware of the cultural diversity which exists within their classrooms, specific suggestions as to how they might effectively interact with International children have been quite sparse. In addition, researchers have not yet begun to assess the efficacy of these limited number of suggestions available for use in classrooms by preschool techers. More generally, however, it is apparent that this area of study has not been developed on the basis of a well-established theoretical foundation (Chu, 1980; Hamilton, 1979; Triandis, 1989).

Some years ago, Snygg and Combs (1949) hypothesized that the behaviors displayed by teachers were a function of the perceptions they held about themselves and others within their classrooms. Applied to teacher preparation programs, this idea suggests that behaviors displayed by preservice teachers in children's classrooms are a function of the manner in which they perceived themselves as teachers and the children they taught.

In spite of its long history, not many teacher preparation programs or its related research have taken seriously these perceptual ideas. In part, this may have been due to the vague quality of Snygg and Combs, (1949) concepts. However, when operationalized within the context of an early childhood teacher preparation program, specific perceptual, theoretical views become relevant and facilitate new suggestions for practice. By utilizing more recent theoretical approaches, such as self-efficacy (Bandura, 1977) and attribution (Weiner, 1985) theories, these ideas become refreshingly sound and relevant for understanding the behaviors of preservice teachers toward International children.

Our review of literature supports this notion, particularly in reference to the relationships between preservice teachers' (1) perceptions about their abilities and skills in teaching International children (e.g., personal teaching efficacy; Gibson & Dembo, 1984), (2) perceptions about the behavioral characteristics of children from various cultural groups (e.g., ethnic attributions; Burt, 1992; Russell, 1982; Weiner, 1979), and (3) behaviors displayed toward children from International cultures (Caldwell & Honig, 1971). Each of these aspects will be discussed briefly, highlighting past theoretical and research studies undertaken. In addition, a section focused on the practical implications of these theoretical and research ideas for the professional preparation of teachers will be presented.

Preservice Teachers' Perceptions of their Skills and Abilities in Interacting with International Children

Research studies focused on understanding the relationship between teachers' perceptions of their abilities in interacting with young children and their actual teaching behaviors have been conducted by Gibson and Dembo (1984), Dembo and Gibson (1985), Mumaw, Sugawara, and Pestle (1991) and Wolfolk and Hoy (1990). In these studies, Bandura's (1977) theory of self-efficacy was used to develop measurement devices to assess the construct of personal teaching efficacy among teachers. This construct of teacher perceptions is of major interest, since the perceptions teachers have about their ability to interact and facilitate desirable learning experiences with young children has been found to be predictive of their performance as teachers (Bandura, 1977, 1979; Gibson & Dembo, 1984; Dembo & Gibson, 1985). This proposition would likely hold true whether applied to International or American children. Some example items used to assess a teachers' personal teaching efficacy related to International children are as follows (Burt, 1992). These were adapted from Gibson and Dembo's (1984) *Teacher Efficacy Scales*.

(1)   When an International child performs at a higher level than she/he usually does, it is usually because I found better ways of teaching that child.

(2)   If an International child in my class becomes disruptive and noisy, I believe that I know some techniques to redirect him/her quickly.

(3)   If I really try hard, I can get through to even the most difficult of unmotivated International children.

Teachers are asked to use these items to rate themselves on a six-point scale from strongly agree to strongly disagree, providing information on the degree to which each of them hold these personal teaching efficacy perceptions. According to Bandura (1977), such personal efficacy perceptions are the most powerful predictors of a teacher's behavior in interacting with International children. When applied to preservice teachers, the proposition would also likely hold true. In addition, these items can be used by supervisors to help preservice teachers reflect upon their own perceptions regarding their ability to interact with and teach International children. Such reflection can serve as a basis upon which more effective ways of communicating with these children and facilitating their learning can occur. The concept of personal teaching efficacy, therefore, is an important construct for study and use in the professional development of early childhood education teachers.

Until recently, researchers have not been able to effectively assess the reasons why teachers hold specific perceptions about the behavioral characteristics of children, particularly those of children from International cultures. On the basis of attribution theory (Weiner, 1979, 1985), researchers have suggested that the reasons teachers give for a child's behavior may be related to the degree to which they hold dispositional biases toward such behavior (Brophy & Rohrkemper, 1981; Cunningham, 1986; Russell, 1982). When considering teachers' perceptions of the behavioral characteristics of International children, therefore, it would appear worthwhile to consider the attributional patterns teachers hold as they judge these children's behaviors.

Assessing a teacher's tendency toward ethnic bias in judging International children's behavior has been a difficult area of study. Often, many teachers do not wish to disclose their biases toward children and adults from other cultures. This seems particularly true in the teaching profession where the ideas of individual human rights, justice, and equity are upheld for all children and adults. However, in order for teachers to develop skills in effectively communicating with children from other cultures, they must be able to examine their own attitudes and beliefs about children from other cultures, so that harmful myths and stereotypes can be eliminated. Asking teachers to identify what they perceive the causes or reasons for the attributions made about International children's behaviors, therefore, may be a less threatening and a more informative way of obtaining their perceptions about these children's behaviors.

To do this, a teacher may be given an International vignette depicting general ethnic profiles of common socialized behaviors associated with a specific culture. For example, a vignette representing a child from the Korean culture (Burt, 1992) may read as follows:

Younghee is a Korean girl who has just arrived from Korea. At preschool she tends to follow others to guide what actions and play activities she may do. She is compliant, unassertive, obedient, dependable, and accepting of authority. Younghee also is observed to be restrained, cautious, and silent toward peers, and tends to look down away from the teacher who seeks her attention. When she speaks, the meaning of what is spoken is unclear and indirect. Peers and teachers need to inquire further about what she means.

After studying such vignettes, teachers are asked to respond to items on a seven-point *Causal Dimension Scale* (Russell 1982), asking them to indicate the degree to which they attribute specific causes to the profiled behaviors. If teachers' attributions of the profiled behaviors are rated toward the end of the scale indicating the causes to be within the child, of a permanent nature, and is something for which the child is responsible, then they would be said to possess a biased dispositional position. On the other hand, if teachers' attributions of the profiled behaviors are rated at the other end of the scale, indicating the causes to be outside the child, of a variable nature, and is something for which no one is responsible, then they would be said to possess an unbiased, situation-based, position.

According to attribution theorists (Brophy & Rohrkemper, 1981; Cunningham, 1986; Russell, 1982; Weiner, 1985), the kinds of attributions teachers make about children's behavior can influence the manner in which they interact with these children. This proposition would hold true for both preservice and professional teachers, and refer to attributions about International and American children. Preservice teachers with relatively unbiased, situation-based dispositional positions would more likely relate to children from all cultures as unique individuals, varying their teaching styles in ways that would adapt to the child's needs, interests, and cultural characteristics rather than attempting to fit all children into one single, stereotypic, cultural mold. Helping preservice teachers to examine their attributions of children from diverse cultural backgrounds, therefore, can aid them in developing their skills for interacting with all children in a manner that takes seriously what is common between them, what makes them unique as a result of their cultural pasts, and what emerges as a result of their interactions together within an early childhood education environment.

In order to fully comprehend how teachers' perceptions (e.g., personal teaching efficacy and ethnic attributions) can influence their interactions with young children, observation studies focused on the actual interactions which occur between teachers and children must be undertaken. Recent research studies are available indicating that young children do make an impact on the behaviors of teachers, which may vary according to such characteristics as children's age, gender, ethnicity, and behavioral stereotypes (Fagot 1978; Grusec & Kuzinski, 1980; Inoff & Halvorson, 1977; Irvine, 1986; Shoopes & Eads, 1977; Stevens, 1980). Likewise, teachers with varying degrees of personal teaching efficacy and ethnic attributions toward children from various cultural backgrounds will have a differential impact on children (Bandura, 1977; Gibson & Dembo, 1984; Dembo & Gibson, 1985; Wolfolk & Hoy, 1990; Brophy & Rohrkemper, 1981; Russell, 1982; Cunningham, 1986; Weiner, 1979, 1985). The direction of influence between teachers and children, therefore, is bidirectional.

A valid and reliable means of observing and coding these interactions is crucial in our attempt at understanding how selected teacher perceptions can influence the interactions which occur between teachers and children, particularly among children from different cultural backgrounds. Caldwell and Honig's (1971) procedures for coding and analyzing the interactional response patterns which occur between teachers and children provides us with a means of accomplishing this goal. This procedure categorizes teacher behaviors resulting from interactions with children into two major categories: (1) Positive Behaviors, and (2) Negative Behaviors.

The Positive Behaviors Category covers such behavioral dimensions as (1) Ego-boosting (e.g., behaviors which encourage a child in a positive manner, such as "I really like the way you listened," while patting the child gently on the back); (2) Teaching (e.g., behaviors which inform, facilitate and/or direct a child to learning activities, such as "Here's a doll," while giving the child a doll); (3) Questioning (e.g. behaviors which asks children about a variety of topics, including "What colors are on this ball?" or "What are the safety rules at school?"); and (4) Attending (e.g., behaviors which involve looking at the child silently, but with interest, as the child participates in an activity, or helping a child with an activity by offering the child additional materials to play with).

The Negative Behaviors Category covers such behavioral dimensions as (1) Commanding (e.g., behaviors which demand that a child act in a particular manner other than directing the child to a learning activity, such as "Get over there and sit down!" or "Be quiet!"); (2) Negatively Reinforcing (e.g., behaviors which forbids, restricts, criticizes and/or threatens a child with statements like "If you don't listen, you won't get to go outside and play!"); (3) Ignoring (e.g., behaviors which involve not responding to a child's solicitations of a teacher's attention); (4) Physically controlling non-verbal behaviors in which the teacher restrains the child's actions by physical means; (5) Combined Behaviors (e.g., behaviors which involve the occurrence of positive and negative behaviors together such as "Don't touch the food! It's hot!"); and (6) Unknown (e.g., behaviors which cannot be categorized in any of the behavior categories described above. The Physically Controlling Category was added based coder agreement during pilot-testing. In using these Positive and Negative Behavior Categories, supervisors can obtain information about the types, duration and quality of behavioral interactions which occur between teachers and children.

Although there are numerous other behaviors that can be studied for an understanding of teacher-child interactions, the behaviors described above were found to occur with consistency in the teacher-child interactions of two- to five-year-olds (Burt, 1992; Caldwell & Honig, 1971; Honig & Witmer, 1986; Witmer & Honig, 1988). In order to use Caldwell and Honig's (1971) *Behavior Coding Categories* effectively, one could select a preservice teacher, two International and two American children of each gender from the larger early childhood classroom, and lead them into a smaller classroom in which they could participate in various curriculum activities.

These curriculum activities could vary from session to session, and include two structured (e.g., reading stories and picture demonstration discussions), and two unstructured (e.g., play dough and blocks) activities. Participation in each of these activities could last approximately 10 minutes per session, with the kind of activity varying at each session. Preservice teachers would, therefore, participate with children from various cultural backgrounds in four, 10 minutes, curriculum activity sessions over a period of several weeks. All of these curriculum activity sessions would be videotaped for later viewing by the supervisor or preservice teacher, using Caldwell and Honig's (1971) behavior coding procedures.

In this manner, supervisors would be able to observe the behavioral response patterns of preservice teachers toward children from both International and American cultures, and design experiences that would enhance their interactions with children, particularly those from International cultures. Furthermore, preservice teachers could observe their own interactions with children over four different sessions, making them aware of the progress they have made in interacting with children from various cultural backgrounds.

Some training is necessary in using Caldwell and Honig's (1971) behavior coding categories; however, once mastered, the procedure is easy to use. Several reliability and validity studies have been conducted for the coding procedures in observing the interactions of preservice and professional teachers with young children (Burt, 1992; Caldwell & Honig, 1971; Honig & Witmer, 1986; Witmer & Honig, 1988).

A MODEL OF TEACHER-CHILD INTERACTIONS

On the basis of our present review of theoretical and research literature, we can now develop a relatively simple model of teacher-child interactions which can help us understand how selected teacher perceptions might influence their behavioral interactions with young children in a multicultural group setting (see Figure 1).

These selected teacher perceptions include preservice teachers' personal teaching efficacy and their ethnic attributions toward children from International cultures. Behavioral interactions refer to behaviors displayed by preservice teachers in their interactions with three- to five-year-old children. Multicultural group setting refers to a small group session in which individual preservice teachers participate with two International and two American children of each gender in selected curriculum activities.

On the basis of past theoretical and research literature just reviewed, it is predicted the preservice teachers' personal teaching efficacy and ethnic attributions toward children from International cultures will significantly contribute to their behavioral interactions with these children. However, the specific manner in which these preservice teacher perceptions will impact upon their behavioral interactions is not fully known at this time. Presently, there are two competing propositions that need to be examined. Some studies suggest that preservice teachers' personal teaching efficacy will have an impact on their ethnic attributions (Bandura, 1986; Covington & Omelich, 1979, 1984; McAuley & Duncan, 1990; McAuley, Duncan & McElroy, 1989) which in turn will have an impact on their behavioral interactions with International children. Other studies, however, suggest that a preservice teacher's ethnic attributions will have an impact on their personal teaching efficacy, which in turn will have an impact on their behavioral interactions (Weiner, 1979, 1985, 1990) with International children.

Presently, we are conducting a research study to examine these propositions, applying path-analytic statistical procedures to data collected on preservice teachers' perceptions and behavioral interactions with International children. Whatever the case might be, it is clear that preservice teachers' personal teaching efficacy and ethnic attributions do contribute to their behavioral interactions with International children. These findings in and of themselves contain important implications for practices which can occur in teacher preparation programs. These implications will be explored in the following section.

IMPLICATIONS FOR PRACTICE IN TEACHER PREPARATION PROGRAMS

What are some of the practical implications of findings regarding the importance of teachers' perceptions in influencing their interactions with children from International cultures that supervisors in teacher preparation programs need to be aware of in facilitating preservice teachers' development? More specifically, how will preservice teachers' personal teaching efficacy and ethnic attributions toward children from International cultures be considered by teacher preparation supervisors in enhancing their abilities and skills in interacting with children from diverse cultural backgrounds? A number of suggestions can be made at this time which supervisors can use with preservice teachers as they interact with children in a multicultural early childhood education program.

Considering Preservice Teachers' Personal Teaching Efficacy

Since preservice teachers' personal teaching efficacy for interacting with International children is a powerful predictor of their interactions with these children, supervisors must take seriously the importance of experiences that will enhance such efficacy in teacher preparation programs. One of the major objectives of teacher preparation programs, therefore, must be:

Objective 1.   To increase preservice teachers' level of personal teaching efficacy in interacting with International children.

A number of strategies can be used to accomplish this objective. First, preservice teachers need to be provided with an opportunity to freely express their concerns and discomforts as well as their joys and successes in interacting with children from diverse cultural backgrounds. This can only occur in an atmosphere of openness and acceptance in which a relationship of trust has been developed between supervisors and preservice teachers.

After such initial discussion has occurred, preservice teachers can be asked to participate in small group sessions with children from diverse cultural backgrounds, participating in simple curriculum activities with them. These small group activity sessions are videotaped for later viewing by supervisors and preservice teachers, during which time the skills and needs of preservice teachers are identified, and plans for the future development of additional skills are made. Once these plans are made, preservice teachers can again interact with children from diverse cultural back-grounds, practising their interactional skills until such time that competence and comfort are acquired.

Since preservice teachers' interactions are videotaped over a number of sessions, supervisors and preservice teachers have the opportunity to view the growth that has taken place among preservice teachers in their interactions with children from diverse cultural backgrounds. Experience and success in interacting with children from a wide range of cultures in a setting consisting of supportive supervisors and peers can provide preservice teachers with an environment that facilitates their personal sense of efficacy (Ruder, 1991). This sense of efficacy can be utilized as the basis upon which positive interactions with children from diverse cultural backgrounds can emerge.

Considering Preservice Teachers' Ethnic Attributions

Like personal teaching efficacy, the manner in which preservice teachers attribute various causes to socialized ethnic behaviors can have a marked impact on the way these teachers interact with children from International cultures. Understanding the reasons why these ethnic attributions are made, therefore, can help preservice teachers to evaluate their currently held perceptions of individuals from diverse cultural backgrounds. A second major objective of teacher preparation programs, therefore, must be:

Objective 2. To increase preservice teachers' level of unbiased attributions toward International children.

As a first step in achieving this objective, preservice teachers can be provided with information about stereotypes, labels, and the reasons why such labels are used to describe people from various cultural groups. Discussion can ensue focused upon the negative consequences of using these labels for individuals who use them, as well as those who are labeled. Knowledge gained from this discussion can also be applied to one's own life, exploring the dispositional labels employed by one's family as well as one's self, examining the consequences that occurred as a result of these labels.

In addition to exploring the meaning of, reasons for and consequences of these labels, it is also important for preservice teachers to obtain accurate information about what various cultural groups are like, and why they behave the way they do (Hildreth & Sugawara, in press). Accurate knowledge of the characteristics of individuals who are part of various cultural groups can pave the way for a more sensitive understanding of differences as well as similarities that exist among people from different cultural backgrounds.

Once this knowledge is gained, preservice teachers can then be asked to observe International children playing in the classroom or actively participate with them in a variety of curriculum activities. In addition, interaction with families from a variety of cultural backgrounds whose children are enrolled in the early childhood education program would be beneficial. Learning from such experiences can be shared with the supervisor and peers as they reflect upon how they view these individuals and the reasons why they attribute certain characteristics to them.

Such interactions, however, will likely destroy previously held stereotypes, allowing preservice teachers to interact with each person as a unique individual with a distinct cultural past, a shared common culture, and a life which has emerged as a result of interactions with them. In this manner, biased ethnic attributions give way to more accurate ones which ultimately preserve the integrity and dignity of individuals from diverse cultural backgrounds rather than maintain the negative stereotypic appraisals which result from limited exposure and interactions.

Considering Preservice Teacher's Behavioral Responses

In addition to becoming aware of the perceptions preservice teachers have about their teaching abilities in interacting with children from International cultures as well as the ethnic attributions they possess, it is important for preservice teachers to also become aware of the behavioral responses they make to children from International cultures. Examination of these behavioral responses are important, because different cultures have different ways of behaving in particular social settings. For example, a Chinese child who never looks into your eyes when you speak to him/her, does not indicate that such a child is not attending to your comments (Jim & Suen, 1990). In fact, among Chinese children, the focus of their eyes to the ground while the teacher is speaking, is made as a sign of respect rather than non-attention. Holding such a child's face up to look at you, or demanding that such a child attend to your remarks may indicate an insensitivity on your part as to the real meaning of the child's behavior. A third major objective of teacher preparation programs, therefore, must be:

Objective 3.   To increase preservice teachers' sensitivity to displaying behavioral responses that communicate an appreciation and understanding of an International child's cultural heritage.

At the onset, preservice teachers need to be provided with information about cultural characteristics that accurately describe how children from different cultural backgrounds react to specific teacher behaviors. For example, among Hawaiians, Native Americans and Mexican Americans, close family ties, cooperation and interdependence are often emphasized (Gillamore, Boggs & Jordan, 1974; Gulick, 1960; Kitano, 1983; Ramirez & Castenada, 1974; Saracho & Hancock, 1983). Teachers who only require children to become involved in curriculum activities that emphasize competition and individual achievement, therefore, are bound to experience a great deal of non-participation from among these children. When experiences are planned in which children are involved in group enterprises that require cooperation, however, participation by these children in a variety of activities is more likely to occur.

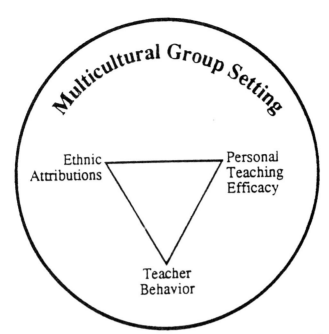

Figure 1   A model of teacher-child interactions includes major perceptual components of teachers' personal teaching efficacy and the teachers' ethnic causal attributions which influence the teachers' behavior toward individual international children.

Likewise, African American children are said to be relational rather than analytical in their cognitive style (Hale, 1983; Hilliard, 1976; Yound, 1970). They tend to view things in their entirety rather than in isolated parts, focus on people rather than objects, and are affective rather than objective in their responses. Interacting with these children in a behavioral style that coincides with their understanding of the world, therefore, is crucial if learning among them is to be facilitated. Furthermore, Asian Americans as a group are known to have a great deal of respect for their teachers (Kitano, 1983; Maldanado, 1976; Pitler, 1977; Sue, 1973). This characteristic coupled with their low verbosity, and emphasis on obedience and deference to authority figures, often places them at a disadvantage in American educational settings, where high verbal ability and active participation in class discussion are often required. Knowledge of these cultural characteristics are important, if preservice teachers are to develop the necessary expertise to effectively interact with children from diverse cultural backgrounds.

In addition to the acquisition of cultural knowledge, preservice teachers can become involved in observing others or themselves via videotaped sessions of their interactions with children from other cultures. An examination of the manner in which teachers respond to children may be important in their attempt at facilitating children's learning. Children from different cultures do not respond to the behavioral styles of teachers in the same manner. Once such knowledge is obtained, adapting one's behavioral responses to children's unique cultural heritages, therefore, may be essential for optimal development to occur.

It is important for preservice teachers to become aware of their own behavioral responses to children, and the manner in which children react to them. Caldwell and Honig's (1971) *Teacher Behavior Coding Categories*, previously discussed, can be used as an effective tool in obtaining such information from videotaped segments of teacher behaviors with International children. The coding categories include a variety of behavioral responses that teachers consistently make in interacting with children in small group activity situations. These include such behaviors as ego-boosting, questioning, informing, reinforcing, attending, ignoring and so on.

In using these teacher behavior categories, however, one should be cognizant not only of how the teacher behaves, but how children respond to such behaviors, and what these behaviors do to children's involvement in learning activities. Furthermore, depending upon the cultural background from which these children come, each of these teacher behaviors may not lead to specific behavioral outcomes among individual children.

These differences in children's reactions to teacher behaviors are important to recognize, if an appreciation of a child's cultural heritage is to be maintained. Such appreciation can go a long way in helping the child feel accepted. This is especially true in an environment that values cultural diversity, opening an avenue through which the child can freely explore the world, acquiring the myriad of knowledge and skills the world of objects and people have to offer, for use in effective social and personal functioning.

SUMMARY

In this manuscript we have explored some of the theories and research related to how selected preservice teachers' perceptions can influence the manner in which they interact with children from International cultures. These selected teacher perceptions included preservice teachers' personal teaching efficacy and attributions of behavioral characteristics associated with children from diverse cultural backgrounds. In addition, we have examined research on the nature of preservice teachers' behavioral responses to interactions with children in a multicultural group setting.

Out of this study, we developed a model of teacher-child interactions from which we drew practical implications for use in teacher preparation programs that takes seriously the role of professional teachers in facilitating the development of children from a wide range of cultural backgrounds. It is hoped that suggestions in this manuscript would prove beneficial to supervisors and preservice teachers in their attempt at developing educational environments that are sensitive to and appreciate the cultural diversity which exists within our early childhood classrooms, so that all children, regardless of cultural origins, can fully benefit from such an experience.

References

Bandura, A. (1977) Self-efficacy: Toward a unifying theory of behavioral change. *Psychological Review*, **84**, (2), 191–215

Bandura, A. (1986) *Social foundations of thought and action: Social cognition theory*. Englewood Cliffs, New Jersey: Prentice-Hall

Bredekamp, S. (Ed.) (1987) *Developmentally appropriate practices in early childhood programs serving children from birth through 8*. (Expanded edition). Washington, D.C.: NAEYC

Brophy, J. & Rohrkemper, M. (1981) The influence of problem ownership on teachers' perceptions of and strategies coping with problem students. *Journal of Educational Psychology*, **73**, 295–311

Burt, L. (1992) *Contribution of personal efficacy and ethnic attribution to the behavior of preservice teachers in a multicultural group setting*. Unpublished manuscript of dissertation proposal. Department of Human Development and Family Sciences, Oregon State University, Corvallis, Oregon

Caldwell, B. & Honig, A. (1971) A procedure for patterning responses of adults and children (APPROACH). *Catalog of Selected Documents in Psychology*, **1**, 13–16

Chu, L. (1980) *Towards a humanistic behaviorism: Self-efficacy in multicultural education*. A presentation in College of Education Dialogue Series. New Mexico State University. ERIC ED 179326

Dembo, M. & Gibson, S. (1985) Teachers' sense of efficacy: An important factor in school improvement. *Elementary School Journal*, **86** (2), 173--184

Fagot, B. (1978) The influence of sex of child on parental reactions to toddler children. *Child Development*, **49**, 459–465

Gibson, S. & Dembo, M. (1984) Teachers' sense of efficacy: An important factor in school improvement. *Journal of Education Psychology*, **76** (4), 569–582

Gillmore, R., Boggs, J. & Jordon, C. (1974) *Culture, Behavior and Americans*. Beverly Hills, CA.: Sage Publications

Grusec, J. & Kuczinski, L. (1980) Direction of effects in socialization: A comparison of the parents' versus the child's behavior as determinants of disciplinary techniques. *Developmental Psychology*, **16** (1), 1–9

Gulick, J. (1960) *Cherokee at the crossroads*. Chapel Hill: University of North Carolina, Institute of Research on Social Science

Hale, J. (1983) Black children: Their roots, cultures and learning styles. In O. Saracho & B. Spodek (Eds.), *Understanding the Multicultural Experience in Early Childhood Education*. Washington, D.C.: NAEYC

Hamilton, D. (1979) A cognitive-attributional analysis of stereotyping. *Advances in Experimental Social Psychology*, **12**, 53–84

Hildreth, G. & Sugawara, A. (in press) Ethnicity and diversity issues in family life education. In J. Schvanefeldt, M. Arcus & J. Moss (Eds.), *Handbook of Family Life Education*. Beverly Hills, CA: Sage Publications

Hilliard, A. (1976) *Alternatives of IQ testing: An approach to identification of gifted minority children*. Los Angeles: California State Department of Education

Honig, A. & Wittmer, D. (1986) Toddler bids and teacher responses. *Child Care Quarterly*, **14** (1), 14–29

Inoff, G. & Halverson, C. (1977) Behavioral dispositions of child and caretaker-child interaction. *Developmental Psychology*, **13**, 274–281

Irvine, J. (1986) Teacher-student interactions: Effects of student race, sex, and grade level. *Journal of Educational Psychology*, **78** (1), 14–21

Jim, E. & Suen, P. (1990) *Chinese parents and teenagers in Canada–Transitions and conflicts*. Canada: Canadian Mental Health Association

Kitano, H. (1973) Japanese American mental illness. In S. Sue & N. Wagner (Eds.), *Asian Americans' Psychological Perspectives*. Ben Lomond, CA: Science & Behavior Books

Maldonado, S. (1976) *Programmatic recommendations and considerations in assisting school districts to serve Vietnamese children*. Urbana, IL: ERIC Clearinghouse on ECE. ERIC Document Reproduction Service No. ED 133 405

Mumaw, C., Sugawara, A. & Pestle, (1992) *Contributions of self-efficacy to global practices and attitudes of home economist high school teachers*. Unpublished manuscript. Department of Human Development and Family Sciences, Oregon State University, Corvallis, Oregon

Pitter, B. (1977) Chicago's Korean American Community. *Integrated Education*, **88**, 44–47

Ramsey, P. (1987) *Teaching and learning in a diverse world: Multicultural education for young children*. New York: Teachers College Press

Ramirez, M. & Castaneda, A. (1974) *Cultural democracy, biocognitive development and education*. New York: Academic Press

Ruder, T. (1992) *Contributions of selected personal and social perceptual factors to the teaching performance of early childhood student-teachers in a multicultural preschool setting*. Unpublished manuscript. Department of Human Development & Family Sciences, Oregon State University, Corvallis, Oregon

Russell, D. (1982) The Causal Dimension Scale: A measure of how individuals perceive causes. *Journal of Personality and Social Psychology*, **42**, 1137–1145

Saracho, O. & Hancock, F. (1983) Mexican American culture. In O. Saracho & B. Spodek (Eds.), *Understanding the Multicultural Experiences of Early Childhood Education*. Washington, D.C.: NAEYC

Shoup, R. & Eads, G. (1977) White pre-service teachers' attitudes toward minority groups. *Psychological Reports*, **40**, 1029–1030

Snygg, D. & Combs, A. (1949) *Individual behavior: A new frame of reference for psychology*. New York: Harper & Brothers

Stevens, G. (1980) Bias in attributions of positive and negative behaviors in children by school psychologists, parents, and teachers. *Perceptual and Motor Skills*, **59**, 1283–1290

Sue, D. (1973) Ethnic identity: The impact of two cultures on the psychological development of Asian in America. In D. Sue & N. Wagner (Eds.), *Asian Americans: Psychological Perspectives*. Ben Lomond, CA.: Science and Behavior Books

Triandis, H. (1989) The self and social behavior in differing cultural contexts. *Psychological Review*, **96** (3), 506–520

Weiner, B. (1979) An attributional theory of achievement, motivation and emotion. *Psychological Review*, **92** (4), 548–573

Weiner, B. (1985) A theory of motivation for some classroom experiences. *Journal of Educational Psychology*, **71**, 2–25

Weiner, B. (1990) Searching for the roots of applied attribution theory. In S. Graham & V. Folkes (Eds.), *Attribution Theory: Applications to Achievement, Mental Health, and Interpersonal Conflict*. Hillsdale, New Jersey: Lawrence Erlbaum Associates, Publishers

Wittmer, D. & Honig, A. (1988) Teacher re-creation of negative interactions with toddlers. *Early Child Development & Care*, **8**, 77–88

Young, V. (1970) Family and childhood in a southern Georgia community. *American Anthropologist*, **72**, 269–288

Professional issues: A perspective on their place in pre-service education for early childhood

ANNE STONEHOUSE and CHRISTINE WOODROW

Faculty of Education, Northern Territory University, Casuarina, NT, Australia

(Received August 1991)

This paper focusses on issues connected with Early Childhood as a profession. Whilst the context is the diversity of service provision in Australia, the issues raised will hopefully contribute to debate in other countries.

Key words: professional issues, pre-service education, early childhood

The early childhood field in Australia operates within a dynamic social and political context. A period of substantial growth in government funding over the past two decades has resulted in rapid expansion of children's services and the placing of child care firmly on the political agenda. This expansion of services has provided graduates in early childhood with more varied options for employment that include not only teaching in traditional sessional pre-school or kindergarten and the early years of school, but also working in a variety of roles in long day care, occasional care, mobile services, out of school hours care, and play in hospital programs, to mention a few.

Early childhood professionals have had to diversify the services that they offer and now work in settings that offer both care and education (Roderick, 1987), and with the increasing professionalisation of child care, some of the distinctions between care and education that have existed in the past have become blurred. This blurring suggests that early childhood professionals must have a perspective that highlights the continuities and commonalities in children's learning and development across the age range, as they are likely to work with children of a variety of ages. They need to be sensitive to the needs of children irrespective of the setting or service and to be confident about meeting those needs in a variety of settings. Across the variety of services that exist currently, there is great diversity among the level and nature of staff qualifications, industrial and working conditions, regulations, employing bodies, and management structures (Watts, 1987), and staff must adjust to this.

In addition there are social factors that influence the work and role of the early childhood professional. These include increasing recognition of the cultural and linguistic diversity of the Australian population, the integration of children with disabilities into mainstream services, increasing numbers of single parent families in the community, and a growth in numbers of women in the work force with young children. These trends have resulted in an increased diversity of users of early childhood services and increased placement of children in multiple early childhood services (Watts, 1987; Ebbeck, 1989). This trend is not confined to Australia.

THE ROLE OF THE EARLY CHILDHOOD PROFESSIONAL

This changing context has precipitated a substantial change in the expansion of roles for the early childhood professional, and along with that, considerable tension and role confusion within the field. In the past many early childhood teachers worked fairly autonomously and their role was relatively well defined, conceived primarily in terms of teaching functions, with a focus on the child and learning — a child development orientation that highlighted the teacher's role in supporting children's development and learning within an educational context. Katz (1977) identified these roles as caretaker, provider of emotional support and guidance, instructor, and facilitator. A comprehensive role analysis of early childhood teaching by Saracho (1984) conceptualised the role as having the following components: decision maker, organiser of instruction, diagnostician, curriculum designer, manager of learning and counsellor/adviser, within the parameters of a child development and learning paradigm. In the contemporary Australian context, such descriptions no longer adequately describe the early childhood professional's role. The role has expanded to include responsibilities to the family, community, and the profession (Ebbeck & Clyde, 1988; Clyde, 1983), and the ability to work effectively as team members with other adults. Current responsibilities include assuming substantial administrative and financial responsibilities, managing and co-ordinating human and material resources, working as part of an inter-disciplinary team, working in meaningful ways to support and involve parents and families, as well as planning and implementing programs to support children's growth and development.

The parameters of the role are ill-defined, with a suggestion that early childhood personnel are increasingly expected to become "all things to all people" (Ebbeck & Clyde, 1988). Weiss (1989) endorses this trend when she states:

Part of the problem arises from the fact that, in seeking to meet new needs as they have arisen, early childhood educators have rarely shrugged off old roles that may no longer be necessary or appropriate. They have simply added new roles to their load. (p. 67)

Weiss asserts that this role overload leads to "at best, confusion and doubt, and at worst to burnout and movement out of the field" (p. 67)

Additionally, early childhood professionals are carrying out these diverse roles in an environment that is characterised not only by uncertainty about roles, but by low status and undervaluing by the community. The early childhood profession has always been attributed low status. The younger the child, the less status is accorded those who work with them, both by the general community and the education profession. Despite kindergarten teachers being among the first educators in Australia to undergo three year rather than two year training courses, it was only in the late sixties that these teachers achieved salary parity with their colleagues in the primary schools. This low status has been compounded by the growth in non school-based early childhood services, most particularly child care, where salaries and working conditions are still poor, and community perceptions have been that it is just "child minding", requiring little more from staff than mothering skills, which any female has. Hence, there exists a demoralising discrepancy between the perception by members of the profession themselves and those outside it of the worth of early childhood personnel. Unfortunately, while there are numerous contemporary analyses of the roles and descriptions of problems and challenges, constructive solutions are not yet forthcoming.

PROFESSIONAL ISSUES

Alongside issues related to the changing and expanding role of the early childhood professional sit additional related complex questions and issues, some of which are as follows:

A.   Is early childhood a profession? If it is not, should it aspire to be, and what strategies can be employed to achieve the status of a profession? If early childhood is a profession, does it meet the standard criteria for a profession or is it a semi-profession or a non-traditional profession?

Feeney (1985) defines a profession in the following way:

1.   A profession involves *specialised knowledge and expertise.*
2.   A profession requires *prolonged training and has requirements for entry* based on this training.
3.   A profession has and requires conformity to *a code of ethics*, which serves to assure clients that the professional services will be rendered in accordance with reasonably high standards and acceptable moral conduct.
4.   A profession adopts *standards of practice.*
5.   A profession has *autonomy*, internal control over the quality of services offered, and it regulates itself.
6.   A profession is characterised by *a commitment to a significant social value*; it uses its knowledge and power for the good of society. (pp. 1-3)

B.   What *is* the profession: is it early childhood, early childhood education, or early childhood care and education?

   The term "early childhood", embracing education and care of children 0-8 years of age, has come to be used to avoid perpetuating the distinction between care and education through the use of either or both of the terms. Traditionally, the term "early childhood education" has been used too restrictively to refer to so-called school based, pre-school, or kindergarten programs, and is seen by many people as not embracing child care. Some people object to calling the profession "early childhood", saying that it is meaningless, as there is not a middle childhood profession or an adolescent profession.

The nature of the discipline of early childhood, or whatever term is used, that is, what comprises its uniqueness, is a source of much debate. The question relates to the extent to which the "specialised knowledge" of early childhood professionals is made up of bits of knowledge from a variety of other disciplines, such as psychology, education, and sociology.

A second major issue relates to the interface between the early childhood profession and the teaching profession — that is, there are some three year trained early childhood teachers who see themselves as having more in common with primary and secondary teachers than with two year trained child care workers.

C.   Who can claim to be an early childhood professional or an early childhood teacher?

Given the array of qualifications available in Australia in early childhood care and education, and the range of people with other qualifications working in early childhood services, there is considerable debate about who can rightly call themselves an early childhood professional or an early childhood teacher. The terminology used highlights the care/education dichotomy — that is, traditionally and currently the title of teacher in Australia, unlike in the United States, has been the exclusive prerogative of those people who have successfully completed an accredited teacher training course. These courses currently are of three years' duration. Graduates of two year Child Care courses are not usually referred to as teachers.

It is obvious from the questions raised above that the most vexing professional issue within early childhood is the dichotomy between care and education, as the disputes and attitudes among people in the field spill over into the community and influence community perceptions about the worth of various types of early childhood programs.

In the rest of this chapter, after a brief overview of early childhood tertiary preparation, the question of why it is appropriate to incorporate the above issues in pre-service courses is addressed. Some strategies for addressing these issues are suggested, with particular attention to the use that can be made of the Australian Early Childhood Associations's Code of Ethics.

PRE-SERVICE EDUCATION FOR EARLY CHILDHOOD

The preparation of specialist personnel for the variety of early childhood settings in Australia takes many forms. Three and Four year diploma and degree courses that typically prepare personnel to work as teachers of children between birth and eight years in settings such as child care, pre-school, and the early years of school are now provided within universities, and are sometimes run alongside of, or as specialisations within generalised courses for the training of primary teachers. Challenges for these courses include ensuring that the needs of the under threes are adequately addressed, and that there is sufficient emphasis on both the commonalities of children's needs irrespective of settings and the unique characteristics and challenges offered by various early childhood settings.

Two year qualifications, generally leading to Advanced Certificates or Associate Diplomas in Child Care Studies, are typically provided in colleges of technical and further education, although more recently three year diploma courses for the preparation of non-school based early childhood professionals have been mounted in some universities.

The provision of pre-service education courses to meet the needs of the field has been a source of great tension throughout the last decade. Battersby (1989) asserts that early childhood teacher education has been and continues to be perceived as the least powerful and most problematic sector of teacher education. A period of significant growth in specialist tertiary early childhood education in the seventies has been followed by a period characterised by struggles to retain the integrity and very existence of courses. In a survey of early childhood teacher education programs, Briggs (1984) suggests that the structure and content of pre-service education for early childhood have moved beyond the control of the profession.

In addition to the pressures created by the amalgamation of courses and institutions, and a perceived diluting of early childhood content, there are some who argue that the orientations of early childhood courses are inappropriate to meet the needs of the early childhood professional in contemporary Australian society. Battersby (1988, 1989) suggests that current courses are characterised by three key elements: a psychological emphasis, a dichotomy between theory and practice, and an orientation that is non-reflective and non-critical. He suggests that these elements create a technical paradigm in which skills and competencies are stressed. He argues:

. . . This emphasis reinforces the simplistic and mistaken belief that the knowledge and practices associated with the professional education of early childhood personnel can be reduced to explicit rules and recipes in the form of a set of skills and competencies. Little or no argument is made of the need to balance this orientation, so that the technical aspects of early childhood education are considered in a critical and reflective way. Such is the need, then, to move towards critical pedagogy in early childhood teacher education. (p. 80)

Brennan and O'Donnell (1986) argue that a psychological focus in courses must be complemented by opportunities to examine political, economic and social structures and issues.

The present and future state of early childhood teacher preparation at the tertiary level is a key professional issue currently. Consequently, the questions raised previously about the state of the profession are made more difficult to answer, and at the same time, answering them is made more urgent, because of changes occurring in tertiary and post-secondary education for early childhood.

SHOULD PROFESSIONAL ISSUES BE DEALT WITH IN PRE-SERVICE COURSES?

A strong case can be made for the importance of addressing professional issues in pre-service education courses despite some contention that beginning teachers and pre-service students are and should be concerned more appropriately with the face-to-face delivery of quality experiences for children and "surviving" the demands of daily interactions with children (Katz, 1972). Additionally, there are those who argue that the chronically low status of the early childhood profession can only be rectified through increased industrialisation of workers, and that this is incompatible with increased professionalism (Almy in Stonehouse, 1989). Others might argue that attempting to deal with the bigger issues within a pre-service program adds yet another pressure to courses, dilutes the content, and results in a destructive sacrificing of depth for breadth.

While it is accepted that any attempt to increase the content of courses necessarily involves some trade-off and compromise, the complexity of issues within the contemporary context demands acknowledgment and more than a cursory treatment from the outset of professional training. If a commitment to professional growth is to be instilled in graduates and to become an ongoing part of their professional life, then the basis must be laid in initial training programs.

The early childhood professional, more than ever, needs to be adaptable, flexible, and reflective. If graduates are to adapt successfully to changing and expanding roles, and are to work successfully towards enhancing their status within the general community, then it is critically important for students to be acquainted with contemporary issues that affect their professional lives and to have the opportunity to examine the impact of these factors on the field, the context in which they operate, and the institutions and factors that are responsible for them. In arguing for a new approach to the training of early childhood personnel, Battersby (1989) asserts that pre-service training should encourage students to reflect critically on the "social, cultural, political and economic factors [that] impact on the lives and experiences of young children" (p. 81). Battersby argues that, after all, "education and schooling are not neutral enterprises, and the act of teaching has a moral and ethical dimension" (p. 81).

However, raising awareness is not enough. To avoid despair and frustration, raising contentious issues must be accompanied by efforts to equip students with some skills and strategies and an attitude of optimism to deal with the demands and issues that they face.

A particular challenge to those who prepare early childhood personnel could be described as addressing the lag between the current role and nature of the work of the early childhood professional and the perceptions of people who choose to train for the profession. That is, it would appear that some people still choose early childhood because they perceive it to offer opportunities to work fairly autonomously rather than as a team member, and to work more with children rather than with adults. These people in some cases may not be comfortable with having to address the politics of early childhood and developing skills of advocacy, teamwork, and effective communication with other adults.

The case for consideration of professional issues in a pre-service program is a strong one. If graduates are to survive in a field that is changing constantly and that is characterised by diversity of service types, varying conditions, low status, tensions and challenges, and if they are to have an impact on its future and any chance of influencing the shape of their own profession, then they must not only have an understanding of the contemporary issues and the forces that shape them, but so too must they have the skills and confidence to work effectively within the community, to advocate for the profession and for children and their families.

Regardless of the answers to the complex questions raised previously about the status of early childhood as a profession, even if it were determined that early childhood is not a profession, it remains important in pre-service education to instil in students a sense of professionalism, that is, the skills, attitudes, values, understandings and beliefs embodied in the work of a professional. In other words, as it is recognised that working in early childhood is complex, it is highly desirable that such workers conduct themselves professionally and that they be aware of issues impinging on their work, regardless of the type and level of qualifications, or even whether or not they have formal qualifications.

SOME WAYS OF ADDRESSING PROFESSIONAL ISSUES AND PROFESSIONALISM IN EARLY CHILDHOOD COURSES

The issues outlined in the beginning of this chapter can be addressed effectively in both direct and indirect ways in pre-service courses.

Course Structure

The very structure, content, and focus of early childhood courses as they relate to the age range covered and the settings that students are being prepared to work in has the greatest potential for breaking down the dichotomy between care and education. Over the past ten years in Australia, there has been a trend in three year early childhood courses to broaden the age range covered from 3-8 or even 5-8 to encompass 0-8, with some allowing for a specialisation in the younger age range (0-5) or the older (3-8) in the second and third years of the course. This enables courses to emphasise commonalities rather than differences in settings.

Requiring students to have practicum experiences across a diversity of settings increases their understanding of the unique challenges and characteristics of each, as well as the commonalities. The authors' experience with Diploma students who plan to teach in pre-schools or the early years of school suggests that a practicum in a child care centre almost always leaves them with a greater respect for child care staff, a more sympathetic attitude toward the complexities of that setting, an appreciation of the substantial obstacles outside the control of the staff that impede the offering of a high quality experience, and a greater understanding of the experiences of the children they will teach.

Special Units or Subjects on Professional Issues

Many courses, even the two year ones, offer at least one compulsory unit on professional issues. These units are an explicit attempt to fill students in on the broader issues that define the context in which they work, including direct attention to the role and status of early childhood. Issues as defined in the questions at the beginning of this chapter can be dealt with directly. Content includes information on such topics as licensing and regulation of services, accreditation of services and personnel, government policy related to children's services, professional development and in-service education, industrial issues, advocacy, community attitudes about early childhood services, the impact of increasing numbers of men entering the profession, legal issues, parent-staff partnerships, professional ethics, work environments, and other current issues.

In addition, in recognition of the changing roles of early childhood professionals, the increasing likelihood of working in a team, the critical importance of having good adult communication skills, and the number of early childhood positions that involve substantial management and administrative responsibilities, most courses have units on human relations, communications skills and management and administration.

Threads or Themes Within Courses

Australia is a multicultural society, and this is reflected in children's services. Hence in most courses there is considerable emphasis on helping students to examine their own attitudes towards people of diverse cultural and linguistic backgrounds in order to offer a program for young children that acknowledges the cultural diversity of the community and aims to help them appreciate the substantial commonalities among people and develop positive attitudes towards differences.

Another assumption that permeates most pre-service education is that early childhood professionals in the nineties and beyond will not only need to be good practitioners, that is, be skilled at engaging in good early childhood practice, but they also will need to be adept at communicating about early childhood philosophies and practices to parents, to unqualified personnel, to policy makers, to people from other disciplines, and to the community at large. It has been said (Stonehouse, 1989) that traditionally early childhood professionals have been better at "doing" early childhood than at talking dispassionately, rationally, clearly, and strongly about what they do and why it is important. This need to be articulate is increasingly recognised in courses, in the assignments given and the ways classes are taught.

Closely related to the previous point is the need to develop advocacy skills in students, to assist them to view one aspect of their professional role as being to promote the rights, interests, and well-being of children in whatever forums they find themselves.

In most courses, efforts are made to assist students to be familiar with and appreciate the contributions to the well-being of young children of other disciplines, professions, and service types. As has been mentioned, increasingly early childhood professionals work in inter-disciplinary teams, and there is growing recognition that early childhood services should not operate in isolation.

An additional theme that pervades early childhood preparation is that pre-service education is just a beginning, that a hallmark of a true professional is a commitment to lifelong learning, ongoing professional development, continual reflection about practices and beliefs.

Tasks and Assignments

In determining methods of assessment and setting tasks and assignments, lecturers are mindful of affording students first hand opportunities to grapple with professional issues. For example, Caldwell (1987) describes three different forms of advocacy:

(1) Personal or "one-on-one" advocacy

(2) Professional advocacy or lobbying

(3) Informational advocacy, or as Caldwell defines it "attempts to raise the general consciousness of the public both about the importance of events that occur during the early childhood period and about the capacity of quality programs to foster growth and development and to strengthen families" (p. 31).

Using these concepts, students can be asked to undertake advocacy on behalf of children and record their experiences in a journal. Current issues, such as is accreditation of services in Australia currently, can be promoted as tutorial or essay topics, and students' work, when it is of a high standard, can be shared with the early childhood community as a valuable resource.

In their practicum experiences in children's services students can be asked to focus on some professional issues as well as issues related directly to children. Students can be asked to participate in and critique meetings of professional associations or to attend in-service education sessions offered in the community. Often there are early childhood activities happening in the community, such as conferences or seminars, which they can contribute to and use the experience in some way to meet requirements for their course. These community based activities have numerous advantages: students are enlightened about professional issues, they get a feeling for what it is like to be a practicing early childhood professional, they become aware of what the issues are and how they are viewed in the community, they begin to build a professional network for themselves, and they make a valuable contribution, thereby strengthening the credibility of the course in the community. Having strong links between the course and the early childhood community is invaluable.

Modelling

As is true with young children, no doubt one of the most effective ways of instilling a sense of professionalism and a concern for professional issues in students is through modelling by lecturers. Traditionally early childhood academics have valued community service highly and most have been very involved in professional organisations, served on community management committees, conducted in-service education sessions on a voluntary basis, and served as informal consultants to services, all activities of a committed professional. However, there is concern now, with the moving of early childhood courses into universities, that early childhood academics will be pressured to pursue academic research and publications and higher qualifications, and that community service will be de-valued as a means of furthering careers.

USE OF CODE OF ETHICS

[Parts of this section are adapted from a paper by Stonehouse, A. and Creaser, B. 'A Code of Ethics for the Australian Early Childhood Profession', to be published in the *Australian Journal of Early Childhood*, January 1991.]

The Code of Ethics of the Australian Early Childhood Association (Appendix) was developed over a period of two years by a National Working Party and included broad consultation with and input from the field. To answer the question of why the Australian early childhood profession needs a code of ethics, the Working Party in its initial proposal used Katz's (1978) definition of a code. She states that "a *code of ethics* may be defined as a *set of statements that helps us deal with the temptations inherent in our occupations* (p. 3)". It includes beliefs about:

● what is right rather than expedient,
● what is good rather than simply practical,
● what acts members must never engage in or condone even if those acts would *work* or if members *could get away with* such acts, acts to which they must never be accomplices, bystanders, or contributors. (p. 4)

There are a number of contemporary pressures on early childhood personnel in Australia which set the context in which they work. These contemporary pressures include the following:

— Increasing demands being placed on early childhood practitioners by funding agencies, parent users, and the general community; that is, an increased requirement for accountability

— Growing emphasis on interdisciplinary approaches to early childhood services, which requires early childhood personnel to work with people with different priorities for and perspectives on the child and the family

— Questioning by sectors of the community of the need for early childhood qualifications in children's services

— Lack of concern outside of the profession for preservation of high quality in early childhood services

— Increasing demand for services, increasing costs, and diminishing resources

— Concern within the early childhood field about whether or not early childhood is a profession, if so, what is its nature, and who is in it?

The development of the Code was based on the assumption that the *process* of determining the key principles which should govern practice would be in itself morale boosting and reassuring, and the *product* would assist in convincing the community of the professionalism of early childhood personnel as well as provide some guidance. It was most relevant for the Australian Early Childhood Association, as the peak early childhood organisation in Australia, to undertake this work. It is intended that the process continue even though there is a Code in place.

In relation to the issues outlined in this chapter, the Code and the material developed to assist in the understanding, use, and implementation of the Code is valuable in at least four ways:

1. The contents of the Code are a guide to both the beliefs and values of the early childhood profession and what constitutes professional behaviour.
2. It is a tool to use to discuss complex ethical issues faced by early childhood personnel.
3. Its existence is one indicator that early childhood is a profession.
4. The Code and the issues around its development and implementation are a focus for discussion of the professional issues raised in the beginning of this chapter, most particularly the issue of the commonalities that unite members of the early childhood profession in spite of the diversity of settings in which members work.

The characteristic of inclusiveness, that is, acceptance and valuing of a range of levels of qualifications and of the worth and contributions of people with no formal qualifications is symptomatic, some would say, of why early childhood does not fit easily into the standard definition of a profession, which is characterised typically by exclusiveness. This perspective is reflected in the Preamble to the Code of Ethics. Rather than applying to a restricted group of specified early childhood professionals with specific formal qualifications, it is hoped that anyone who works with or on behalf of young children will base their work on the Code. Needless to say, it is recognised that people with formal early childhood qualifications will be able to apply the Code more thoroughly and with more understanding than those with no formal qualifications or formal qualifications in other fields. In addition, formal enforcement of the code, with penalties for violations, the most serious of which is expulsion from the profession, has been rejected in favour of informal adoption, further evidence of an attitude of inclusiveness about the field.

A number of strategies were devised by the Working Party to engage people in thinking about the Code. These included generating lists of practices they disapproved of as a beginning step towards developing a list of core values, an ethical pursuits game, where participants are asked to defend a pre-determined position on an ethical issue, and keeping a journal of ethical issues faced. The Code, because it does not provide "right" answers or solutions to complex problems, enables students to gain some understanding of at least one aspect of operating as a professional, namely, not having a list of prescribed answers, but having responsibility to rely on one's own judgment. The fact that the Code was developed for people who work in all early childhood settings emphasises the commonalities among early childhood personnel.

It would be appropriate for early childhood preparation to contain considerable attention to the Code, its development and use, as these embrace all of the issues focussed on in this chapter.

CONCLUSION

More than ever, young children need committed, strong, articulate professionals. In a time of great change, as characterises the early childhood field in Australia currently, it is critical that pre-service education for early childhood addresses the broader political, social, and professional issues that establish the context in which early childhood personnel operate. It also strengthens the profession, as a view of oneself as a professional is established from the beginning of one's preparation is likely to be maintained and strengthened throughout one's professional life.

It is imperative the people preparing to enter any profession understand the internal issues that affect its status and effective functioning. As was asserted previously, perhaps the most debilitating and vexing internal professional issue in the early childhood field in Australia currently is the care/education dichotomy. The issue and the challenge has been expressed eloquently by Cameron (1989):

. . . I have always been somewhat perplexed by the preoccupation of early childhood professionals with the terms 'care' and 'education' and with their ingenuity in investing these terms with whole families of meanings, to the extent that they can be used with telling effect for disparagement and abuse and for avoiding the need to listen to contrary points of view. It is easy to see why this preoccupation emerged and to laud the contribution it has made to the clarification of roles and the evolution of client responsive services but, to outsiders like me, a continued preoccupation seems unproductive. I say this because I accept as a truism that education and care are interlocked and mutually dependent dimensions of the services we are required to provide all children, whatever their age.

. . . Elements of the current preoccupation with supposed differences have less to do with the quality of the services we provide and much more to do with the maintenance of past orthodoxies and outmoded boundaries, much more to do with rigidity and concern for the status quo and less to do with flexibility and sensitivity or response in a rapidly changing environment. (p. 64)

The range and complexity of professional issues within the field of early childhood offer a substantial challenge to those responsible for educating new people entering the profession, for the future of the profession depends in large part on how these issues are addressed. The profession can ill afford to be divided from within, and there is a critical need for the profession to modify perceptions, work with each other more, and speak with a united voice.

References

Battersby, D. (1988) Towards critical pedagogy in early childhood education. Proceedings of the Australian Early Childhood Association 18th National Conference, Canberra

Battersby, D. (1989) The need for reform in early childhood teacher education, *Unicorn*, **15**, (2), May, 78–83

Brennan, D. & O'Donnell, C. (1986) *Caring for Australia's Children*, Allen & Unwin, Sydney

Briggs, F. (1984) A survey of early childhood teacher education courses in Australia. *Australian Journal of Early Childhood*, **9**, (1), 5–13

Caldwell, B.M. (1987) Advocacy is everybody's business, *Child Care Information Exchange*, March, 29–32

Cameron, J. (1989) Reflections, in A. Stonehouse Ed. *Care and Education — You Can't Have One Without the Other*. Northern Territory University, Darwin

Clyde, M. (1983) Early childhood courses in Australia: Patchwork eclecticism or ideological pluralism? *Australian Journal of Early Childhood*, **8** (1), 19–26

Ebbeck, M. & Clyde, M. (1988) Early childhood teaching: the disintegrated profession? *Early Childhood Development and Care*, **34**, 279–285

Ebbeck, M. (1989) Preparing early childhood personnel to be pro-active, policy making professionals. Paper presented at the XIXth World Assembly and Congress of O.M.E.P., London

Feeney, S. (1985) Thoughts about early childhood education as an emerging profession. Paper given to the Hawaii AEYC Conference on the Arts and Young Children

Katz, L. (1972) Developmental stages of preschool teachers. *The Elementary School Journal*, **23** (1), 50–54

Katz, L. (1977) *Talks with Teachers: Reflections on Early Childhood Education*, National Association for the Education of Young Children, Washington, D.C.

Katz, L. (1978) Ethical issues in working with young children. In L. Katz and E. Ward *Ethical Behavior in Early Childhood Education*. National Association for the Education of Young Children, Washington, D.C.

Roderick, J.A. (1987) Who shall teach young children in multiple settings? *Childhood Education*, **63** (3), February, 177–180

Saracho, O. (1984) Perception of the teaching process in early childhood education through role analysis. *Journal of the Association for the Study of Perception*, **19** (1)

Stonehouse, A. (1989) Nice ladies who love children: the status of the early childhood professional in society. *Early Child Development and Care*, **52**, 61–79

Stonehouse, A. & Creaser, B. (in press) A code of ethics for the Australian early childhood profession, *Australian Journal of Early Childhood*, January, 1991

Watts, B. (1987) Changing families — changing children's services: Where are the children going? Are kindergarten teachers ready to do too? *Australian Journal of Early Childhood*, **12** (3), 4–12

Weiss, G. (1989) From missionary to manager: the changing role of the early childhood educator, *Unicorn*, **15** (2), May, 67–72

AUSTRALIAN EARLY CHILDHOOD ASSOCIATION

CODE OF ETHICS

[Note: The code of Ethics of the National Association for the Education of Young Children in the United States was an invaluable point of reference for the development of the Australian Code. Some of the items in the Australian code are worded similarly to items in the NAEYC code. Permission has been requested and is expected to be received in the near future for using some similar wording.]

Preamble

A code of ethics is a set of statements about appropriate and expected behaviour of members of a professional group and, as such, reflects its values. The Code that follows was developed by a National Working Party of the Australian Early Childhood Association, with considerable input from the field, and therefore, is a Code that is owned by the field, not imposed upon it. The Code has been developed to inform and guide the decisions and behaviour of all personnel involved both directly and indirectly in the provision of early childhood services for children between birth and eight years of age. Although oriented towards those who are in daily contact with children and their families, the Code is also intended as a guide for those who work in other capacities, for example, as tertiary educators, administrators, policy makers and advisory staff. Their work impacts significantly on the ethical behaviour of early childhood personnel in the field.

Young children are especially vulnerable. They have little power over their lives and few skills with which to protect themselves. This places early childhood personnel in a relationship of special trust, one that is powerful, important, and easily violated. The vulnerability and powerlessness of young children and the recognition of the multi-faceted dimensions of the role of early childhood personnel serve to highlight the special importance of a code of ethics. As early childhood personnel carry out their work with and on behalf of young children and their families, they often face situations that involve a conflict of their responsibilities and professional values. A code of ethics is not intended to, and could not possibly, provide easy answers, formulae, or prescriptive solutions for the complex professional dilemmas they face in their work. It does provide a basis for critical reflection, a guide for professional behaviour, and some assistance with the resolution of ethical dilemmas.

Adherence to this code necessarily involves a commitment to:

- View the well-being of the individual child as having fundamental importance

- Acknowledge the uniqueness of each person

- Consider the needs of the child in the context of the family and culture, as the family has a major influence on the young child

- Take into account the critical impact of self esteem on an individual's development

- Base practice on sound knowledge, research, and theories, while at the same time recognising the limitations and uncertainties of these

- Work to fulfil the right of all children and their families to services of high quality.

I. In relation to CHILDREN, I will:

1. Acknowledge the uniqueness and potential of each child.
2. Recognise early childhood as a unique and valuable stage of life and accept that each phase within early childhood is important in its own right.
3. Honour the child's right to play, in acknowledgement of the major contribution of play to development.
4. Enhance each child's strengths, competence, and self esteem.
5. Ensure that my work with children is based on their interests and needs and lets them know they have a contribution to make.
6. Recognise that young children are vulnerable and use my influence and power in their best interests.
7. Create and maintain safe healthy settings that enhance children's autonomy, initiative, and self worth and respect their dignity.
8. Help children learn to interact effectively, and in doing so to learn to balance their own rights, needs, and feelings with those of others.
9. Base my work with children on the best theoretical and practical knowledge about early childhood as well as on particular knowledge of each child's development.
10. Respect the special relationship between children and their families and incorporate this perspective in all my interactions with children.
11. Work to ensure that young children are not discriminated against on the basis of gender, age, race, religion, language, ability, culture, or national origin.
12. Acknowledge the worth of the cultural and linguistic diversity that children bring to the environment.
13. Engage only in practices that are respectful of and provide security for children and in no way degrade, endanger, exploit, intimidate, or harm them psychologically or physically.
14. Ensure that my practices reflect consideration of the child's perspective.

II. In relation to FAMILIES, I will:

1. Encourage families to share their knowledge of their child with me and

reciprocate by sharing my knowledge of children in general with parents so that there is mutual growth and understanding in ways that benefit the child.

2. Strive to develop positive relationships with families that are based on mutual trust and open communication.

3. Engage in shared decision making with families.

4. Acknowledge families' existing strengths and competence as a basis for supporting them in their task of nurturing their child.

5. Acknowledge the uniqueness of each family and the significance of its culture, customs, language and beliefs.

6. Maintain confidentiality.

7. Respect the right of the family to privacy.

8. Consider situations from each family's perspective, especially if differences or tensions arise.

9. Assist each family to develop a sense of belonging to the services in which their child participates.

10. Acknowledge that each family is affected by the community context in which it operates.

III. In relation to COLLEAGUES, I will:

1. Support and assist colleagues in their professional development.

2. Work with my colleagues to maintain and improve the standard of service provided in my work place.

3. Promote policies and working conditions that are non-discriminatory and that foster competence, well-being and positive self esteem.

4. Acknowledge and support the use of the personal and professional strengths which my colleagues bring to the work place.

5. Work to build an atmosphere of trust, respect and candour by:

- encouraging openness and tolerance between colleagues
- accepting their right to hold different points of view
- using constructive methods of conflict resolution, and
- maintaining appropriate confidentiality.

6. Acknowledge the worth of the cultural and linguistic diversity which my colleagues bring to the work place.

7. Encourage my colleagues to accept and adhere to this code.

IV. In relation to the COMMUNITY AND SOCIETY, I will:

1. Provide programs which are responsive to community needs.

2. Support the development and implementation of laws and policies that promote the well-being of children and families and that are responsive to community needs.

3. Be familiar with and abide by laws and policies that relate to my work.

4. Work to change laws and policies that interfere with the well-being of children.

5. Promote co-operation among all agencies and professions working in the best interests of young children and families.

6. Promote children's best interests through community education and advocacy.

V. In relation to MYSELF AS A PROFESSIONAL, I will:

1. Update and improve my expertise and practice in the early childhood field continually through formal and informal professional development.

2. Engage in critical self-reflection and seek input from colleagues.

3. Communicate with and consider the views of my colleagues in the early childhood profession and other professions.

4. Support research to strengthen and expand the knowledge base of early childhood, and, where possible, initiate, contribute to and facilitate such research.

5. Work within the limits of my professional role and avoid misrepresentation of my professional competence and qualifications.

6. Work to complement and support the child rearing function of the family.

7. Be an advocate for young children, early childhood services, and my profession.

8. Recognise the particular importance of formal qualifications in early childhood studies, along with personal characteristics and experience, for those who work in the early childhood profession.

9. Act in the community in ways that enhance the standing of the profession.

The future of teacher education in the changing world

OLIVIA N. SARACHO

University of Maryland, College Park, Maryland, USA

(Received February 1992)

Critical issues in the field of teacher education are identified and related to concerns for the preparation of early childhood teachers and the search for professionalism. A concern for quantity and standards and the clarification of professional knowledge are identified as issues of international significance.

Key words Teacher education, the future

Teacher education in many nations is currently in a state of flux. Although we are almost at the threshold of the 21st century, the future direction of these programs is hard to determine. Higher education institutions, teacher organizations, national organizations, and national and state education authorities have called for ways to improve teacher education so high quality educational personnel will be provided for the schools.

For more than three decades, the field of teacher education has grappled with the following critical issues:

— How can we ensure the quality of teacher education programs? What standards should we use? How should they be established? By whom?
— Who will be responsible for preparing early childhood teachers? What roles should the schools, both public and private play? Should it continue to be the primary responsibility of higher education institutions?
— How can we maintain the supply of early childhood teachers to the field? Should we seek out special populations to increase their participation in early childhood education?
— How do we ensure equity in early childhood programs and in early childhood teacher education programs?
— How do we continue the professional development of early childhood teachers beyond their graduation from pre-service teacher education program?

While these concerns about the preparation of early childhood teachers seem universal, different approaches to their resolution will have to be found in each country. All of them are related to the nature of professionalism in the field of early childhood education. Spodek, Saracho and Peters (1988) identified some of the concerns for professionalism in the United States. Building upon these, we present the following:

1. *There is a need to establish standards of quality for practice.* A fundamental set of knowledge, skills, understandings and values must be expected of all practitioners. This should be universal for all early childhood agencies, irrespective of the service that is provided or the ages and developmental levels of the children served. Standards are maintained through some type of license permitting individuals to practice in their profession. Teachers who work with children under five may have to meet different requirements from those who work with children five through eight. This division is set mainly because older children are educated in public schools, while the younger ones are not. Nevertheless, the field of early childhood education needs to be concerned with the needs of all children and should establish standards for all practitioners working with children in kindergartens, primary classes, child-care centers, or other institutions. Competent practice and the criteria for entry into the profession must be defined to ensure that early childhood practitioners are competent and caring. Thus the issue of specialization in early childhood education will have to be addressed.

2. *Reasonable standards of early childhood professionalism must be determined and applied.* Applying the term *professional* may suggest the need to identify several levels of professionalism. Some differential of levels may suggest different standards of preparation for different positions in the field, even at the entry point. Identifying different levels of professionalism may also indicate different stages in an early childhood practitioner's career. In most nations and states two different authorities — an education agency and a social welfare agency — determine the minimal qualifications for early childhood practitioners and the ways in which practitioners receive their professional preparation. A social welfare agency decides the qualifications for practitioners in child care centers. These are often embedded in licensing standards for centers. Education authorities establish qualifications for teachers in schools. Too often these standards are different for each agency. Only as these different standards begin to come closer to one another will universal standards for practice be established in early childhood education.

3. *Alternative ways to enter the field must be provided.* Traditionally early childhood practitioners have come from many different fields: education, child development and social work, to name but a few. This diversity of backgrounds has enriched the field. Ways need to be found to maintain that diversity even as the field becomes increasingly bureaucratized. Ways need to be provided to allow individuals from different socio-economic levels and different ethnic and cultural backgrounds to enter the field. Participation must be sought to allow members of nation's minority groups to become early childhood practitioners.

4. *We need to determine how to apply standards and who should do it.* As noted above, different agencies establish and apply standards for different practitioners.

Professional organizations need to find ways to influence standards for early childhood teacher education programs, though they may not be responsible for creating and implementing these standards. It is essential that the public at large be educated about the importance of high-quality early education programs staffed by competent, professional practitioners and how the creation of standards serves young children.

5   *We need to find ways to deal with gender and economic issues.* Gender and economics concerns in the field of early childhood education are intertwined with those in the larger society. Men make up a small proportion of the practitioners in the early childhood field. Men, more than women, have upwardly mobile careers in the field, transferring rapidly from positions as classroom practitioners to supervisors, administrators, and teacher educators. Another concern is that salaries are lower in the early childhood education than in other professions that require equal preparation. There is also a limit on services provided to young children since too often parents must pay the fees for early childhood services for children below school age. It is essential that in establishing standards of professionalism the issue of professional compensation be addressed.

6.   *We need to define professional knowledge and values for the field.* In establishing professional standards, one assumes that a body of knowledge, skills and values needs to be shared among practitioners. Research suggests that teachers must have a repertoire of behavioral skills and a set of principles with which to support their actions, although how teachers think about practice may not be as important. It is essential that, in establishing standards, that teachers' basic cognitive processes related to problem solving and decision making within the realm of early childhood educational practice be addressed.

People's feeling concerning their actions and their values regarding children reflects a set of ethics for early childhood educators. A code of ethics that integrate such values separate competent practitioners — professionals — from laypersons.

Values continuously change as societies change. Cohesive, stable values which can be predicted and be taught in scarcely exist. Pragmatic values, which assist in making "working" decisions, prevail. Pragmatism and opportunism, which differ from individual to individual, may be considered fundamental contemporary values. Thus, society frequently encounters controversy.

There is one final concern that needs to be' addressed. Raising the level of professionalism in early childhood teacher education may increase its costs and its benefits. Obstacles may develop for early childhood practitioners, restricting those who join the field. All of these must be dealt with in the debate in association to the professional status of early childhood practitioners.

This book has attempted to describe the different teacher education programs in several countries throughout the world. Generally where the society, the university and the student are committed to the fullest development of research and teaching in an atmosphere of academic freedom, and where adequate resources are available in the form of faculty, libraries, laboratories and financial support.

Frequently, teacher educators consider programs in their own country and believe that they represent the total range of possible alternatives. However, the organization and implementation of teacher education in other countries can be far different from what is familiar to those of a single country. Saracho and Spodek (1990) examined how early childhood teachers are prepared in several countries, both developed and developing countries. They were interested in learning about the many possible conceptions of an early childhood teacher, many possible goals of teacher education programs, and many possible ways of achieving common goals. They found a number of similarities among the countries including the United States in regard to preparation of early childhood teachers. Apparently, these countries have traditions from those in the United States in the areas of early childhood and teacher education, although they have all been influenced by American early childhood education theories and practices. Most of the countries had different preparations for their kindergarten teachers, child care workers, and elementary school teachers. Presently, the United States is shifting in the direction of requiring post-bachelors degree education as part of the preparation of early childhood teachers. Reforms in teacher education (e.g., Holmes Group and the Carnegie Forum) are not only being contemplated in the United States; similar concerns are also being heard in other countries.

Cooperative efforts in teacher education throughout the world are likely to be more productive in the long run than a reliance on unilateral approaches. College-based teacher educators, which are often considered armchair experts in an ivory tower, are generating equal partnerships with practitioners. Teachers are pursuing self-renewal beyond their immediate peer group. State departments of education are delegating responsibility by developing which include other sections of the education profession.

The quality of early childhood programs is highly dependent on the quality of their teachers. Teacher education programs contribute to the quality of the teachers. As countries attempt to improve their teacher education programs they should focus on programs that serve young children, even though no direct relationship exists between outcomes in teacher preparation programs and outcomes in children's programs.

The improvement of early childhood education and the preparation of its practitioners is an international phenomena. Although enhancements will vary from country to country, there is also a degree of consistency among them. It is significant that nations throughout the world striving to enrich programs that prepare teachers of young children, and to manage pressing problems that endure in early childhood education and the preparation of early childhood teachers (Saracho & Spodek, 1990) >

Standard, certificates and diplomas are controlled by those who have power in the educational system. They are generally administrators of schools and teacher education institutions. This "old establishment" has recently been challanged by administrators of liberal arts colleges and by those in higher education who compete with teachers' colleges. Standards set by higher education are publicly debated.

Teacher education programs throughout the world are responsible for the following:

1. They communicate in their own unique manner the cultural heritage (e.g., the history, the scientific knowledge, the literature) of their society and of the world culture of which their society is a part.
2. They prepare teachers to successfully join the elite in their societies to exercise skills in science, technology, management and instruction.
3. They foster the individuals' ability to provide leadership and obtain a sense of responsibility to their country fellows.
4. They develop their critical skills which can help them to introduce changes and simultaneously appreciate their heritage.

Universities' major responsibility is to award new knowledge to the world's pool of knowledge and inspire students to contribute creative and original ideas. They must perform these functions to become independent rather than being parasitic on the university systems of other countries and unable to manage national development tasks.

In seeking ways to improve early childhood teacher education programs, it is important to study what happens to the students within universities, how those who receive a "modern" education and who have joined the intellectual classes envision their society and its authority system after they have left university. At firsthand, little reliable data have been found regarding the adults' attitudes who have experienced the intellectual classes.

References

Saracho, O. N., & Spodek, B. (1990). Early childhood teacher preparation in cross-cultural perspective. In B. Spodek & O. N. Saracho (Eds.), *Yearbook in early childhood education: Early childhood teacher preparation* (Volume 1) pp. 102 -- 117. New York: Teachers College Press

Spodek, B., Sarachol, O. N., & Peters, D. L. (1988) Professionalizing the field: The tasks ahead. In B. Spodek, O. N. Saracho & D. L. Peters (Eds.), *Professionalism and the early childhood practitioner* pp. 189 -- 194. New York: Teachers College Press

Notes on contributors

MICHAEL BUCKINGHAM
Michael Buckingham, until recently an Assistant Dean of the Faculty of Education at Roehampton Institute. Currently a visiting lecturer and freelance consultant in information technology.

LINDA M. BURT
Linda M. Burt is an early childhood specialist and Doctoral candidate in the Department of Human Development and Family Sciences, Oregon State University, Corvallis, OR. 97331, USA.

MIRA CHOUDHRY
Mira Choudhry is Reader in Education, National Council of Educational Research and Training, Department of Preschool and Elementary Education, New Dehli, 110016, India.

JAN DUFFIE
Jan Duffie is at the Institute for Early Childhood, Macquarie University, Sydney, New South Wales, Australia.

ROY EVANS
Roy Evans is Assistant Dean, Inservice and Research, Roehampton Institute, London SW15, UK.

ANNE FINDLAY
Anne Findlay is an Assistant Dean in the School of Education, Roehampton Institute, London SW15, UK.

EMIKO HANNAH ISHIGAKI
Emiko Hannah Ishigaki is Dean and Professor of Early Childhood Education, Graduate School, Seiwa College, 7 – 54 Okadayama, Nishinomiya 662, Japan.

GEORGE LEWIS
George Lewis is at the Institute for Early Childhood Education, Macquarie University, Sydney, New South Wales, Australia.

YU-WEI LIN
Yu-wei Lin is at Taipei Provincial Teachers College, Taiwan.

ELANA N. NEGNEVITSKAYA
Elana N. Negnevitskaya is at Moscow Pedagogical Institute, Moscow, Russia.

ISAAKI NOGUCHI
Isaaki Noguchi is Professor, Deparment of Preschool Education, Faculty of Education, Hirosaki University, 1 Bunkyocho Hirosaki, Aomori, 036, Japan.

LINDA POUND
Linda Pound previously a Senior Lecturer in Early Childhood Education at Froebel College, Roehampton Institute, is presently a Senior Inspector of Schools with an Early Childhood brief with the London Borough of Greenwich.

PHILIP ROBINSON
Philip Robinson is Dean of the Faculty of Education and Pro-Rector, Roehampton Institute, London SW15, UK.

OLIVIA SARACHO
Olivia Saracho is Professor of Early Childhood Education, Department of Curriculum and Instruction, College of Education, University of Maryland, College Park, Maryland 20742 1175. USA.

WENDY SCHILLER
Wendy Schiller is Dean, Institute of Early Childhood, Macquarie University, New South Wales, Australia, 2109.

KELVIN L. SEIFERT
Kelvin L. Seifert is at the University of Manitoba, Department of Educational Psychology, Winnipeg, Manitoba, R3T 2N2, Canada.

BERNARD SPODEK
Bernard Spodek is Professor of Early Childhood Education, Department of Curriculum and Instruction, University of Illinois and Urbana-Champaign, 1310 South Six Street, Champaign, Illinois 61820 6990, USA.

ANNE STONEHOUSE
Anne Stonehouse is Associate Professor, Faculty of Education, Northern Territory University, PO Box 40146 Casuarina NT, Australia 0811.

BERTIL SUNDIN
Bertil Sundin is in the Department of Education, University of Stockholm, S-106 91 Stockholm, Sweden.

ALAN I. SUGAWARA
Alan I. Sugawara is Professor, Deparment of Human Development and Family Sciences, Oregon State University, Corvallis, OR 97331, USA.

R. MURRAY THOMAS
R. Murray Thomas is Head of the Programme in International Education, Department of Education, University of California, Santa Barbara, California 93106, USA.

CHRISTINE WOODROW
Christine Woodrow is in the Faculty of Education, Northern Territory University, PO Box 40146 Casuarina, NT, Australia 0811.

Index